Sports Law in Bulgaria

Sports Law in Bulgaria

Second Edition

Boris E. Kolev
Tzvetelin Z. Simov

This book was originally published as a monograph in the International Encyclopaedia of Laws/Sports Law.

Founding Editor: Roger Blanpain
General Editor: Frank Hendrickx
Volume Editor: Michele Colucci

Wolters Kluwer

Published by:
Kluwer Law International B.V.
PO Box 316
2400 AH Alphen aan den Rijn
The Netherlands
Website: www.wolterskluwerlr.com

Sold and distributed in North, Central and South America by:
Wolters Kluwer Legal & Regulatory U.S.
7201 McKinney Circle
Frederick, MD 21704
United States of America
Email: customer.service@wolterskluwer.com

Sold and distributed in all other countries by:
Quadrant
Rockwood House
Haywards Heath
West Sussex
RH16 3DH
United Kingdom
Email: international-customerservice@wolterskluwer.com

Printed on acid-free paper

ISBN 978-90-411-9313-1

e-Book: ISBN 978-90-411-9345-2
web-PDF: ISBN 978-90-411-9376-6

This title is available on www.kluwerlawonline.com

Printed and Bound by CPI Group (UK) Ltd, Croydon, CR0 4YY.

The Authors

Boris E. Kolev was born on 2 September 1977 in Sofia, Bulgaria. He holds an LLM in International Business Law from the Central European University (Budapest, Hungary, 2004), a *Magister Juris* degree from the University of National and World Economics (Sofia, Bulgaria, 2002) and a Ph.D. from Paisii Hilendarski University of Plovdiv. He completed a Post Graduate Research Project in 2006 at ASSER College Europe titled 'Harmonization of the Legal Status of Professional Football Players within the European Union: *Lex Sportiva and Lex Mercatoria*'. Boris Kolev has extensive practice as a corporate lawyer, which he gained with leading Bulgarian law firms. Between 2008 and 2013, he was a member of the Advisory Board of the *International Sports Law Journal* issued by the International Sports Law Centre of the ASSER Institute in The Hague. Currently, he is a Managing Partner at KOLEV TODOROVSKA Law Firm. Boris Kolev has numerous publications on sports law issues, as author or co-author of such articles as *TV Rights in Bulgarian Football* and *Player's Contracts in Bulgarian Football* in the *International Sports Law Journal*. He contributed the chapter on Bulgaria in the book *Players' Agents Worldwide: Legal Aspects* (T.M.C. Asser Press, 2007). Together with Tzvetelin Simov he co-authored the chapter on Bulgaria included in *The International Guide to the Taxation of Sportsmen and Sportswomen* issued by NOLOT BV. In 2013, together with Tzvetelina Petkova he published the monograph 'Bulgaria' in *International Encyclopaedia of Laws: Media Law*.

The Authors

Tzvetelin Z. Simov was born on 2 March 1977 in Sofia, Bulgaria. He holds a *Magister* degree in Accountancy and Control from the University of National and World Economics (Sofia, Bulgaria, 2000). He is a Managing Partner of the accountancy and business consultancy company Business Logic Ltd. He has had extensive practice as a business consultant since 1995 and has largely specialized in the fields of taxation, social security, accountancy, finance and investments. Together with Boris Kolev he is author of the article *Player's Contracts in Bulgarian Football* published in issues 1–2 of the *International Sports Law Journal* in 2006, as well as co-author of the chapter on Bulgaria included in *The International Guide to the Taxation of Sportsmen and Sportswomen* issued by NOLOT BV. For this monograph, he contributed the parts dealing with taxation and social security of the Bulgarian athletes.

Table of Contents

Table of Contents

List of Abbreviations

AFL	Amateur Football League
BBF	Bulgarian Basketball Federation
BFU	Bulgarian Football Union
BGN	Bulgarian Lev
BNSF	Bulgarian National Sports Federation
BNT	Bulgarian National Television
BOC	Bulgarian Olympic Committee
BST	Bulgarian Sports Totalizer
CABFU	Court of Arbitration with BFU
CAS	Court of Arbitration for Sport
CBA	Collective Bargaining Agreement
CEM	Council of Electronic Media
CEV	Confederation Europeenne de Volleyball
CPC	Commission on Protection of Competition
ECJ	European Court of Justice
ECT	The Treaty of the European Communities
EEA	European Economic Area
EU	European Union
FC	Football Club
FIBA	International Basketball Federation
FIFA	Fédération Internationale de Football Association
FINA	International Amateur Swimming Federation
FIVB	Federation Internationale de Volleyball
GNP	Gross National Product
IOC	International Olympic Committee
LLM	Law on Labour Migration
LLMLM	Law on Labour Migration and Labour Mobility
LOC	Law on Obligations and Contracts
LPDP	Law on Personal Data Protection

List of Abbreviations

LPOPCSE	Law on Public Order Protection at Conduction of Sports Events
MYS	Ministry of Youth and Sports
NSSI	National Social Security Institute
PFL	Professional Football League
PPP	Public Private Partnership
SAC	Supreme Administrative Court
UEFA	Union of European Football Associations
UNESCO	United Nations Educational, Social and Cultural Organization
VAT	Value Added Tax
WADA	World Anti-doping Agency
WADC	World Anti-doping Code

Acknowledgements

This monograph has been particularly challenging to write since it is the first ever comprehensive study on the various legal aspects of the Bulgarian sports movement. I would like specially to thank Dr Robert Siekmann from the ASSER International Sports Law Centre for telling me about the Sports Law section of this spectacular undertaking in the area of law called the International Encyclopaedia of Laws and for encouraging me to contribute.

I am very thankful to Professor Darina Zinovieva, Ph.D. in Administrative and Medical Law, for her help especially with respect to the Doping in Sport part of the monograph, to Viktor Kirkov from the Professional Football League for his kind and timely assistance in finding relevant information and documents necessary for the writing and to Darina Prodanova from the State Agency of Youth and Sports for providing me access to files and documents available with that agency.

Further I would like to thank my friends and colleagues Anastasia Dyulgerova, Violeta Ananieva, Marina Uzunova, Plamena Stoykova, Svetla Stoykova, Teodora Tsenova, Zlatina Rousseva, Lyubomira Gramcheva, Anton Petrov and Dimitar Dimitrov for the lovely discussions we had on the fascinating subject of the Bulgarian Sports Law.

Last but certainly not least, I thank Dr Michele Colucci for supervising my work and my very good friend Tzvetelin Simov for contributing the taxation and social security parts of the monograph. I really enjoyed working with them and hope that we will have many other joint projects in the future.

Sofia, 2 June 2017
Boris E. Kolev

General Introduction

Chapter 1. Introduction

1. Sport is a perfect example of a bottom-up kind of pressure on the national legal systems where certain members of the society in result of their activity transcending national borders choose by themselves the kind of law they wish to apply. In sport, the simultaneous application of legal norms at different levels of governance (global, European Union (EU), national and regional), without rules regarding the hierarchy of those norms, would result in confusion with judges and consequently a threat to undermine fundamental principles of national or international legal systems depending on which rules would ultimately take precedence.

2. This controversy stemming from the application to athletes of various legal norms deriving from different sources, with often-conflicting legal rules, is one of the biggest issues of international sports law today. This was the reason athletes found themselves in a 'legal jungle', according to the popular metaphor used by Dr Roberto Branco Martins. Merely reconciling the conflicting provisions under the conventional theory of the hierarchy of the sources of law where national law shall take supremacy over the rules of the international sports associations would not correspond to the current trend for simultaneous application of legal norms at different level of governance.

3. National legal systems should respond to the process of internationalization of the law in general, as clearly demonstrated by the example of sports law, and cope with today's legal reality where legal rules are the product of large international communities, rather than being made by the competent authorities of the individual States. Reconciling the conflicting rules and the creation of one truly international, coherent and harmonious system of legal order in the field of sport, where judicial decisions would be predictable to a larger possible extent, should be a priority issue for the sports academics and researchers in the coming years.

4. One valuable means for achieving a high level of congruence and even harmonization, between rules pertaining to different legal orders might turn out to be the idea about the emergence of 'world law'. A definition of the term 'world law' is given by the late Harold Berman – a prominent professor from Harvard University and chairman of the World Law Institute of the Emory University in Atlanta. According to Berman, 'world law' means the common features of the legal systems of the world, and especially the body of customary law that is gradually being created by the people of the world in their transnational interrelationships. Included are many aspects of world economic law, universal criminal law administered by the International Criminal

Court, much of intellectual property law, much of human rights law as well as the world sports law enforced by the Court of Arbitration for Sport (CAS).

5. The idea for the emergence of such world sports law, called *lex sportiva*, in result of the development of the jurisprudence of the CAS and the uniform application and interpretation of legal rules in sport due to the activity of that arbitration body, is recently gaining popularity. *Lex sportiva* is deemed to be an autonomous body of rules having a non-national character. The concept of *lex sportiva* draws an analogy with the concept of *lex mercatoria* as a non-national legal system.

6. *Lex sportiva* may apply to relations in sport, first, if incorporated in the national laws; second, as an autonomous body of law, which is to be recognized as such by national laws; and third, as mandatory rules reflecting a public policy so commanding that they must be applied even if the general body of law to which they belong is not made competent by application of the relevant rule of conflict of laws.[1] However, there is currently a need for making the legislative and decision-making process in sport more democratic and transparent in order to give legitimacy to *lex sportiva* as a transnational law made by the world community of sportsmen and enforced by CAS.

7. The Sports Law section of the project International Encyclopaedia of Laws with its monographs on sports law comprising various countries in the world and published by Kluwer Law International is a unique source of information for legal writers, scholars and researchers interested in comparative sports law. It allows the identification of provisions of national legislations that are inconsistent with the international legal regulation of sport, evidences the extent to which national legislations incorporate *lex sportiva* and demonstrates how national legal systems cope or fail to comply with the process of internationalization of the sports law.

8. The present country monograph on the Bulgarian sports law also invokes quite interesting and challenging issues for future discussions.

1. P. Mayer, *Mandatory Rules of Law in International Arbitration*, 2 Intl. Arb. J 274, 275 (1986).

Chapter 2. Historical Overview of Sport and Its Legal Regulation in Bulgaria

9. The first comprehensive piece of legislation on sport in Bulgaria was the Law on Physical Education and Sports of 1933.[2] This law provided for mandatory physical education for all Bulgarian youngsters up to the age of 21. The law announced the release from physical education of the sick and disabled persons as well as married women.

10. Pursuant to the Law of 1933, every institution and enterprise, whether State or private, had the obligation to take care for the physical education of its personnel.

11. Particularly noteworthy are the provisions in the Law of 1933 regarding the sports pitches. Every municipality was obliged to designate places for pitches and other sports sites ranging from one to one and a half hectares for the municipalities with population up to 20,000 inhabitants. In respect to municipalities with more than 20,000 inhabitants, additional three square metres per inhabitant had to be provided. Pursuant to Article 21, all those designated places were deemed the property of the physical education organizations and the respective municipality was obliged to issue a notary deed of ownership. Moreover, upon that law entering into force, all pitches and other sites for sport existing in the country, granted for temporary use or donated to physical education organizations by the State or the municipalities, were deemed the property of those organizations.

12. The above provisions are nowadays used as arguments by today's sports clubs to acquire the ownership with respect to the sports sites used by them, but owned either by the State or by the municipality. Most of the current sports sites and facilities were built during the socialist period between 1945 and 1989 where only the State could own them.

13. Another noteworthy provision of the Law of 1933 was the one exempting all organizations, unions and federations for physical education from imposition of any kind of taxes, fees and liabilities.

14. During the socialist period, sport used to have a privileged standing. Sport was perceived as an instrument for promotion of socialist values in the society and opportunity for demonstration of the competitiveness and the merits of the socialist system. With the abolishment of the bourgeois laws following the end of World War II and the establishment of the communist regime in Bulgaria, including the abolishment of the Law on Sports of 1933, sport as activity remained largely autonomous and free from any special legal regulation and intervention.

15. In the years of socialism, sportsmen had the status of amateurs, that is, sport was considered as an activity exercised without payment having mostly recreational and leisure character.

16. In the late 1950s and during the 1960s, football as the most popular sport experienced some sort of professionalization although this development was not legally recognized. Football clubs (FCs) from the capital Sofia were affiliated with the

2. The Law on Physical Education and Sport of 1933 in State Gazette issue No. 273 of 10 Mar. 1931 and issue No. 32 of 13 May 1933.

administrative regions of the city and the State at that time. Companies registered with the respective regions were responsible for paying the salaries of the players. This way, football players were on paper workers in the metal, fur and other industries and received salaries above the average for the country.

17. Later in the 1970s, football players were recognized as employees of their clubs. The status of the clubs at that time was particularly noteworthy – they were organizational units within public institutions such as the Bulgarian Army, the Ministry of Interior and the like. Consequently, football players were granted with military ranks within said institutions and could progress in the hierarchy depending on their performance on the pitch. Some of the most honoured players at that time even reached the rank of lieutenant-colonel.

18. The big advantage of the militarization of football players from legal perspective was the equation of their working activity to Category 1, according to the then effective categorization of labour. For instance, workers in the mines also fell within the first category. Said categorization entailed as the most important implication the right of football players to retire after thirteen and half years, which was especially beneficial with a view to the short, as a rule, sporting career. The attachment to public institutions triggered also social benefits such as the right of players to rent or buy apartments from the housing fund of the particular institution at preferential prices.

Chapter 3. Statistics

19. According to the statistical information published on the website of the Ministry of Physical Education and Sports, which, as of 2 August 2013 was renamed to the Ministry of Youth and Sport (MYS) the number of the elite sportsmen in Bulgaria tends to decrease. The main reason is pointed to be the absence of young talents capable of reaching high sporting results and winning awards at international competitions. The trend for decrease in the number of highly qualified coaches willing to work in the country has been observed as well.

Chapter 4. Institutions

20. Bulgaria used to have a special State agency dealing with sports during the mandate of the government of Sergei Stanishev between 2005 and 2009. Until August 2013, sport was administered by the Ministry of Physical Education and Sport, currently renamed to MYS.

Chapter 5. Sports Law as Branch of Law

21. In the Western legal doctrine, there are various opinions whether sports law is an independent branch of law called Sports Law or one may speak only about existence of legal rules applicable to sports. In other words, the issue is mainly whether there is Sports Law as such, or it will be more correct to call the applicability of the law in the field of law as Sports and the Law. In Bulgaria, this issue was addressed by Rumen Nekov in his article Sports Law – Emergence, General Characteristics and Specifics.[3] He referred to the definition of branch of law as provided in Bulgarian legal doctrine by Professor Rossen Tashev. According to Tashev, branch of law shall be understood as unification of groups of legal rules, grouped in institutes, which regulate a certain circle of social relations by means of specific legal methods and which have internal unity. The main features of the branch of law serving for its demarcation are the existence of individual subject for regulation as well as the existence of specific methods for legal regulation. The legal rules included in a branch of law enjoy internal unity and, at the same time, they are autonomous with regard to the legal rules belonging to other branches of law.

22. Nekov noted that the legal rules applicable in the field of sport do not show internal unity and autonomy. In fact, legal rules from administrative law, commercial law, property law, competition law and other recognized branches of law apply in the sports realm. The legal regulation of the latter is also lacking specific method in comparison to the public and private branches of law where the methods of superiority and equality, respectively, are clearly visible. However, Nekov invokes the formation of complex branches of law as a result from the development of the public relations and the tendency for complication of the legal matter. These new branches of law emerge after certain heterogeneous legal rules, which have already found their systematic places within the traditionally existing branches in accordance with the criteria, are united in a new relatively autonomous and relatively independent new legal establishment, which constitutes a kind of superstructure over the already built system of law. Nekov provides the bank law as an example for such complex branch of law, which is already recognized officially as such in Bulgaria. Therefore, Nekov concludes, sports law must be likewise attributed to this category of branches of law. I concur with Nekov's opinion.

---

3. R. Nekov (Sports Law), *Emergence, General Characteristics and Particular Features*, in *Modern Law: Problems and Tendencies* (Krassimira Sredkova ed. SIBI press 2011).

Part I. Organization of Sport

Chapter 1. Public Regulation

§1. Introduction

23. Bulgaria qualifies as an interventionist[4] country in terms of regulation of sport since it has adopted a specific piece of legislation aiming to regulate various aspects of sport movement. The main and most significant legislative Act governing sport in Bulgaria is the Law on Physical Education and Sports (the Law on Sports) enacted by the Bulgarian National Assembly in 1996.[5]

24. Sports is mentioned also in the Constitution[6] in the provision concerning the right of citizens to health protection, which right is included within the scope of the main rights of citizens of the Republic of Bulgaria. Article 52, paragraph 3 of the Bulgarian Constitution reads as follows: 'The State shall protect the health of its citizens and provide incentives for development of sport and tourism.' This way, the importance of sport for the state of public health is recognized by the State in its supreme legislative Act and its protection amounts to carrying out of a public function.

4. The term 'interventionist' was introduced by the Study on National Sports Legislation in Europe conducted by the Council of Europe in 1999. Pursuant to this study, 'interventionist' is a country that has 'specific legislation on the structure and mandate of a significant part of the sport movement'.
5. Law on Physical Education and Sport of 9 Jul. 1996 in the State Gazette issue No. 58 of 9 Jul. 1996.
6. Constitution of the Republic of Bulgaria of 13 Jul. 1991 in the State Gazette issue No. 56 of 13 Jul. 1991.

§2. Regulation of Sports under the Law on Sports of 1996 and the Regulations of the Council of Ministers Implementing the Law on Sports of 2001

I. General Principles of the Physical Education and Sports System

25. Article 3 of the Law on Sports lays down the general principles of the system of physical education and sport, which are determined as:[7]

- interaction and coordination of the efforts of the State and public institutions for establishing and efficient functioning of the system of physical education and sport;
- overall binding of physical education and sport to health care, holiday activities, education and culture, so that a united functional system is established for the purpose of increasing its balanced impact with respect to all strata of the population;
- providing democracy and self-governance to the associations of citizens and providing choice of means and methods for practising physical exercises, sport and tourism;
- applying regularity, a scientific and differentiated approach with respect to practising physical exercises and sport during the entire human life cycle; and
- complying with the generally recognized worldwide principles of the physical education and sport and the international sport cooperation.

II. The Role of the State

26. The State shall promote the development of physical education and sports by certain actions enumerated in a non-exhaustive list set forth in Article 4 of the Law on Sports.

27. The promotion shall result in acknowledgement on the part of the State that practising physical exercises, sport and tourism is a necessity inherent to every Bulgarian citizen who has the right to maintain and improve his motive abilities.

28. The State is obliged to provide possibilities and appropriate conditions to all citizens to practise sport for health and long life without discrimination based on age and social status.

29. The State is further under obligation to create the legislative framework for the development of physical education and sport in the country, to create conditions and support sport for children and youth sport, sport in schools and universities as well as the overall socially beneficial sport activity aiming at the improvement of the state of health of the whole nation, to create conditions for the development of sport for high achievements and provide for the training and participation of the international and Olympic teams of Bulgaria in international competitions and Olympic Games.

---

7. Regulations Implementing the Law on Sports of 18 Jul. 2003 in the State Gazette issue No. 64 of 18 Jul. 2003.

30. The State plays also a role with respect to the constructing, maintaining, modernizing and managing sports sites and facilities that are State owned and shall control the conditions and the procedure for their use in accordance with their designation.

31. The State exercises certain regulatory and controlling functions with respect to the activities of the sports organizations, participates in the fight against doping by undertaking measures for observing the anti-doping rules, enforces rules for ensuring safety at sporting events as well as undertakes measures against violence at stadiums and sport halls and against hooliganism on the part of spectators of sports events.

32. The State supports and promotes the non-profit organizations for implementation of socially beneficial sports activities through tax, credit interest, customs and other financial and economic relief, and finances such programmes and projects approved following the respective order. Training sports specialists, assisting the improvement of their qualification, carrying out of scientific, research, informational and advertising activity and creating conditions for development of public-private collaboration constitute other activities of the State, via which the State may perform its role for promotion of physical activity and sport.

III. The Role of the Municipalities

33. Pursuant to Article 4(a) of the Law on Sports, the municipalities shall promote the development of the physical education and sport by adopting legislative framework, approving and financing programmes for the development of local sports activities in compliance with the national programme; constructing, maintaining and modernizing sport sites, facilities and sites for social tourism, which are in municipal ownership; assisting the organization of sport competitions on the territory of the municipality; exercising financial, economic and control functions with respect to the municipal sport activity; supporting the activity of the sports organizations, registered as non-profit legal entities for performance of activity in public benefit, which provide free of charge classes with physical activity and sport for children, pupils, students and persons in unequal position through financing their activities, programmes and use of sports sites and facilities in municipal ownership; establishing sport academies for kids, youngsters and students on the territory of the respective municipality individually and/or in cooperation with sports organizations, registered as non-profit legal entities for performance of activity in public benefit; and creating conditions for development of public-private collaboration.

IV. State Bodies for Management of Physical Education and Sport

A. Council of Ministers

34. The Council of Ministers approves the basic trends of the national policy in the field of physical education and sport, proposes for adoption by the National Assembly a national strategy for development of the physical education and sport for a period of ten years and adopts the national programme for development of physical education and sport for a period of four years coinciding with the Olympic cycle and reports about its fulfilment by submitting for adoption by the National Assembly a report on it. The Council of Ministers shall also provide annually relevant funds for the development of the physical education and sport through the law of the State budget of the Republic of Bulgaria.

B. MYS

35. Pursuant to Article 2, paragraph 2 of its Statute, the MYS is the administration which shall assist the Minister of Youth and Sports for the performance of his powers and obligations and provide the necessary technical assistance with regard to his activity as well as administrative services to citizens and legal entities. The Ministers and other State bodies shall interact in the area of the physical education and sport and social tourism with the Minister of Youth and Sports. The Statute[8] of MYS determines the organization, activity, functions and the number of personnel of the Ministry and its organizational structures and administrative units.

C. The Minister of Youth and Sports

36. The government body responsible for the management, coordination and control of the implementation of the State policy in the field of physical education, sport and social tourism is the Minister of Youth and Sports, who manages and represents MYS. The powers and obligations of the Minister of Youth and Sports comprise the exercise of the functions described below.

37. The Minister of Youth and Sports prepares and proposes to the Council of Ministers a national strategy for a period of ten years and national programme for the development of the physical education and sports for a period of four years. In 2014 a new provision was inserted empowering the Minister of Youth and Sports to adopt annual national programmes in performance of the said national programme.[9] His/her activity comprises interactions with different bodies and organizations, such as the State and municipal bodies for the purpose of development of physical education and sport, sports organizations during the process for implementation of the national strategy and the aforementioned national programmes, sports federations and Bulgarian Olympic Committee (BOC) for the purpose of the joint financing of the programme for preparation and participation of Bulgarian athletes at the Olympic Games.

38. The Minister of Youth and Sports further coordinates the activity of sports organizations with the State and municipal bodies. He/she supervises the activity of sports organizations for compliance with the Law on Sports and supports the activity of sports organizations registered as non-profit legal entities for implementing socially beneficial activities for the realization of the State policy in the field of sport and social tourism.

---

8. Structural Regulations of the MYS of 8 Jul. 2013 in the State Gazette issue No. 62 of 12 Jul. 2013.
9. Amendment of the Law on Physical Education and Sport in the State Gazette issue No. 21 of 8 Mar. 2014.

39. The Minister of Youth and Sports exercises also certain powers stemming from the State ownership over certain sports sites and facilities. More particularly, the Minister of Youth and Sports is the body responsible for the management of such facilities, provided that the latter have been entrusted to MYS in accordance with the respective procedure and relevant needs.

He exercises the powers of the State as a sole owner of the registered capital in one person-owned commercial companies as well as the powers of shareholder of the registered capital in limited liability companies or companies limited by shares, wherein the State participates and controls the observation of the regime for use of the national sports facilities owned by the State in compliance with the needs of physical education, sport and social tourism.

40. The Minister of Youth and Sports grants, renews, refuses and revokes licences to sports federations and national sports organizations for performance of sport activity. He appoints the management bodies of the Bulgarian Sports Totalizer (BST) and proposes its statute for adoption by the Council of Ministers. The Minister of Youth and Sports represents the Republic of Bulgaria before other States and international organizations for the purpose of negotiating and concluding international treaties for cooperation in the sports activity within its competence as granted by the Council of Ministers. He permits the organization of regional, European and World championships in conformity with the requirements of the international sports organizations and following coordination with other States and municipal bodies.

41. The Minister of Youth and Sports is granted certain powers and obligations with regard to the fight against use of doping in sport. He/she shall organize the prevention and control as well as fight against violence in sport. Further, he/she shall assist the other competent State and municipal bodies and their administration and interaction therewith, adopt and support programmes for the qualification enhancement, professional realization and requalification of sports pedagogical personnel.

42. The Minister of Youth and Sports shall adopt the criteria, conditions and procedure for awarding athletes, sports specialists and activists as well as talented children and young people in the area of sports. He/she shall organize and support the activity of the State and local authority bodies and sports organizations related to the problems of physical education and sport for the purpose of realization of the State and local policy.

43. In his/her capacity of a primary administrator with budget credits, the Minister of Youth and Sports is entitled to confirm a plan in coordination with the Minister of Finance for allocation of the receipts from the BST and to distribute them for the development of the physical education and sport in compliance with the national programme adopted by the Council of Ministers.

44. The amendment of the Law on Sports in the end of 2010[10] implemented new powers and obligations of the Minister of Physical Education and Sports: he/she shall propose to the Minister of Education, Youth and Science the opening, reconstructing and closure of the State's sports schools and shall appoint their directors. The Minister is also entitled to grant the status of high-grade athlete to athletes with significant sport results.

10. Amendment of the Law on Physical Education and Sport in the State Gazette issue No. 96 of 7 Dec. 2010.

V. Sporting Bodies for Organization of Sports Activities

A. Sports Organizations

45. The main role for the organization of sports activities in Bulgaria is played by sports organizations. The latter are legal entities that carry out training, competition, organizational and administrative activities in one or several kind of sports as well as develop and popularize physical education and sports. Sports organizations may be sports federations, sports clubs and national sports organizations. The role of the State is to encourage the establishment and functioning of the sports organizations as indicated in Article 10 of the Law on Sports.

B. Sports Federations

46. Sports federations are defined in Article 14 of the Law on Sports as voluntary associations of sports clubs engaged in one sport or more sports similar to each other, which shall coordinate the development, practising and administration of the respective sport at national level on the territory of the country and shall represent the member clubs before State and international sports organizations.

47. One of the main implications of the interventionist model in the field of sport is that the powers of sports federations are considered public powers originated from the State and conferred to the sports federations by issuance of a special licence to that end by the Minister of Youth and Sports.

48. The issue about the delegation of State powers to organizations operating under the private law has also a constitutional aspect. The Constitutional Court of the Republic of Bulgaria developed the principal position that the transfer of public functions of the State to private organizations is in compliance with the Constitution in certain cases where it is done by virtue of the law.[11]

49. However, there are some further considerations taken by the Court in the latter's analysis – the legal nature of the persons entrusted with the performance of State functions, the designation of the particular State functions as well as the extent to which the transfer respects, corresponds or contradicts the democratic virtues and principles laid down in the Constitution. The Court underlined that, as a rule, a transfer of State functions to non-State organizations is constitutionally compliant if such organizations have the legal form of non-profit organizations.

50. In another decision, the Constitutional Court distinguished two groups of State functions, and only the functions of the second group were capable of being transferred to organizations other than State bodies.[12] The first group comprises functions of the State bodies pertaining to safeguarding the security of all persons on the territory of the country such as maintaining public order, protecting citizen's fundamental rights, life and property, managing public State property, imposing taxes, enacting laws and other similar functions. The second group of functions is directed to the creation of

11. Decision No. 10 of 1994 under constitutional file No. 4 and Decision No. 3 of 2000 under constitutional file No. 3 rendered by the Constitutional Court of the Republic of Bulgaria.
12. Decision No. 5 of 10 May 2005 under constitutional file No. 10 of 2004 rendered by the Constitutional Court of the Republic of Bulgaria.

conditions for improvement of the welfare, promotion of democratic principles of management, justice and equality in all fields of public life. Said functions may be transferred to other non-State bodies, provided that the State retains the control thereof.

51. The transfer of State powers to non-State organizations in the field of sport meets all the requirements set by the Constitutional Court. The powers are indicated in and transferred by virtue of the Law on Sports. Sports federations are non-profit organizations, and the powers transferred belong to the second group of State functions as classified by the Constitutional Court.

52. The majority of the powers granted to the sports federations holding a sports license by virtue of the Law on Sports are of regulatory, disciplinary and jurisdictional nature.

53. Sports federations are entitled to develop and implement specific normative, methodological, and administrative regulations for managing their respective sports; to adopt rules and exercise sports adjudication and technical arbitration; to grant, terminate and withdraw the competition rights of athletes; to stand as beneficiaries of State and municipality aid for the public sports services performed by them; to hold advertisement and broadcasting rights for the sporting events organized by them while providing percentage of the revenues to the participating sports clubs, to sanction athletes and officials who have admitted to the use of doping and application of doping methods in training and competition activities.[13]

54. Further, sports federations enjoy some purely sporting competences such as the right to organize the championships of their respective sports at State level, to designate the champions in the respective age groups, to award titles to sportsmen, coaches and sports specialists, to propose to the Minister of Youth and Sports to award status of a high-grade athlete to athletes with significant sport results, to select the members of the national teams representing Bulgaria in international competitions and organize the training process thereof, to train special technical and administrative staff to deal with their respective sport.

55. Sports federations are prohibited from setting requirements that limit the participation in the State championships to professional athletes and/or professional clubs pursuant to Article 19, paragraph 2 of the Law on Sports.

56. Sports federations are registered under the legal form of non-profit legal entities for conducting socially beneficial activity within the meaning of the Law on Non profit Legal Entities.[14]

57. Sports clubs engaged in sports having tourist-sport and military-technical character, motor, hunting and fish catching sports, sports clubs of disabled people and veterans as well as clubs established at administrative division and industry level are entitled to unite themselves in multi-sports federations. Similar multi-sports federations may be established also for the promotion and development of sport in the secondary and high schools and military sport following the conditions and procedures determined by the respective ministers and coordinated with the Minister of Youth and Sports.

---

13. All powers of sports federations are enumerated in Art. 19 of the Law on Sports.
14. Law on Non-Profit Legal Entities of 1 Jan. 2001 in the State Gazette issue No. 81 of 6 Oct. 2000.

C. *Sports Clubs*

58. Sports clubs are members of licensed sports federations and are not subject to direct licensing by the Minister of Youth and Sports apart from the licensing of sports federations. They are defined as voluntary associations of citizens, registered as non-profit legal entities, which shall develop and popularize the physical education and sport as well as carry out training and competition activity in one or more kind of sports. For achieving their objectives sports, clubs shall exercise the following activities.

59. Pursuant to Article 11 of the Law on Sports, sports clubs shall support sports exercises of the citizens and organize them for practising physical exercises and sports activities; organize and carry out training and sport and competition activity; build, maintain, manage and use sports facilities; exercise preparation of sportsmen; perform other activities related to the development and promotion of sport.

60. In general, sports clubs are registered as non-profit associations (sports associations) under the Law on Non-Profit Legal Entities. Professional sports clubs, however, may be registered either as sports associations or as companies limited by shares (sports companies) in accordance with the Law on Commerce.[15]

61. All types of sports clubs are explicitly authorized by virtue of their membership with the respective sports federations to exercise the following activities:

- to propose to the respective sports federations the granting, termination and withdrawal of the competition rights of the athletes;
- to carry out transfer of sportsmen;
- to hold advertisement rights, rights of TV and radio broadcasting of sports events, organized by them under terms and conditions specified by the respective sports federation; and
- to render sports services, which are defined as paid services associated with the specific sports activity, such as training services, lease of sports facilities and so forth.

62. Further, sports clubs acquires the following rights by virtue of their membership with the sports federation:

- to participate in the State championships and international competitions; – to organize amateur and professional teams;
- to receive State aid; and
- to use sports facilities that are in State or municipality ownership following a procedure established by the law.

D. *United Sports Clubs*

63. Sports clubs running different kinds of sports may unite themselves in united sports clubs by registering as legal entities with non-profit purpose. The requirements to the united sports clubs are set forth in Article 5 of the Regulations implementing the Law on Sports (Implementing Regulations). Members of such united sports club

15. Law on Commerce of 1 Jul. 1991 in: the State Gazette issue No. 48 of 18 Jun. 1991.

retain their legal independence. Only sports clubs having valid membership with licensed sports federations may avail of this right for association with other clubs under the form of united sports club. The purpose of the united sports clubs encompasses promoting physical education and sports among the population and supporting their members for more fulfilling practice and development of sport.

64. The fact that the provisions concerning the united sports clubs are contained in the Implementing Regulations of the Law on Sports, that is, in a sub-legislative Act shall be noted. The discussions about the amendments of the Law on Sports included proposals for their regulation in the basic law and not in the regulations. Nevertheless, the last amendments of the Law on Sports and its Implementing Regulations do not provide changes in this legal situation.

E. Sports Clubs at Schools and Universities

65. Sports clubs may be established with secondary schools and universities under conditions and following procedure set forth by the respective minister coordinated with the Minister of Youth and Sports. Schools' and universities' sports clubs are structures of the schools' and universities' sports federations and associations.

VI. National Sports Organizations

66. National sports organizations are voluntary associations of sports clubs and/or sports federations, which shall coordinate the activity of their members in the specified field of the system of physical education, sport and social tourism and interact with the State and the international sports organizations for the purpose of forming and implementing the national sports policy. The national sports organizations shall take part in the preparation, realization and reporting on the results of the implementation of the national programme for development of physical education and sports. National sports organizations are registered as non-profit associations for the public benefit pursuant to the Law on Non-Profit Legal Entities. Only one national sports organization in the respective field of the physical education, sports and social tourism may be granted a sporting licence. The particular fields are enumerated in an exhaustive list in the Implementing Regulations of the Law on Sports and they are seven in number:

(1) physical education and sport at schools;
(2) physical education and sport at the armed forces;
(3) physical education and sports in the system of the Ministry of Interior;
(4) physical education and sport for all;
(5) social tourism;
(6) interaction of sports organizations running similar types of sports; and
(7) physical education and sport for children with special educational needs and for children at risk.

VII. The BOC

67. The BOC is a non-profit legal entity, which shall exercise the powers and competences related to the development of the Olympic movement and popularization of the Olympic ideas within the country. BOC is governed in its activity by the provisions of Bulgarian legislation and the rules of the Charter of the International Olympic Committee (IOC) as stated in Article 16, paragraph 2 of the Law on Sports. BOC is the only institution that may authorize the use of the Olympic symbols and signs.

VIII. Physical Education and Sports in Schools, the Armed Forces, the National Security Service, and the Ministry of Interior

68. The public regulation of amateur sport affects also the physical education and sport in schools, the armed forces, the National Security Service, and the Ministry of Interior. Chapter 4 of the Law on Sports is dealing specifically with physical education and sport at said institutions.

A. Physical Education and Sport in Schools

69. The Law on Sports sets a minimum threshold for the classes in physical education and hikes, which shall not be less than three hours a week or used for other purposes.

70. Schools shall create conditions for classes designated for physical exercises and sport having medical purpose as well as conditions for classes with adapted physical exercises and sport for students having special educational needs.

B. Extracurricular Sports Activities

71. Along with the mandatory physical education classes, schools are further obliged to provide conditions for continuation of the sports classes beyond the mandatory physical education. Such extracurricular sports activities are voluntary. They shall be organized in the classes of the optional education through special sports sections and clubs established within the school with the consent of the director of the respective school and under the supervision of teachers and coaches having a professional qualification in the respective kind of sport with the support of the school board of trustees. The extracurricular training and competition activities of students are organized by sports clubs at schools, schools' sports sections and teams, student sports academies with the support and assistance of schools' board of trustees following a procedure, specified by the Minister of Education and Science and coordinated with the Minister of Youth and Sports.

72. Student sports academies are extracurricular units established on territorial principle, where students may continue the development of their physical qualities as well as the special knowledge, skills and habits attributed to a particular kind of sport. The student sports academies are opened, restructured and closed with an order by the

Minister of Education and Science as stated in Article 10, paragraph 6 of the Law for the Public Education.[16]

73. Schools shall encourage the participation of students in schools' sports clubs and schools' sports sections and teams, shall construct, maintain and develop the necessary equipment and facilities for the practice of physical activities and sports and shall provide conditions for their adequate use within the mandatory programme and the extracurricular activities of the physical education and sports. The financing of the activities shall be provided from the State budget, by the municipalities and by natural and legal persons.

C. Sports Schools

74. Pursuant to Article 23 of the Law on Sports, students may continue their education in V, VI, VII, and VIII grade of the sports schools after checking up of their abilities in the relevant type of sport. The sports schools shall provide common educational, specialized – and after finishing VIII grade – also vocational preparation. The education of the students for acquiring vocational qualification shall be conducted under the conditions and the procedure of the Law on the Vocational Education and Training.[17]

75. There are two types of sports schools: *State* and *municipal*. This classification is legally provided and is significant to the sources of financing, the order of opening, restructuring and closing of sports schools and the procedure for appointing of their directors. Besides opening of special sports schools, the Law on Sports lays down the possibility for the regular schools to establish specialized classes in one or more types of sports.

76. The *State* sports schools shall be funded by the State budget through the MYS and shall be opened, restructured and closed by an order of the Minister of Education and Science upon proposal of the Minister of Youth and Sports in accordance with conditions and following a procedure as well as in compliance with criteria set out in the Implementing Regulations of the Law on Sports. The directors of the State sports schools are appointed by the Minister of Youth and Sports on the basis of a competition, conducted as provided by the Labour Code and under the conditions determined by the Implementing Regulations of the Law on Sports.

77. The opening, restructuring and closing of *municipal* sports schools, on the other hand, shall be done by an order of the Minister of Education and Science in coordination with the Minister of Youth and Sports under conditions and following the procedure specified in the Law of the Pre-school and School Education. These sports schools are financed by the municipal budgets. Directors of these schools are appointed by the head of the regional inspectorate on education following competition held under the conditions and procedure set in the Labour Code and the Implementing Regulations of the Law on the Public Education.

16. Law for the Public Education of 18 Oct. 1991 in the State Gazette issue No. 86 of 18 Oct. 1991.
17. Law on the Vocational Education and Training of 30 Jul. 1999 in the State Gazette issue No. 68 of 30 Jul. 1999.

78. The applicants for directors of sports schools shall have master's degree and at least three years teaching or professional experience in the field of the physical education and sports.

79. The Minister of Youth and Sports shall confirm by way of an order the State Admission Plan for the State and municipal sports schools in coordination with the Minister of Education and Science. The Minister of Youth and Sports, again in coordination with the Minister of Education and Science, shall adopt an ordinance for the terms and procedure of the admittance and specialized preparation of the students in the sports schools. With the amendments of the Law on Sports in 2014 the directors of the state sports schools were obliged to consult with the Minister of Youth and Sport the provision of the activities related to the education and training, sports and competition, and recreational process of the students. Furthermore, following the same amendments the sport schools were declared as centres for preparation of reserve of the sport for high achievements, in which the so-called Olympic units of students having outstanding sports talent shall be created and developed.

D. Sport at Higher Schools

80. The physical education and sport in the higher schools are an integral part of the education of the students. They are included therein under the form of obligatory and optional classes, with certain duration of the obligatory classes dependent on the pursued educational and qualification degree, 'Bachelor' or 'Master'.

81. The academic programmes for physical education and sport shall be worked out in compliance with the higher school's profile and the proposals of the Student Council. The grade system for the physical fitness of students shall be determined by the higher school.

82. The training and competition activity in the higher schools is voluntary, and it shall be carried out by the students' sports clubs. The higher schools shall promote the establishment and development of students' sports clubs and shall assist their socially beneficial sports activity. Higher schools shall provide the possibility for combining the training and competition activities of outstanding athlete students with the requirements of the academic process. Special scholarships can be determined for outstanding athlete students in the higher schools. The Minister of Youth and Sports may propose to the academic councils of the respective higher schools to accept without competition examination sports people with medals won at Olympic Games, world and European competitions. Such category sports people may be accepted in higher schools after explicitly issued decision of the academic council. Pursuant to Article 26, paragraph 5 of the Law on Sports, they are separate from those confirmed by the Law on the Higher Education yearly number of students for acceptance in universities.

E. Physical Education and Sport at the Armed Forces, the National Security Service, and the Ministry of Interior

83. Physical education and sport in the armed forces, the National Security Service and the Ministry of Interior constitute a compulsory element of military training, educational process and motive regime of the military staff, the officers, and the sergeants of the National Security Service and of the employees of the Ministry of Interior. The classes for physical exercises and sport are given pursuant to schedules approved by the Minister of Defence, the Head of the National Security Service, and the Minister of Interior, respectively. The higher military schools shall provide annual evaluation and require State examination in physical training.

84. Persons serving in the armed forces including civilians and employees thereof as well as the employees of the National Security Service and the Ministry of Interior may become members of sports clubs set-up within the systems of the Ministry of Defence and the Ministry of Interior as well as with the National Security Service, following conditions and procedures specified by the respective heads. Such sports clubs are free to be joined also by other persons. Sports clubs, except for those set up within the system of the mentioned bodies may include in their name notions related to their activities only after receiving permission by the respective head of the body. The Minister of Defence, the Head of the National Security Service, and the Minister of Interior shall approve the procedure and the way of organization and holding of sport competition activities for the employees of the armed forces, the National Security Service, and the Ministry of Interior, respectively.

85. Students in military high schools, persons serving in the armed forces, civil servants as well as the employees of the National Security Service and the Ministry of Interior who play for the national teams of the country or participate in the State championships in a given sport shall train and compete under procedure specified by the respective heads of the bodies. For this purpose, the latter are entitled to form special units carrying out training and competition activity. Athletes included in the aforementioned special units shall be proposed by the licensed federations and may keep their club belonging registered before their inclusion therein.

86. The regional and national championships for students at schools and universities as well as within the system of the armed forces shall be organized by schools, universities and military clubs, and federations in interaction with the respective ministries, institutions and MYS.

IX. Sport for All

87. Sport for all is defined in point 1 of the additional provisions of the Law on Sports as a system of widely accessible means, methods and forms of motive activity for maintaining health, physical development and physical fitness of people through individual or group sports practices.

88. Physical education, sport and social tourism are recognized as basic means for strengthening the health and physical fitness of the nation, and they shall be promoted and assisted by the municipalities and the State accordingly. The creation of conditions for practising and development of the physical exercises and sport by the population is an integral part of the social policy of the municipalities with respect to the populated areas under their authority.

89. The municipalities shall determine the procedure and shall provide suitable conditions for use of the municipal sports facilities by citizens for practising physical exercises and sport for all. Institutions and sports organizations, using State or municipal sports facilities, shall provide coaches, methodological and medical aid to the citizens who practise physical exercises and sport for all, under conditions determined by the respective State and municipal bodies.

90. The municipalities shall assist the development of the sport for all and the social tourism by creating and maintaining rest areas, health routes, children's sports platforms, bicycle lanes and suitable infrastructure to the mountain and high-mountain huts, camping lots and shelters. Organizations and persons who manage and use tourist huts, hostels, tourist dormitories, camping lots and shelters shall maintain the tourist marking in their adherent regions and shall provide facilities to the individual and organized tourists while observing the instructions of the Mountain Safety Office with the Bulgarian Red Cross regarding the safety conditions. Employers shall create and provide conditions for physical education, sport and active rest of the workers and employees. Funds necessary for this purpose shall be determined by Collective Bargaining Agreements (CBAs).

X. Sport for Disabled Persons

91. Physical education and sport for disabled persons shall aim the improvement of the quality of living and shall contribute to the rehabilitation and social integration of the disabled persons. The Law on Sports contains in its Article 33 a representation that all necessary conditions for practising sport in all its varieties shall be provided for disabled persons. MYS is obliged to support the training process and participation of disabled athletes at Olympic Games, World and European championships by providing expedient resources to that end. Disabled athletes are further entitled to use free of charge the State and municipal sport facilities and do not pay entrance fees for competitions. By the amendments of the Law on Sports in 2014 a new paragraph 3 to Article 33 has been inserted providing for support by the MYS of the activities of sports organizations related to the adapted physical activity of the disabled persons.

XI. Social Tourism

92. Pursuant to point 2 of the additional provisions of the Law on Sports, 'social tourism' is a form of motive activity in the open for improvement of the physical working capacity and emotional enrichment of the personality through organization of free time, leisure, relaxation and physical recovery of the citizens.

93. Social tourism shall be practised by the citizens individually or through participation in tourist associations. The latter are registered as non-profit legal entities for the public benefit within the meaning of the Law on Non-profit Legal Entities. Their main scope of activity shall be the arrangement of social tourism. Tourist associations may unite on territorial and national levels. Only one association may be established on a national level. Such association shall have a status of a national sports organization and shall be licensed under the provisions of Article 17 of the Law on Sports. Other persons may also organize particular tourist events and provide related services in compliance with the order determined by the Law on Sports.

94. Social tourism shall be carried out through tourist activities using the created material basis consisting of categorized tourist huts, shelters, houses, accommodation facilities and study centres, marking and other tourist sites and facilities. The Council of Ministers, the respective ministries, the competent State bodies and public organizations shall assist the practising of the social tourism by the citizens of the Republic of Bulgaria. The Minister of Education and Science in coordination with the Minister of Youth and Sports shall determine the mandatory requirements for the practising of tourism for children and students, organized by the institutions within the system of the pre-school and school education.

XII. Sport for Top Achievements

95. The Law on Sports introduces another category of sport – the so-called sport for top achievements, which is defined as a specialized system of means, methods and forms of motive activity of persons, registered as athletes in order to achieve maximum performance during preparation and participation in competitions organized and controlled by sports organizations.

96. The State and the municipalities, jointly and in cooperation with sports organizations shall support and develop sport for top achievements, for increasing its prestigious, integrating and educational functions as factors of sports development. More particularly, said activity shall comprise the following: discovering and supporting sports talents, educating coaches and general development of educational and training process, supporting sports medicine and sports science and granting suitable facilities for training and competitions to sports organizations. Further, the sport for top achievements shall be developed by showing due respect to sports ethics, health protection, and the moral and physical immunity of the athletes.

97. The training and competition activities for top sports proficiency shall be carried out by persons registered as amateur or professional athletes under the supervision of coaches pursuant to Article 35 of the Law on Sports.

XIII. Administration of State Sports Championships

98. Training process and participation in competitions included in the State and international sports calendar are the joint responsibilities of the sports clubs and the sports federations.

99. Sports federations are obliged to adopt regulations for the organization of regional and State championships and the competitions included in the State calendar for the respective sport. Further obligations of sports federations in relation to the administration of the State championships are provided for in the Implementing Regulations.

100. Every sports federation is obliged to organize and financially support the organization of State championships in the respective sport administered thereby on the territory of Bulgaria. State championships shall be organized in a way taking into account the different age groups and distinguishing between the two sexes in conformity with the specifics of the different kinds of sports. Sports federations may organize regional championships as stages of the State championships in the various kinds of sports. The particular way of organization shall be dependent on the number and the geographical location of the sports clubs – members of the respective sports federation.

101. When organizing and administering the State championships in different kinds of sports, the sports federations can establish professional groups (leagues), where only professional athletes or professional teams participate as both the Law on Sports and the Implementing Regulation provide for. The principal one sport – one professional league is set in the Implementing Regulations. Such a league does not enjoy independent legal capacity and shall function as an auxiliary body of the sports federation. Its activity shall be governed by regulations approved by the sports federation.

XIV. Participation of Sportsmen in National Teams and National Olympic Teams

102. Pursuant to Article 47 of the Implementing Regulations sports federations shall select on annual basis the squads of the national teams divided according to age group and sex. The selection shall be solely merit-based, that is, dependent on the achieved sporting results. Planning and organization of the training process of the national representative teams for the purpose of participation in world and European championships as well as in other competitions included in the international sports calendar shall be also prerogative of the sports federations but shall be further supported by the State and municipalities.

103. The participation of athletes, coaches and specialists in the national Olympic teams of the Republic of Bulgaria shall be recognized as a mission of the public interest and prestige, and it shall be subject to a special aid and guarantees on part of the State as proclaimed in Article 36, paragraph 4 of the Law on Sports.

104. The Implementing Regulations contain additional provisions concerning the obligations of the respective bodies as well as the programmes for Olympic preparation. The Minister of Physical Education and Sports shall further approve the programme for preparation and participation of Bulgarian athletes at the Olympic Games acting upon proposal of BOC and following coordination with the sports federations. Said programme shall include the obligations of MYS related to the training process and participation of Bulgarian athletes at the Olympic Games, the criteria for selection of the individual athletes and teams to be included in the programme for Olympic training; scientific, medical and information support; material and technical support; sports equipment and facilities provided for Olympic training; accountability and control.

105. The programme for Olympic preparation shall be implemented according to annual and stage training plans, which shall be prepared by the sports federations. Sports federations shall be responsible for carrying out the programme on the ground of agreements for Olympic preparation concluded with the Minister of Youth and Sports. Sports federations shall further prepare expert analysis and reports for the performance of the different stages of the preparation as well as an annual report.

XV. Policy Towards Young Promising Athletes and Disabled Athletes

106. The Implementing Regulations used to set forth provisions on the State policy with respect to young promising athletes as well as disabled athletes in Article 48. The said article was revoked with the amendment of the Implementing Regulations of the Law on Sports in force as of 1 January 2011.

107. The preparation and participation of sportsmen having disabilities at Olympic Games, World and European championships shall be organized by the respective sports federations and supported by expedient funds from the budget of the MYS.

XVI. Scientific Activity in the Field of Physical Education and Sport

108. Chapter 7 of the Law on Sports is dealing with the scientific activity in the field of physical education and sport. This activity is carried out on the basis of a national programme for development of the physical education and sport in Bulgaria. The main body responsible for the scientific activity is the Expert Council on Physical Education and Sports established with the Minister of Youth and Sports and composed of representatives of the MYS, the Ministry of Education and Science, the Ministry of Health, the Ministry of Environment and Water, the Ministry of Labour and Social Policy, the Bulgarian Academy of Science, the Ministry of Defence, the Ministry of Interior, the National Security Service, the National Municipality Association in the Republic of Bulgaria, the universities, the National Sport Academy, the BOC, sports schools, sports organizations, other legal non-profit persons with subject of activity in the area of the physical education and sport and the social tourism as well as distinguished experts in these areas.

109. The scope of powers of the Expert Council on Physical Education and Sports are listed in Article 8(a), paragraph 3 of the Law on Sports and comprises discussions and delivering opinions on the national strategy and the national programme for development of the physical education and sport and the annual national programmes for the implementation of the national program, the drafts of legal Acts in the field of the physical education and sport and on the research, methodological, experimental and development activity in the system of physical education and sport. The Expert Council also participates in the process of development and endorsement of criteria for public introduction of the types of sport and social tourism aimed at effectiveness of the system of physical education and sport.

110. The conduct of strategic scientific research in the field of the physical education and sport is attributed to the National Sport Academy 'Vassil Levski' in coordination with specialized sports departments existing with other higher schools, MYS, the Bulgarian sports federations and other stakeholders in physical education and sport pursuant to Article 54 of the Implementing Regulations.

111. The scientific and implementation activity related to the control of the educational and training process in the field of sport for top achievements shall be carried out by a special administrative unit with MYS as provided in Article 55 of the Implementing Regulations.

112. Pursuant to Article 56 of the Implementing Regulations, the experimental and implementation activity in the field of the physical education and sport shall be carried out by specialized teams formed with the respective institutions and organizations.

XVII. Preparation of Sports Specialists

113. The MYS jointly with the Ministry of Education and Science shall work out and submit for approval the State requirements for training of specialists in the field of physical education and sport. The training and qualification of the sports pedagogical and coach specialists shall be carried out by the higher schools, which provide specialized education in the field of physical education and sport. The Minister of Education and Science, in coordination with the Minister of Youth and Sports, shall submit for approval the number of the sport and pedagogical specialists, whose education in the higher schools shall be financed by the State.

114. MYS shall examine the needs for sport and pedagogical specialists in the field of physical education and sport. For such specialists shall qualify teachers in physical education, coaches in various kinds of sport, sports methodologists and instructors.

115. Obtaining professional qualification and capacity by sport pedagogues, coaches and managing staff shall be carried out only in high schools with specialized education in the sphere of the physical education and sport. The said qualification and capacity may be also obtained by coaches, sport methodologists or instructors with secondary education under the procedure set forth in the Law on Vocational Training and Education and in compliance with the ordinance under Article 6, paragraph 2 of the Law on Physical Education and Sport. The conditions and the procedure for recognizing professional qualification obtained in other countries with the purpose of education, training and management of the physical education and sport shall be carried out in compliance with the domestic legislation.

116. Sports federations shall organize courses and seminars on a regular basis for education, training and qualification improvement of referees, and specialized technical and administrative specialists in various kinds of sports.

XVIII. Sports Ethics

117. Article 41 from Chapter 8 of the Law on Sports as well as the Implementing Regulations provide for certain common obligations of the State, MYS and the sports organizations with respect to sports ethics.

These obligations are set out below:

- protecting and developing moral and ethical bases of sport;
- protecting the sport and the athletes against exploitation for political, commercial and financial interests as well as from harmful and humiliating treatment;
- promoting and supporting sports organizations and persons, who have demonstrated solid ethical principles in their work in the field of sport;

- undertaking suitable public educational measures for popularizing the sport ideals, the principle of fair play, the promotion of the mutual respect between spectators and athletes, as well as for the increase in the number of sport practitioners; and
- taking measures against the acts of violence during sports competitions, the use of doping and all forms of social discrimination.

118. Sports ethics further constitutes a principle, which shall be observed during sports events by the athletes, sports officials, technical and managing persons and spectators.

119. The particular role of MYS with regard to sports ethics amounts to creation of conditions for preservation and development of the moral and ethical bases of sport through performance of certain actions set out in Article 60 of the Implementing Regulations.[18]

120. Article 61, paragraph 1 of the Implementing Regulations provides elaborated rules on the obligations of the sports organizations with regard to sports ethics.[19]

121. All individuals participating in the organization and management of physical education and sport are obliged to comply with the generally accepted ethic rules by providing example through their own daily activity pursuant to Article 61, paragraph 2 of the Implementing Regulations.

XIX. Medical Control

122. Chapter 9 of the Law on Sports contains provision on the medical control in sport. The Minister of Health, in coordination with the Minister of Education and

18. Such actions are: interacting with other State bodies and sports organizations for the purpose of promotion of high ethical norms in all fields of public life related to the physical education and sport; supporting the sports organizations in the latter's activity for promotion of sports ethics and supporting those sports organizations that are laying efforts for combating the doping and violence in sport; providing incentives such as monetary and material awards to athletes and coaches who have proved to have high sporting moral, who observe the principles of the fair play and to whom no penalties in the course of the training and competition activity have been ever imposed; preparing educational programmes for popularization of the ideals and the principles of fair play; supervising the sports organizations in order not to admit use of doping and violence, discrimination based on race or nationality and other forms of humiliating attitude towards persons; organizing information campaigns jointly with other institutions for the purpose of popularizing the principles of fair play and prevention of the spectators' violence and misconduct.
19. These obligations are the following: to work out and popularize unambiguous rules and criteria for ethical conduct and provide suitable incentives; to organize studies with athletes for improvement of their sporting culture and cultivation of spirit of respect to the rival; to create sport and technical as well as material conditions for participation of all athletes in the training and competition activity while observing their needs and personal dignity; to work together with the representatives of the fen clubs for popularizing the sport virtues and to promote mutual respect among the fens of the various clubs or teams; to provide assistance to the specialized State bodies in the latter's efforts to combat the violence at the sport fields; to fight against the use of doping and unfair conduct during the training and competition activity and to impose penalties with respect to the guilty persons.

Science and the Minister of Youth and Sports shall determine the medical rules and requirements for the physical education and the extracurricular sports activity of students.

123. The medical control of the training and competition activities shall be carried out in the sports medical establishments appointed by the Council of Ministers at the proposal of the Minister of Health and the Minister of Youth and Sports, under conditions and by an order determined by the Council of Ministers.

124. Children and students in the general education schools, special schools and higher schools shall be subject, annually, to prophylactic medical examination and assessment of their physical development. Right to participation in regional, State and international competitions shall only be given to athletes who have passed the obligatory medical examinations.

125. The sports organizations cannot use, in their activities, forms and methods leading to damage to the health of the athletes. The use of doping and the applying of doping methods in the training and competition activities shall be prohibited. The Council of Ministers shall determine the conditions and procedure for carrying out doping control during the training and competition activities as well as the prevention and the fight against use of doping in sport. The amateur and professional athletes shall be obliged to meet the requirements for doping control established by acts of State authorities and the recognized international organizations in this field.[20]

126. The organizers of sports competitions and tourist events shall provide medical care for the participants and shall be liable for that. The specialized control bodies of the Ministry of Health and of the Mountain Safety Office with the Bulgarian Red Cross shall stay for sports competitions and tourist events if medical care and mountain rescue are not provided. Not admitted or removed from training and competition shall be the persons who have not passed obligatory medical examination according to a decree of the Minister of Health.

127. More detailed rules on the medical control in sport are provided in the Implementing Regulations. The medical control covers obligatory prophylactic medical examinations of the persons, exercising physical education and sport as well as provision of medical insurance with respect to sports competitions and sport and tourist events. The medical control shall be carried out for the training and competition activities of the athletes, during the classes with physical exercises and sport at schools and in case of organization of out of classes and extracurricular sport activity.

128. The persons exercising physical education and sport shall be subject to obligatory initial, periodical and pre-competition examinations.

129. The purpose of the initial medical examinations is the acknowledgement of the health conditions of the persons, engaged in physical education and sports activities in order to exclude diseases incompatible with their participation in training and competition activity. Each person who has passed such initial medical examination shall receive a medical certificate having certain term of validity.

130. The periodical medical examinations shall be carried out for establishment of the impact of the training and competition activity on the health of the persons dealing with physical education and sport.

20. *See* Part 3, Doping in Sport, *infra*.

131. The pre-competition medical examinations shall be carried out for establishment of the current health condition of the persons signed up for participation in sports competitions. The pre-competition medical examination is clinical and, depending on the results therefrom, permission or prohibition for participation shall be given.

132. The medical insurance at sports competitions and tourist events encompasses designation of medical persons and teams on duty, inspection of the sanitary and hygienic condition of the used sport sites and facilities, checking of the medical documents of the participants in the various competitions and, if needed – provision of medical aid for athletes, officials or spectators.

133. The control for the use of forbidden substances or methods in the training and competition activities is a prerogative of the Anti-doping Centre. Sports federations are obliged to support doping control by watching their member clubs as well as the national teams not to use in their activities substances and methods to the detriment of the health of the athletes.

XX. Licensing of Sports Organizations

134. Sports organizations that are subject to the requirement to obtain a licence, that is, sports federations and national sports organizations, shall meet certain conditions precedent for this purpose.

They must:

- be registered as a not for profit legal person for performing activity for the public benefit with the purpose of organizing and conducting training and competitions in a specific or similar types of sports;
- have an established structure as an association of at least seven sports clubs registered in no less than three administrative regions of the Republic of Bulgaria;
- have adopted rules for holding competitions included in the State sports calendar in the sport or the similar types of sports that will be developed and managed;
- have an adopted development programme in the respective subject area of physical education and sport and social tourism;
- have categorized the sports clubs in its membership according to the criteria set by the Implementing Regulations.

135. The amendments of the Law on Sports in 2010 brought some changes in the regulation of the procedure for licensing of sports organizations. The regulation of the procedure is much more detailed, thanks to the explicit provisions in the matter of granting, renewal, refusal for granting and revocation of the sports licence. The legal characterization of the latter is given below.

136. The content of the sports license is determined in Article 17, paragraph 3 of the Law on Sports. The sports licence is issued for a two-year term by the Minister of Youth and Sports. It includes acknowledgement on the part of the State that the respective sports organization is competent to perform the activities specified in the Law on Sports. The sports license contains permission to the sports organization to perform administrative functions, related to the regulations of the respective type of sport. The sports licence also includes the right of the sports organizations to organize and hold competitions, to register sports results, to award titles and to determine the composition of the national teams. Further, sports license entitles the licensed sport organizations to receive State and municipal aid with respect to the public benefit activities carried out by them. National teams and championships selected and organized by licensed sports organizations are acknowledged by the State exactly by virtue of the sport licence.

137. A sports licence may be issued only to one national sports organization in the respective subject area of physical education, sport and social tourism as already mentioned in Part I, Chapter 1, section 2, VI.

138. Furthermore, a sports licence may be granted only to one sports federation running a particular sport or similar kinds of sports and one multi-sports federation, established in accordance with the respective uniting feature.

139. Applications for issuing sports licences and the documents attached thereto shall be submitted to the Minister of Youth and Sports who is obliged to issue or refuse the issue of a sports licence by a well-motivated order within one month from the submission of the application. The Minister of Youth and Sports shall refuse to issue a sports license when the sports organization does not comply with the requirements of the Law on Sports or has failed to comply with the procedure on the submission of an application and the attached documents; when it engages in sports activities for which another sports organization has been issued a sports licence or when carries out a sport activity which may not be defined as a sport one; when it has not adopted a sports calendar or a budget. The last two juridical facts that lead to refusal for issuing a sports licence are lapsed liabilities of the sports organization to the State and/or the municipalities and the cases of instituted insolvency or liquidation proceedings for sports organizations or when such have been declared insolvent. In case of refusal for issuance of a sports license the respective sports organization may file another application after the expiry of one year following the entrance into force of the order, by virtue of which the issuance of the sports licence has been refused and the removal of the reasons for the refusal.

140. Further, the licensed sports organizations shall be subject to attestation for renewal of the licence once per every four years. The applications for renewal of sports licences and the documents thereto shall be submitted at least two months prior to expiration of the validity of the licence in force. The attestation shall be carried out by a commission appointed by the Minister of Youth and Sports under the following requirements:

(a) For a sports organization which has:

- complied with the rules adopted by it and the applicable laws in organizing and conducting the training and competition activities during the period under assessment;
- held annual State championships in the sport or similar types of sports managed by it;

- achieved a level of public promotion of the respective types of sports measured through a system of sport development indicators: number of athletes by age groups, participants in training and competition activities, coaches, sports experts, sports referees, established sports clubs, arranged competitions, sport achievements and developed network of sport services for the citizens;
- undertaken particular measures for the development of sports for children and adolescents, including for discovering and supporting of sport talents;
- complied with and popularized the humane principles of sports and sports ethics and has taken the necessary measures not to allow the use of doping and violence before, during and after holding sports events.

(b) For a national sports organization which has:

- members of at least two-thirds of the sports clubs and/or sports federations carrying out activities in the respective subject field of the system of physical education, sport and social tourism;
- fulfilled the programme for sport development in the respective subject field of the physical education, sport and social tourism;
- maintained cooperation with the State authorities, municipalities and international sports organizations for protection of the interests of its members and settlement of occurring disputes;
- complied with and popularized the humane principles of sport and sports ethics and has taken the necessary measures not to allow the use of doping and violence before, during and after holding sports events.

141. The Minister of Youth and Sports may refuse to renew a sports license when one or more of the following conditions refer to a sports organization:

- it has not submitted an application for renewal of the sports licence within the set term unless there are justifiable reasons thereof;
- it has not submitted the required documents that should be attached to the application;
- in case one or more of the requirements following the attestation have not been met;
- it has not adopted a sports calendar or a budget;
- it has got overdue liabilities to the State and/or municipalities or such liabilities that derive from the use of sports sites and facilities owned by business companies with fifty and more than 50% of State or municipal share in the capital stock;
- it is undergoing insolvency or liquidation proceedings or has been declared insolvent.

142. Pursuant to Article 17(c) of the Law on Sports, the Minister of Physical Education and Sports is entitled to revoke a sports license if he/she establishes that the sports organization:

- does not observe or violates the requirements of the Law on Sports;

- does not observe or violates the terms and procedures for licensing of sports organizations;
- has not adopted a sports calendar or a budget;
- has got overdue liabilities to the State and/or municipalities, unless extension of the deadline for the payment or deferral of the liabilities have been admitted or such liabilities that derive from the use of sports sites and facilities owned by business companies with fifty and more than 50% of State or municipal share in the capital stock;
- is undergoing insolvency or liquidation proceedings or has been declared insolvent;
- breaches its statute;
- has illegally expended funds extended under the procedure of the Law on Sports;
- has not complied with one or more of the requirements following the attestation.

143. Furthermore, the law describes three juridical facts that lead to an automatic termination of the validity of a sports licence: a written request of the sports organization, termination of the legal entity and expiry of the license validity if it has not been renewed.

144. The Minister of Youth and Sports shall organize the establishment and keep a national registry of the licensed sports organizations and their member sports clubs.

145. The orders by which the sports licences are granted, renewed, refused or revoked shall be subject to appeal through the procedure provided for in the Administrative Procedure Code.[21] A new provision in force as of 9 November 2012 provided that the appeal shall not have suspensive effect with respect to the orders referred to in the previous sentence.

XXI. Sports Sites and Facilities

A. Historical and Legal Background of the Problem with the Use of Sports Facilities in Bulgaria

146. The use of the sports sites and facilities by the sports organizations is currently the hottest and highly debatable issue for all stakeholders in sport in Bulgaria. The condition of the existing sports sites and facilities is very poor and the need for their modernizing is compelling.

147. The collapse of socialism and the numerous changes followed led to separation of the sports clubs from the State and administrative bodies, to which they used to belong, and their registration as non-profit organizations pursuant to the then effective Law on Persons and Family. However, the same did not happen with respect to the ownership over the existing sports sites and facilities, which remained in the domain of the State, although sports clubs continued using them due to the status quo.

148. Prior to the changes in 1989 and the beginning of the transition period to market economy, the property could be owned by the State, cooperatives and other

21. Administrative Procedure Code of 12 Jul. 2006 in the State Gazette issue No. 30 of 11 Apr. 2006.

public organizations (socialist property) as well as by individuals (personal and private property). With the amendments of the Law on Property promulgated in the State Gazette, issue 31 of 17 April 1990, the property could be owned by the State, municipalities and other legal entities and citizens.[22]

149. Upon the enactment of the Law on Local Self-Governance and Local Administration on 17 September 1991, certain properties having been in State ownership up to that moment passed to the municipalities. Such properties include, *inter alia*, the sites of the municipal infrastructure of local importance, designated to serve the administrative needs of the municipalities as well as for health, educational, cultural, commercial, daily, sport and communal services.[23] Under the effect of this provision, the ownership with respect to certain sports sites and facilities of local importance was transformed from State into municipal.

150. For the period between 1990 and 1996, the State and the municipalities were entitled to transfer or lease their property to legal entities and citizens.[24] This way, sports clubs being non-profit organizations under the then effective Law on Persons and Family could avail of this legal ground in order to continue using the stadiums, on which they were playing their host matches.

151. By the enactment of the special Law on the State Property and the Law on the Municipal Property in 1996, the demarcations between public State and private State property, on the one hand, and between public municipal and private municipal property, on the other hand, were introduced.[25]

152. Public State property are, *inter alia*, properties designated as such by virtue of the law or by an Act of the Council of Ministers properties, conceded to the administrative bodies for exercising their functions as well as properties of national importance, designated for regular meeting of public needs of national significance through common use and determined by the Council of Ministers.[26] All other properties that do not qualify as public State property under the categorization made with the Law on the State Property shall be considered to be private State property pursuant to Article 2, paragraph 3 thereof. The main implication of the demarcation of the State property is the ban stated in Article 7, paragraph 1 of the Law on the State Property for the public State property to be subject to sale and other acts of disposal or to acquisition by way of adverse possession.

153. Public municipal properties under Article 3, paragraph 2 of the Law on the Municipal Property are:

– designated as public municipal property by virtue of the law;

22. Article 2 of the Law on Property of 16 Nov. 1951 in the State Gazette, issue No. 92 of 16 Nov. 1951.
23. *See* §7, point 6 of the Law on the Local Self-Governance and Local Administration of 17 Sep. 1991 in the State Gazette, issue No. 77 of 17 Sep. 1991.
24. Article 7 of the Law on Property in its version as of 1990, issue No. 31 of the State Gazette.
25. Article 2, para. 1 of the Law on the State Property of 21 May 1996 in the State Gazette, issue No. 44 of 21 May 1996 and Art. 3, para. 1 of the Law on the Municipal Property of 21 May 1996 in the State Gazette, issue No. 44 of 21 May 1996.
26. Article 2, para. 2 of the Law on the State Property; the other cases are not mentioned because sport sites and facilities cannot fall within these categories of public State properties.

- designated for the performance of the functions of the bodies of the local self-governance and the local administration; or
- designated by the Municipal Council aiming at the permanent meeting of the public needs of local significance.

154. Consequently, all other municipal properties shall be considered private municipal property.

155. The implications of the division between the two forms of municipal properties are similar to the ones in the case of State property. Article 7 of the Law on the Municipal Property clarifies further that public municipal property shall not be alienated and encumbered as in the latter case an exception could be provided only by virtue of the law.

156. The Law on Sports entered into force in 1996 delegated to the Council of Minister the power to designate the sports sites of national significance (in 2000, this power was clarified as the power to determine the status of the sports sites of national significance). The amendment of the Law on Sports in 2008 revoked this power of the Council of Ministers and implemented explicit criteria which the sports sites and facilities shall meet in order to be given the status of national significance. The sports sites and facilities must:

- be intended for training and educational activities and used by sports federations for developing sport for top achievements;
- meet the conditions for holding of national and international sports competitions; and
- meet the internationally established requirements for the different types of sports.

157. The sports sites and facilities of national significance and those for social tourism of national significance are specified in the Attachments of the Law on Sports. The latter may be amended by the National Assembly upon a proposal of the Council of Ministers. The prohibitive norm of Article 47(a), paragraph 4 of the Law on Sports forbids such sites and facilities to be provided for use through concessions. The sports sites and facilities having national significance have been defined in the last version of Article 47a of the Law on Sports in 2011 as such being in ownership of the State, the municipalities or commercial companies, in which the State or a municipality is the sole owner of the registered capital and which serve for permanent satisfaction of common national needs in the field of physical education and sport as well as meet at least one of the following requirements:

- they are designated for education and training activity and are used by sports federations for development of sport for high sporting proficiency;
- they meet the conditions for organization of national and international sports competitions;
- they meet the internationally specified requirements for the various types of sport.

Likewise, the sites and facilities for social tourism of national significance have been defined as such in State or municipal ownership or in ownership of commercial companies, in which the sole owner of the registered capital is the State or a municipality, which serve for permanent satisfaction of common national needs in the field of the social tourism. The sports sites and facilities in public State ownership provided for use to the National Sports Academy 'Vassil Levski' are also considered to be of national significance.

158. The Law on Sports empowers the Council of Ministers to designate the sports sites and facilities or individual parts thereof granted to the State bodies for performance of their functions in the field of physical education, sport and social tourism and, therefore, being in public State ownership pursuant to the Law on the State Property as referred above. Also, the Council of Ministers is entitled to designate those sports sites, which subject to coordination with the respective municipal councils shall become ownership of the municipalities.

B. Number of Sports Sites and Facilities

159. Pursuant to the analysis of sport in Bulgaria stated in the National Programme for Development of Physical Education and Sport in the period 2013–2016, the total number of the registered sports sites and facilities for social tourism as of 2010 is 3,096; and 90% of the registered sites are managed by the respective municipalities, 7% are in state ownership and 3% in private ownership. Further, according to the list specified in the Attachment No. 1 of the Law on Sports the number of the sports sites of national significance is nineteen. It has to be mentioned that the MYS is obliged to keep a public register of the sports sites and the social tourism sites. The register has informative functions and provides options for search of the information contained therein by typing the name of the site, its location, the type of the site or the facility, the municipality, and the sport, for which it is used. Pursuant to Article 97 of the Implementing Regulations, the public register shall consist of documents on paper and a computer database. The latter is already accessible online through the website of MYS.

C. Providing for Use of Sports Sites and Facilities

160. Pursuant to Article 50 of the Law on Sports the sports sites and facilities owned by the State and the municipalities in Bulgaria shall be used for meeting the needs for physical education and sport and the auxiliary and servicing activities related thereto. In addition, such sites and facilities shall be used for the training and competition activity of the sports organizations and the sports schools, by students from the National Sports Academy 'Vassil Levski', by the national teams in the various types of sport, for school, out of school and students' sport, for sport in the armed forces, in the National Security Service and in the Ministry of Inferior, for sport for all and for sport for disabled people. The State and the municipalities are obliged to provide, free of charge, entirely or partially, for certain period of time, sports and tourist sites and facilities to the institutions within the system of the pre-school and school education and to the high schools for realization of activities related to physical education, sport, and tourism as well as for training and competition activity of primary, secondary, and high school students, under conditions and following a procedure determined by the respective bodies. The sports sites and facilities owned by the State, the municipalities and the schools shall be used also by the primary, secondary, and high students' sports clubs for implementation of the programmes for development of physical education, sport, leisure, and tourism of such students. The municipal councils are responsible for specifying the procedure, under which the sports sites and facilities in municipal ownership shall be used by citizens for reaching the objectives of the physical education and sport.

161. Article 51 of the Law on Sports contains some conditions and limitations with respect to the sports organizations and other legal entities, to which such State and municipal sorts sites and facilities might be provided for use as we as regarding the way of their use. Such sports organizations and legal entities are obliged to use such sites and facilities in accordance with their designation and in the view of the needs, for which they have been provided for. Organizations, which have used preferences from the State or the municipalities for the construction of sport sites and facilities, are obliged to coordinate in advance the designs for their construction with the respective State and municipal bodies and are not allowed to use them for purpose other than their designation. Only by way of exception, State and municipal sports sites and facilities may be used for cultural and other needs and events of public interest, under conditions and procedure, specified by the respective department and municipal council, if such use is not harmful to the general sports activity, and the said sports sites and facilities would not be damaged. The provision of State and municipal sports sites and facilities for gratuitous use to legal entities and individuals, performing economic activity, is strictly forbidden under the Law on Sports. Units of State and municipal sports sites and facilities designated for servicing and auxiliary activities may be provided against payment to legal entities and individuals for organizing the infrastructure for servicing sports activities, with the exception of the advertising rights over them, only in cases where no obstacles occur for their use according to their main designation.

162. The Law on Sports, further in its Chapter X titled Sports Sites and Facilities, deals with certain specific forms of providing for use of such sites and facilities – lease, concession, and Public Private Partnership (PPP). All these forms together with the option for providing of gratuitous right of construction will be discussed below in historical context. This approach is needed because none of the above forms of use existed at the time of the enactment of the Law on Sport and they were gradually included therein throughout the years as a result from particular problems and developments. That is why also examples of particular sports sites and facilities will be used.

D. *Lease of Sports Sites*

163. The Law on the State Property in its initial version as of 1996 prohibited the sites in public State ownership from being subject to lease agreements. This provision questioned the legal ground for the use of the sports facilities, which were registered as public State property but used by sports clubs exactly on the ground of lease agreements. This was the case with the stadium Bulgarian Army used by the FC CSKA Sofia. An exception from this rule was inserted in 1998 stipulating that in exceptional cases public State properties as well as parts thereof may be subject to lease agreements for a period not exceeding three years, provided that they are used in accordance with their designation and the exercise of the activities, for which they are granted, is not disturbed. Said lease period was extended twice – to five years in 2005 and to ten years in 2009.

164. The stadium Bulgarian Army was leased to FC CSKA Sofia in 2005 exactly for a period of five years according to the information provided by club's officials. The management of the stadium as public State property was granted to the Ministry of Defence, which had the capacity of a lessor under the agreement. The lease agreement expired in 2010.

165. Pursuant to the Law on the State Property, the procedure for the lease in such exceptional cases is to follow the one set with respect to the private State properties, that is, by way of a public tender. This reference was provided for with the amendments in 2005 along with the extension of the lease period to five years. Although the reported period of the lease under the lease agreement between the Ministry of Defence and FC CSKA Sofia was five years, that is, in line with the amendments in 2005, it is highly unlikely that such a tender had been organized.

166. The lease of sports sites had to follow the procedure set by Article 74 of the Implementing Regulations which provides for two methods for designation of the lessee – direct (available only for licensed sports organizations or sports clubs members thereof) or through competition. Pursuant to Article 50(a) of the Law on Sports, the sports sites and facilities which are public State and public municipal property (except those which have the status of national significance) may be leased under the terms of the Law on the State Property and the Law on the Municipal Property only to non-profit legal entities for performing activities for the public benefit, the main activity of which shall correspond to the purpose of use of the property. The private State and municipal properties, on the other hand, may be leased only to sports clubs, sports federations and national sports organizations. The lease period for the sports sites and facilities in public and private ownership is maximum ten years.

167. The properties listed above may be provided to licensed sports organizations by the heads of institutions, regional governors or municipal councils upon coordination with the Minister of Physical Education and Sports following the procedure set in the Implementing Regulations.

168. The situation with the use of the stadium 'Georgi Asparouhov' by the other big Bulgarian FC Levski Sofia also deserves a special note due to the fact that it reveals other elements and nuances, which were not present in the case of CSKA. Apart from the total mess caused by the existence of two deeds of ownership attributing the ownership simultaneously to the State (the Ministry of Interior was in charge for managing the stadium) and to the Sofia Municipality, it is currently accepted that stadium 'Georgi Asparouhov' is private and not public State ownership. This status of the stadium entails also a different regime for its lease.

169. In general, the main and most important implication of the status of private State property is the possibility for such property to be subject to sale and other acts of disposal as well as to acquisition by way of adverse possession. In the particular case of sports facilities, this means that such stadiums may be sold or contributed in-kind to the registered capital of the respective sports club, provided that the latter is registered under the form of a company limited by shares. The option for acquisition by way of adverse possession is inapplicable for sports clubs as far as they all have the capacity of lessees and neither own, nor even pretend to own their stadiums.

170. The specificity of the case with the 'Georgi Asparouhov' stadium is the indication placed on the Deed of State Ownership, issued on the ground of the Decree on the State Property of 1975, that the use and the operational management of the stadium was granted to FC Levski Sofia for an indefinite period of time and free of charge.[27] This status quo was to be addressed by paragraph 6 of the Transitional Provisions of the Law on the State Property providing for reduction of such right of use to ten years, which is the maximum period under the new law. However, the Constitutional Court proclaimed the anti-constitutionality of said provision,[28] which provided the ground for the officials of FC Levski Sofia to conclude that the club's right of use for an indefinite period of time and free of charge has continued to exist. This way, according to the representatives of FC Levski Sofia, the club has not paid anything for the use of the stadium, unlike FC CSKA Sofia, which reported the amount of Bulgarian Lev (BGN) 25,000 per month payable as a rent for the use of the Bulgarian Army stadium.

171. Nonetheless, the lack of any ownership rights of the already private sports clubs with respect to their stadiums and, furthermore, the unclear rules for their use including the duration of such a use seriously affected the incentive of the sports clubs' owners to invest in modernizing sports sites and facilities. This caused a long lasting deadlock, which was still present at the time of writing this monograph. In result, the single refurbishment of the stadiums for all these post-socialist years was the change of the old metal seats with new plastic ones in accordance with the Union of European Football Associations (UEFA) requirements and under the threat for prohibiting the clubs using stadiums with metal seats from playing their home matches from the UEFA tournaments there. In fact, only four of the club stadiums in Bulgaria have licences for playing home matches from the UEFA tournaments at the time of writing. The last more significant repairs of stadiums were carried out by PSFC Chernomoretz and by PFC Litex. These two clubs invested in their home stadiums by changing the turf and the seats, constructing and reconstructing of the grandstands, etc. The home stadium of FC CSKA Bulgarian Army is also currently under repairs; the 'Georgi Asparouhov' stadium, on the other hand, underwent small repairs in 2010.

27. This information is provided by the officials of FC Levski Sofia and cited by the media. The authors have not been able to verify the information by independent check of said Deed of State Ownership.

28. Decision of the Constitutional Court of the Republic of Bulgaria No. 7 of 10 Apr. 2001 under constitutional file No. 1 of 2001. The Court found contradiction with the provisions of the Constitution concerning the immunity of the private property (the Constitution envisages compulsory alienation of property including both ownership and right of use but only after observance of certain cumulatively present conditions precedent), the protection of free entrepreneurship and economic investments of the Bulgarian and foreign citizens and legal entities, the guaranteeing of equal opportunities for economic activity for all citizens and legal entities and the principles of the lawful State.

E. Initial Attempts for Overcoming the Deadlock

172. The strategy employed by FC CSKA Sofia for the purpose of overcoming the deadlock included convincing the Ministry of Defence (and then SAYS[29] to which the management of the stadium was ultimately transferred) to initiate the deregistration of the stadium Bulgarian Army as public State ownership, to transform it to private State ownership and then contribute it under the form of in-kind contribution to the registered capital of the club being a company limited by shares against acquisition of the respective shares corresponding to the amount of the contribution. In consideration of this contribution, the president of CSKA Sofia at that time promised to invest in a new modern stadium the amount of BGN 120 million.

173. This scenario was completely possible under the then effective law. The transformation of the property from public State to private State property could occur pursuant to decision of the Council of Ministers upon proposal of the respective minister headed the ministry, under which umbrella the particular property has happened to be. The Council of Ministers is also entitled to set forth the procedure for transactions with private State sports properties.

174. However, this scheme invoked many objections due to the effect of 'hidden' privatization caused by the circumvention of the Privatization Agency that was considered as an abusive practice. The financial losses for the State inflicted by such schemes were also raised as an argument against the in-kind contribution of the Bulgarian Army stadium. Although similar schemes had already taken place in the Bulgarian economic life at that time, the public discontent towards them in combination with the attractiveness of the stadium and its position in the spotlight of the public attention forced the government to be extremely cautious and, ultimately, to refuse to make the contemplated contribution.

175. The disposal of sports sites and facilities – private State and municipal property shall be carried out by the heads of the respective administrative bodies or by the regional governors. The disposal is such juridical Act with which one real right is transferred, altered, restricted or terminated.[30] Pursuant to Article 70 of the Implementing Regulations, the disposal is set as an exception and may be carried out only when the sites have not been used in accordance with their purpose for a period longer than three years. The regional governors shall dispose with the sports sites which are real estate upon written consent of the Minister of Regional Development and Public Works. The heads of the respective administrative bodies are entitled to dispose with the sports sites and facilities that are personal estate. In all cases of disposal, there has to be an advanced coordination in written form with the Minister of Physical Education and Sports. Further, a statement by the respective sports federation is required for those sports sites and facilities that are used for holding of State championships of a definite type of sport. Opinions have been already expressed that instead of explicit prohibition concerning such sports sites, it would be better for all sports sites and facilities to be

29. Since 2009 SAYS has been abolished and replaced by the MPES, which was renamed to MYS in 2013.
30. Decision No. 91 of 1 Oct. 1974 of the Supreme Court of Cassations under civil case No. 63 of 1974.

registered as public State property and public municipal property, respectively, which automatically would entail the same prohibition.

176. Another argument, which happened to be against the interests of FC CSKA Sofia, was the need for balancing also the interests of the members of the Bulgarian Army, who used the sports facilities under the umbrella of the Ministry of Defence for training and preparation as well as the interests of other sports (for instance, the stadium comprises also a track for running and generally provides conditions for light athletics and other sports).

177. The failure to provide the conditions precedent for the investment plans of the president of CSKA Sofia, allegedly caused his withdrawal of the presidency and the purchase of the club by the Company Global Steel owned by the Indian businessman Pramod Mital in December 2006. The attempts of the new president to transform the stadium into private State ownership also did not meet with success.

178. The position of the representatives of FC Levski Sofia to the problem with the sports facilities was naturally influenced by the peculiar unlimited-term and gratuitous right of use with respect to the Georgi Asparouhov stadium, which status they wanted to maintain and further to have it confirmed by the new piece of legislation in the field of sport. During the discussions about the then draft for amendment of the Law on Sports FC Levski Sofia officials suggested the insertion of a provision entitling FCs having a right of use as of 1996 based on a legal ground, having continued to exercise said right at the time of the amendment and having invested in such facilities to be granted a gratuitous right of use for the period of thirty-five years. The insertion was allegedly justified with the need for compliance of the future law with the decision of the Constitutional Court and the need for legalization of the existing status quo.

179. However, the proposal of FC Levski Sofia representatives encountered a serious opposition due to reasons such as the conflict with the rule already laid down in the Law on Sports that sports companies, registered pursuant to the Law on Commerce, that is, all big FCs are not entitled to use sports facilities without payment as well as some other reasons such as the need for the use of the stadiums for sport for all and also for sports other than football. The attempts of the FC Levski Sofia to contest the aforementioned rule, claiming that the registration of FCs as commercial companies was at a time a single legal organization form provided for in the law, which was naturally retained despite the later introduced alternative for their registration as non-profit organizations, were not successful and, ultimately, the proposal was not included in the final draft submitted for the discussions in the Parliament.

180. In 2008, a new provision 50a of the Law on Sports was inserted[31] allowing the lease of the sports sites and facilities, which are public State and public municipal property, except the ones included in the respective lists of the sports sites and facilities as well as social sites of national significance, only to non-profit legal entities for performance of activity in public benefit, which main activity coincides with the designation of the property. In addition, such lease shall comply with the terms and conditions set in the Law on State Property and the Law on Municipal Property, respectively. This meant that given sites and facilities in public state ownership could be leased following a tender for a period of up to ten years provided that they would

31. Amendment of the Law on Physical Education and Sport in the State Gazette issue No. 50 of 30 May 2008.

be used in accordance with their designation and the activities, for which such sites and facilities have been granted, would not be disturbed. The lease contract is concluded on the basis of the results from the tender. The terms and conditions for the lease of public municipality properties were analogical whereas the decision for starting the procedure for lease would be taken by the respective municipal council, which is also the body to determine the lease fees. Also, in the case of municipal State property a competition could be conducted as the second alternative option to the tender.

181. By way of the same amendment in 2008, the lease option was introduced also with respect to the sports sites and facilities, which are private State and private municipal property. The terms and conditions for the lease were identical to the ones applicable to the public State and public municipal properties, however, the potential lessees could be only sports federations, national sports organizations and sports clubs as defined in the Law on Sports.

182. Pursuant to the third paragraph of Article 50a of the Law on Sports all sports sites and facilities, notwithstanding their particular title of ownership, may be leased to licensed sports organizations by the head of departments, the regional governors or the municipal councils after coordination with the Minister of Youth and Sport and following the procedure specified in the Implementing Regulations. It should be noted that the aforementioned paragraph uses the term 'licensed sports organizations', which is narrower in comparison to 'non-profit legal entities for performance of activity in public benefit' as referred to in paragraph one of the same article dealing with the sports sites and facilities in public State or municipal ownership. However, the contradiction is only ostensible because the third paragraph of Article 50a only indicates that the cases of lease of sports sites and facilities to licensed sports organization should be dealt with under the procedure specified in the Implementing Regulations. The main difference between the said procedure and the procedures provided in the Law on the State Property and the Law on the Municipal Property, respectively, is the possibility for lease of sports sites and facilities via direct contracting or via competition. This means that the procedure provided in the Implementing Regulations is only applicable to the licensed sports organizations. Other non-profit legal entities for performance of activity in public benefit such as, for example, non-profit legal entities constituting associations of sports clubs running different kinds of sport, may apply under the procedures in the respective property laws. The option for establishment of such associations is expressly provided in Article 11, paragraph 3 of the Law on Sports.

183. In case two or more applications have been submitted, priority shall have the candidate which is a licensed sports organization and develops the sport, for which the property is intended. Under other equal conditions priority shall have the applicant, which has proposed a financially secured investment programme of a higher value for maintenance and improvement of the property and has fulfilled correctly its obligations under preceding contracts for its use. The public contribution of the candidate to sports shall be assessed in the course of evaluation. When a sports facility is a multifunctional one, the terms for using the facility, parts thereof and/or of facilities from other sports organization carrying out sports activities therein, shall be determined in the lease contract.

184. In 2009, FC CSKA was sold to the private limited company 'Titan Sport'. The new management paid up the liabilities of the club to MYS. In an interview in the press at that time, the president of CSKA Sofia expressed the club's will to apply for the procedure for lease of the stadium. However, the proven impracticability of the lease formula for the development and modernization of the sports sites and facilities in Bulgaria necessitated the finding of a better legal form for their use and management.

F. *Concessions of Sports Sites*

185. The highly recommended form in all cases where the State or the municipalities are not capable of effectively managing their property is privatization. However, in the field of sport due to the latter's specificity privatization is not the panacea, which it might be in other sectors of the economy. Despite its commercial aspects and possibilities to be organized as a business, sport has further social, recreational and health protection functions, which are essential for the society and could not be left to depend solely on the constantly fluctuating economic and business circumstances. Sport is not so economically sound in comparison to other sectors of the economy and potential shift to other businesses for the businessmen engaged in sport is very likely. This fact caused the concerns of State officials that the designation of the sports sites and facilities would be changed immediately after their potential privatization and, therefore, the State must not lose the ownership.

186. The exclusion of the two turned out to be marginal forms for dealing with the problem – privatization and retention of the central management of the sport sites and facilities by the State normally led to discussions of the possibilities for establishment of public-private partnerships and decentralization through the increase of the role of the municipalities in the development of sport. And also normally the discussions focused on the single form of public-private partnership regulated in details by the Bulgarian legislation at that time – the concession.

187. Article 16(a) of the Law on the State Property provided for the option certain objects of public interest within the meaning of the Law on Concessions[32] to be granted to third parties through concession. This option also amounted to exception of the general rule for the prohibition of granting public State property to third parties similarly to the lease option. This provision of the Law on the State Property was revoked in 2013 upon the coming into force of the Law on PPP.[33] Pursuant to Article 5 of the said law lands, buildings, facilities, movable assets as well as industrial property rights which are owned by the state and designated for sport may serve as objects of public-private partnerships as far as services of public interest are provided through the maintenance of such sites. However, it must be noted that one of the mandatory conditions precedent for establishment of public-private partnership set in Article 3, paragraph 2, section 2 of the said law requires that the assignment of the activity of public interest could NOT be realized through concession because there are no revenues from the customers of the service of public interest or from other third persons in relation with the activity of public interest and if there are such revenues it is not envisaged that the private partner will have rights over them. Upon the coming into force of the Law on PPP in the very beginning of 2013, Article 50b of the Law on Sports was actually replaced by a new provision saying that the financing as well as

32. Law on Concessions of 2 May 2006 in the State Gazette issue No. 36 of 2 May 2006.
33. Law on PPP of 1 Jan. 2013 in the State Gazette issue No. 45 of 15 Jun. 2015.

the construction and/or the management and/or the maintenance of sports sites and facilities and such for social tourism in state or municipal ownership or in ownership of public law organizations may be carried out via PPP under the terms and conditions and following the procedure under the newly at that time enacted Law on PPP.

188. Concession is defined in Article 2, paragraph 1 of the Law on Concessions as a right of exploitation over object and/or a service of public interest, granted by concedent to equity commercial company – concessionaire, against the obligation of the concessionaire to construct and/or manage and maintain the object of the concession at own risk. The Law on Concessions distinguishes three forms of concessions according to their subject – concession for construction, concession for extraction and concession for service. Only the latter is relevant for those sports facilities, which have been already built and need renovation, that is, for all currently existing sports sites and facilities in Bulgaria.

189. The concession for service comprises management of the object of the concession. Pursuant to Article 4 of the Law on Concessions, the concession fee is consisted of the right of the concessionaire to exploit the object of the concession or of said right plus compensation payable by the concedent for covering part of the costs. The concession for service may also include performance of partial construction and mounting works in the cases when there is need for accomplishment of pending construction or partial expanding, partial reconstruction, partial rehabilitation or repair of the subject of the concession, which might be the case with a sports facility.

190. As of 1 July 2006, the Law on Sports provides the options for concessions of the sports sites and facilities in public State or public municipal ownership to natural and legal persons under the procedure set in the Law on Concessions. Pursuant to Article 50(c) of the Law on Sports, sports sites and facilities in State or municipal ownership or owned by governmental organizations may be granted under concession for construction and/or concession for service. The conditions for public access and use of the site and its facilities shall be specified with the decision for opening the procedure for granting concession. In the contract for granting concession, the obligations of the concessionaire for fulfilment of the conditions for public access and use of the site and its facilities as well as the consequences from their breach shall be indicated including the contract termination.

191. The Law on Sports used to settle a specific advantage for the sports organizations that develop the particular sport for which the sports facility is mainly intended. Such organizations had priority when the applicants for concession were more than one and had submitted equivalent financial offers. However, with the most recent amendments, this advantage was abolished.

192. It shall be noted that the option for concession with respect to sports sites and facilities under the Law on Sports at first was available only for those in public ownership either State or municipal. At the same time, the Law on Concessions made the provision that private State and private municipal properties used for economic activity may be also subject to concessions. The amendment of the Law on Sports in 2008 implemented the generic term 'state or municipal ownership', thus overcoming the contradiction and including the option for sports sites and facilities in private State or municipal ownership to be subject to concessions.

193. One of the main reasons for the initial reluctance of all sports clubs to commence the procedure for receiving the stadiums under concession agreement is the very long and complicated procedure provided for in the Law on Concessions including performance of preparatory activities, implementation of the procedure for granting the concession (adoption of decision for opening the procedure, conducting open procedure, limited procedure or competition dialogue for granting the concession, determining the concessionaire) and conclusion of the concession agreement.

194. FC CSKA was the first sports club, which in April 2007 officially announced its interest in receiving concession with respect to the sports sites and facilities currently used by the club including the Bulgarian Army stadium. At that time, pursuant to Article 11, paragraph 1 of the Law on Concessions, the object of the concession could also include the adjacent infrastructure and belongings, existing or which will be constructed by the concessionaire. In 2012, the wording of that article was entirely changed. However, a new provision of Article 13, paragraph 3 was inserted saying that the object of concession may include one or more belongings, existing or which will be constructed by the concessionaire.

195. FC CSKA further expressed its willingness to commence and go through all the stages of the respective procedure. The envisaged term of validity of the concession agreement was thirty years as the maximum period set in Article 10, paragraph 1 of the Law on Concessions for granting concession is thirty-five years. The club prepared investment plan envisaging very serious amount of investments. In 2010, the new at that time owners of the club also expressed the club's willingness to build a modern stadium by investing BGN 100 million only if the club was granted concession. On 27 March 2012, the long-waited contract for granting concession was officially announced to have been signed between FC CSKA and the MYS. The term of the concession as reported on the media was twenty years. Unfortunately, the concession obtained did not lead to any improvements of the stadium, and its terrible condition caused the loss of the licence even for playing matches from the domestic championship, and FC CSKA was forced to host its home matches at other stadiums. In July 2013, the club again encountered change in the ownership and in October the process for urgent repairs of the stadium was resumed. The new owner of the club stated publicly that the contract for concession signed in the beginning of 2012 was totally disadvantageous for the club, that it should be terminated and, instead, the state let the stadium to FC CSKA gratuitously similarly to the situation with FC Levski Sofia. The example of FC CSKA Sofia as the first and the single FC which used the concession formula for the renovation and development of the sports sites and facilities in Bulgaria is, therefore, negative.

G. *Gratuitous Right of Construction*

196. The amendment of the Law on Sports in 2010 implemented a new option for development of the sports sites and facilities in Bulgaria – creating of gratuitous right of construction (gratuitous superficies). The right of construction is a limited real right which provides the opportunity for the owner of the land to cede to another person the right to construct a building on his/her land, whereby the other person becomes owner of the building. Further, the owner of the land may also transfer independently from the land the ownership of an already existing building. The general provisions of this right are laid down by the Law on the Ownership. The specific procedure for constituting a right of construction on a real estate that is in private State ownership is set by the Law on the State Property and respectively for those in private municipal ownership – by the Law on the Municipal Property.

197. Pursuant to the specific norm of Article 50(d) of the Law on Sports a gratuitous right of construction may be established in favour of sports federations for the purpose of constructing of sports sites and/or facilities. Said real right may be established on a real estate – public and private State or municipal property, except for those determined as exclusive State property. Superficies shall be granted for a period of up to thirty years.

198. Sports federations have to meet the requirements set in paragraph 2 of the same article in order to be granted the gratuitous right of construction. They must:

- have been licensed under the procedure of the Law on Sports and have operated at least four years;
- not be undergoing insolvency or liquidation proceedings;
- have no lapsed liabilities to the State or the municipalities unless they have been rescheduled or postponed;
- have no lapsed liabilities that derive from the use of sports sites and/or facilities owned by business companies with fifty and more than 50% of State or municipal share in the capital stock;
- have provided financing or financially secure investment programme for constructing the sports site and/or facilities as well as for their maintenance and management during the period for which the superficies is granted; and
- have presented a preliminary design for construction of the sports site and/or facility.

199. The applications for establishment of gratuitous right of construction shall be submitted to the Minister of Youth and Sports and shall be announced in one daily newspaper and also on the webpage of MYS within seven days from their receipt. The superficies on real estate – private or public State property, is established by the regional governor at the location of the real estate on a basis of a decision of the Council of Ministers. The Minister of Youth and Sports shall prepare a motivated report in that matter. On the other hand, the right of construction on property in private or public municipal ownership shall be instituted by the mayor of the municipality without public tender or a competition after a decision of the municipal council and submitted opinion of the Minister of Youth and Sports.

200. The sports federation that is granted the right of construction undertakes to construct and start exploitation of the sports site and/or facility for a term of up to five years, considering the date of which the contract came into force. The expenses related to the planning, designing, constructing and starting exploitation of the sports sites and facilities shall be taken over by the respective federation. There is an explicit prohibition for the sports federations to cede the right of construction to third persons as well as to dispose with the constructed sports site or facility. Further, the superficies cannot be used as collateral for securing obligations of the sports federation or third parties.

201. The Law on Sports sets three juridical facts that lead to termination of the right of construction before the expiry of the contract. The right is terminated by the regional governor or by the mayor of the municipality on a basis of a decision of the Council of Ministers or the municipal council when:

- the Minister of Youth and Sports has revoked or refused to renew the sports licence of the sports federation;
- the sports federation have violated the provisions of the Law on Sports or the terms of the contract for creating of superficies; or
- the construction has not started for three years after creating of the right of construction or when the sports site and/or facility has not been finished for five years.

202. In such cases, the expenses related to the acquisition of the ownership by the State or the municipality shall be taken over by the sports federation.

203. The gratuitous right of construction implemented by the 2010 amendment of the Law on Sports is a clear attempt for stimulating of the construction of brand new sports sites and facilities in Bulgaria.

204. Although it is too early to make comments on the realization of this formula, it should be noted that it would hardly solve the problem with the ruining stadia. In order to achieve effective results, the members of the sports federations have to be united and there have to be consistent policy and clear financial strategy. The systematic interpretation of Article 50(d) of the Law on Sports and the relative provisions of the Implementing Regulations draws the conclusion that the right of construction of sports sites and facilities comprises only the legal possibility for the owner to cede to another person the right to construct a building on his/her land, whereby the other person becomes owner of the building. The legal possibility set in Article 63, paragraph 2 of the Law for the Ownership for the owner of the land to transfer the ownership of an already existing building independently from the land, thus remaining owner of the land, is excluded. This means that the ownership of already existing sports sites and facilities – State or municipal property, may not be transferred to sports federations.

205. Furthermore, it turns out that the sports federation is a fictive owner of the sports site and/or facility because of the explicit prohibition to dispose with the constructed sports sites and facilities. Although the right of construction is ceded gratuitously by the owner of the real estate, which in this case is the State or the municipality, all the expenses related to the constructing of the sports sites and facilities are taken by the sports federations. It also should be mentioned that by virtue of Article 58, paragraph 5 of the Law on the State Property and Article 37, paragraph 3 of the Law on the Municipal Property when the constituted right of construction is of a definite term, upon expiration of the term of constitution the constructed site shall be transferred gratuitously as property of the State or the municipality. This legal base will give the sports federations plenty to think about: will they risk investing in something they really will not have the chance to own in the future? Will there be any retrieval of the investments?

H. Latest Developments

1. The Situation with CSKA Sofia and the Use of the Bulgarian Army Stadium

206. Although PFC CSKA Sofia finished the first half of the 2014/2015 season as a leader in the Bulgarian A group, the financial problems, which were unresolved for years, was paving the way to the inevitable financial collapse of the club. In the spring of 2015, the club's shares were acquired by two of the CSKA main creditors, to whom they were pledged. The creditors were not willing to invest in the club and cover its debts so the shares were transferred to a company, allegedly formed by and representing the club's fans. The idea was that the fans should find investors and save their club. However, this turned out to be the mission impossible and the club failed to cover the licensing criteria and had to start the next 2015/2016 season from the highest amateur division – the so-called C group of the domestic championship. At the same time also a procedure for declaring the club's insolvency was opened with the Sofia City Court and a court appointed trustee took the management of the club together with its executive director. Under the applicable chapter of the Law on Commerce there was an option (after the preparation of the list with all creditors having debts admitted by the trustee) that reorganization plans would be submitted by interested parties aiming the gradual repayment of the debts and the club's full recovery. During the court proceedings CSKA continued competing in the C group and using the Bulgarian Army stadium on the ground of the effective agreement with the MYS. It was remarkable that even from the C group CSKA managed to create a true miracle and won the Cup of Bulgaria in 2016 after defeating two clubs from the A group at the semi final and the final. However, in July 2016 the MYS terminated the agreement with CSKA for the use of its home stadium due to the club's failure to perform it under the precise terms and the conditions thereof. The termination of the agreement made all attempts for the recovery of the club doomed and the two reorganizational plans submitted to the Sofia City Court within the insolvency proceedings remained without any further consideration. This way, the club was left with no hope for survival. CSKA was not able to form a team for the next 2016/2017 season and, in practice, seized to exist as a FC only waiting for the final declaration of the insolvency, the public sale of its assets and its official deregistration.

207. In the summer of 2016, in parallel with the above-described events, the club Chavdar from the town of Etropole, which was developing mainly youth football via its well-known youth academy in Bulgaria, changed its name from Chavdar to CSKA 1948. Then, the renamed club (which as a legal form was a joint stock company) acquired the shares of the famous Bulgarian FC Litex Lovech – four times champion and four times holder of the Cup of Bulgaria in its history and, also, having good results in the European tournaments especially in the first decade of this century such as 1/16 finals for the UEFA Cup in 2001 and 2006. At the time of the acquisition, Litex Lovech was bearing its sanction imposed by the Bulgarian Football Union (BFU) being exclusion from the A group due to intentionally leaving the pitch during its match with Levski Sofia and was supposed to start the next championship in the B group. Litex was similarly renamed to CSKA-Sofia and changed its seat and address of the management from the town of Lovech to the address of the Bulgarian Army Stadium in Sofia. In the summer of 2016, a reform in the structure of the Bulgarian championship was made and a new First Professional League was established. The participation in the new league was not made subject to sport merits but rather dependant on financial, infrastructural and administrative criteria. This way, the new club CSKA-Sofia (former Litex Lovech) was allowed to apply for participation in the newly formed league. Before the official start of the 2016/2017 season the BFU officially announced the right of the renamed club to participate in the First Professional League claiming that all legal and other conditions were duly met. After the termination of the agreement between the authentic CSKA and the MYS the use of the Bulgarian Army stadium was temporarily provided to the renamed Litex Lovech pending the organization of a tender.

208. In the very beginning of 2017, the Council of Ministers changed the type of ownership of the Bulgarian Army stadium from public state into private state and contributed it to the registered capital of the state company National Sports Base as an in-kind contribution. The officially announced reasons for the transformation of the ownership were the need for better management and for attracting private investments. After eleven years of desperate searching for the best formula for the development of the sports sites and facilities in Bulgaria, the State decided to give up from its public ownership and leave this matter to negotiations between a State owned company and the interested parties from the private sector.

2. The Situation with Levski Sofia and Georgi Asparouhov Stadium

209. In October 2012, the executive director of Levski Sofia officially announced the plans for full reconstruction of Georgi Asparouhov stadium. The envisaged reconstruction was planned to pass through three stages – sector A and B until may 2014, sector C – 2015, and sector D – 2017. According to the plans only the pitch and a small part of the old platforms were supposed to stay untouched. In February 2013 the works for the destroying of sector A started with detonating the massive cover and the concrete construction. The sector was supposed to be opened in the end of May 2014 on the occasion of the club's 100 years jubilee, however, this happened only on 23 April 2016 and the sector had no cover and still, as of the time of writing, does not have such. The official capacity of the platform is 6,000 spectators and it was announced to have cost BGN 11.5 million, approximately EUR 5.75 million. At the time of writing there is no official plan or idea how the reconstruction works are going to continue. The club is under the heavy pressure of financial problems and is not far away from the destiny of its historical rival CSKA Sofia. Despite of the status of private State ownership of the Georgi Asparouhov stadium and the right of Levski Sofia to use for an indefinite period of time and free of charge, this fact did not suffice for the completion of the process of modernization of the site and, instead, burdened the club with more financial obligations.

3. The Example of PFC Ludogorets Razgrad and Its Stadium

210. PFC Ludogorets Razgrad became a champion of Bulgaria for five years in a row starting in the 2011/2012 season. Moreover, this club managed to reach the group stage of the Champions League in 2013/2014 and 2016/2017 seasons. After finishing at the third place in its group in the latter participation, the club even managed to qualify for the play-offs of the UEFA Europa League in the beginning of 2017. Apart from that, PFC Ludogorets signed and developed some promising talents, whose market value increased significantly. The positive and successful business model of PFC Ludogorets had beneficial impact also on the development of the club's home site – the stadium Ludogorets Arena. The stadium is owned by the Municipality Razgrad and obtained its current name in 2011. The stadium underwent a repair in 2011. In May 2015 a new platform of the stadium was built and named after the defender Kosmin Motti, who was the hero of the team qualifying the club for the first time in the Champions League after saving as a goalkeeper two penalties from the shootouts and scoring one penalty himself. In 2016, the Municipality Razgrad opened a procedure for granting concession regarding the stadium having as subject 'Reconstruction and Modernization of Ludogorets Arena, its Management and Maintenance after Entering into Exploitation'. The concession formula should lead to the completion of the construction of the stadium, which will meet the requirements for qualifying as forth category according to the classification of the UEFA. The capacity of the stadium will be 12,500 seats. The example of Ludogorets shows that concession can still be effective decision for modernization of the sports sites provided that the main activity of the FC to use the stadium is well structured as a business and the site can be effectively exploited economically following purely market reasons and logic.

4. The Sports Base of the Bulgarian National Football Team

211. On 17 November 2016, the new sports base of the Bulgarian national team, including the new administrative building of the BFU, was officially opened. The base was announced to have cost EUR 10 million and EUR 9.5 million of its value was covered by the various projects of the *Fédération Internationale de Football Association* (FIFA) and UEFA. This example demonstrated that the financing of construction and investment in new sports sites and facilities is actually possible through external financing.

5. Construction of New Sites and Facilities

212. The above conclusion is also confirmed by the fact that the new sports sites and facilities in Bulgaria are mainly constructed by the use of EU funding and, most often, under the EU programs for regional development. This way, there are very good sites and facilities in remote areas or areas, where there is shortage of population at young age to be able to use them. As regards sports sites and facilities in the biggest cities, the majority of them continue being in ruins and the situation is even much heavier for the sports other than football, which are totally dependent on the State financing.

XXII. Public Financing of Sport

A. Eligibility for Public Financing

213. Certain sports activities and objectives enumerated in Article 58 of the Law on Sports are eligible for financing with the resources of the State budget such as:

- the construction, reconstruction and modernization of sports sites of national importance and facilities for social tourism of national importance as well as of sports sites and facilities and facilities for social tourism that are State and municipal property;
- the expenses for educational and training and competition activities as well as for maintenance and development of sports and material and technical basis in the sports schools;
- the scientific, research and applied activity in the sphere of physical education and sport;
- the medical and doping control;
- activities and measures of the national programme for development of the physical education and sport;
- other activities in the sphere of physical education, sport and social tourism, determined by a law or by an Act of the Council of Ministers;
- a programme for Olympic training;
- a programme for development of the sport for top achievements; and
- the preparation and organization of world and European championships hosted by the Republic of Bulgaria.

214. The resources, described above, shall be provided on an annual basis by the Law on the State Budget of the Republic of Bulgaria. Further, the Law on Sports makes provision for an expedient subsidy for maintenance and development of the sports base at schools of the national education system and in higher education that shall be allocated annually to the budget of the Ministry of Education and Science.

215. Likewise, the municipalities shall finance and support:

- programmes and activities of the physical education, sport and social tourism of children from the kinder gardens and the students from the schools and the centres for support of the personal development;
- the creation of conditions for practising by the citizens and, most of all, of the children and youth, of physical exercises, sport and social tourism and the development of the sport for all; and
- the construction, reconstruction, modernization, and management of the municipal sports sites and facilities and the tourist basis, provided for social tourism in the mountains and remote regions, by a decision of the municipal council.

216. The municipalities can further support sports organizations, sports schools and tourist associations, whose headquarters and activities are on the territory of the municipality.

217. The municipal councils shall adopt municipal programmes for development and promotion of the physical education, sport and social tourism.

218. In addition, financial resources are accumulated in the budget of the MYS from sources such as: expedient subsidies on annual basis for the development of the physical education and sport at the amount of the tax for the previous year deposited in the State budget by the BST due under the Law on Corporate Income Taxation; donations, wills and sponsorship by Bulgarian and foreign individuals and corporate bodies; and other sources determined by a law or an Act of the Council of Ministers.

219. Pursuant to Article 59(a) of the Law on Sports the so accumulated resources of the budget of MYS are eligible to be spent for:

- financing the activity of the MYS;
- construction, reconstruction and modernization of sports sites and facilities and facilities for social tourism of national importance as well as of sports sites and facilities and facilities for social tourism that are State and municipal property;
- support of talented children and young people with abilities to progress in their sports;
- support of expedient programmes and projects of sport and tourism among pupils, students and people with disabilities;
- financing expedient programmes and projects of physical education, sport and social tourism of the disabled and the sport for all;
- stimulation and awarding high-grade athletes, medal and prize winners from European and world championships and Olympic Games and from similar championships and games for the disabled;
- social support for athletes, disabled sportsmen and veteran sportsmen and coaches;
- other sports activities and activities in the field of social tourism;
- realization of the basic tasks of the national programme for development of the physical education and sport;
- supporting projects for construction and maintenance of tourist markings along the European walking routes passing through the Republic of Bulgaria;
- financing activities on a programme for Olympic training and activities on a programme for development of the sport for top achievements;
- financing activities related to medical and doping control;
- support of the scientific, research and applied activity in the sphere of physical education and sport;
- assisting the preparation and holding of world and European competitions hosted by the Republic of Bulgaria; and
- providing insurance for athletes in cases of events causing damages of their immaterial good or death in the process of their sport and competition preparation and participation at Olympic games, World and European championships.

B. Financing Sports Organizations

220. Public financing is available only for those sports organizations that are registered as non-profit legal entities for the public benefit. The State shall support the sports activity of the licensed sports organizations and their members, as well as the educational and training and sports and competition activity in the state sports schools under conditions and in line with a procedure determined by the Minister of Youth and Sports. The State and the municipalities can also support non-profit associations and organizations that organize and encourage children and youngsters to practise physical exercises, sport, sports games and tourism.

221. Article 62 of the Law on Sports further lists the possible sources of financing for the sports organizations which are non-profit legal entities for the public benefit as set out below:

- membership fees and individual and team taxes;
- transfer of athletes;
- receipts from participation in sport competitions;
- receipts from sports services;
- receipts from advertising, television and other rights of circulation;
- donations and sponsorship;
- resources, submitted by the State and/or the municipalities;
- receipts from the management of own property;
- resources submitted by international sports organizations; and
- other receipts from activities of physical education and sport.

222. The sports organizations shall account for and prove the expediency of the spent resources, received from the State and the municipalities following a procedure determined by the Minister of Youth and Sports and the municipal councils.

C. The BST

223. It is already a common practice in Bulgaria that the State establishes public companies operating in a way similar to a fund in order to stimulate certain sectors of the economy, which, as a rule, do not attract serious investors' interest due to low profitability and long gestation period of the investment. At the same time, such sectors are considered vital for the economy or other important interests of the country are at stake, or the State is obliged to provide conditions for their growth and sustainable development. Therefore, the State very often avails itself of its right to set-up State companies under Article 62, paragraph 3 of the Law on Commerce.

224. Said companies are not commercial companies in either of the forms provided for in the Law on Commerce. They are sui generis companies, which have to be established by virtue of a special law or by insertion of a special provision for their establishment in the existing laws governing the relationships in the particular sector of the economy. Such companies have been already formed for sectors such as environmental protection, all kinds of transport – air, railway and marine, prison activity and are envisaged for establishment in the sectors forests and fisheries.

225. The main functions of a State company, its management structure, financial sources, objectives and other elements are provided for either in the law itself or the law authorizes the Council of Ministers to adopt the statute of the State company where all requisites are provided for or further elaborated on the basis of the provisions of the law. As a rule, such State companies do not have registered capital and normally, they have the obligation to reinvest all profits gained in the course of their business activity for pursuing the objectives, for which they have been established.

226. The legal ground for the establishment of BST was contained in section 11 of the Transitional and Concluding Provisions of the Law on Gambling, which was replaced by the new Law on Gambling. The latter entered into force on 1 July 2012. Article 14 thereof is titled 'Gambling games organized by the state' and stipulates that the State can organize traditional lottery, lottery games with numbers, instant lottery and betting about the results of sports competitions and races with horses and dogs through the State company BST established with the MYS. BST is not a commercial company and the State holds all rights therein. In general, State is entitled under Article 4, paragraph 1, section 3 of the Law on Gambling to organize gambling games only for the purpose of supporting sport, culture, health protection, education and social activity.

227. Article 14, paragraph 2 of the Law on Gambling authorizes the Council of Ministers to adopt the BST statute following a proposal of the Minister of Youth, and Sports, which is the body to appoint and release its corporate bodies. The BST statute adopted by the Council of Ministers in the year 2000 and lastly amended in July 2014 determines its structure, way of management, games organized by BST, its funds, the raising and distribution of the resources, and provisions on international cooperation.

228. Pursuant to its statute, BST accumulates its funds from the proceeds of the organized gambling games and also from donations and revenue from other activities, which support, pursued or supplement its main scope of activity. The proceeds from the gambling games organized by BST shall be allocated as follows:

- not less than 50% – for payment of winnings to the persons, who provided tokens, slips of forms, checks or other signs confirming the winning, which they materialize; and
- not less than 17% for support and development of the BST.

229. The difference between the proceeds from the gambling games, reduced by the taxes charged thereon and the other fees due by virtue of the Law on Gambling as well as by the above stated amounts, shall be used for the needs of the physical education and sport and for maintenance, repair, reconstruction, complete renovation or creation of new sports sites and/or sports facilities in the state and municipal schools. The particular distribution of the resources is an obligation of the Minister of Youth and Sports. The formed sum of winnings that are not claimed within the established terms shall be used for stimulating the development of the BST as well as for realization of the activities under the Law on Sports. The resources for these activities shall be provided following a decision of the BST management board, which must be coordinated in advance with the Minister of Youth and Sports after the accountancy conclusion in every three months.

230. The use of the income from the BST activity after taxation and deduction of the expenses and the paid winnings shall be approved by the Minister of Youth and Sports in coordination with the Minister of Finance with respect to the funds directed for support of the physical education and sport and those for maintenance, repairs, reconstruction, full innovation and establishment of new sports sites and/or sports facilities in the State and municipal schools. In the latter case, the Minister of Youth and Sports in accordance with the financial resources shall comply with the annual programme, proposed by the Minister of Education and Science.[34]

231. Article 59(b) of the Law on Sports determines the objectives, for which the resources accumulated in result of the BST activity may be used:

- activities of licensed sports organizations and their members as well as of sports clubs;
- organizing domestic championships and international competitions on the territory of the country, included in the State and international sports calendar;
- preparation and participation of Bulgarian sportsmen and sportswomen in European and world championships and Olympic Games and in similar championships and games for people with disabilities;
- construction, reconstruction and modernization of sports sites and facilities and social tourism facilities of national importance as well as of sports sites and facilities and facilities for social tourism that are State and municipal property;
- granting lifetime monthly premium for Olympic medallists who have ceased their active competition activity;
- education and training and sports and competition activity in the State sports schools as well as for maintenance and development of the sporting and material and technical basis;
- granting lifetime monthly premium for the personal coaches of the Olympic medallists, who have obtained the right of pension for social security service and age in the context of the Social Security Code;
- granting lifetime monthly premium for the head coaches of the combined Olympic teams in the respective sport, who have obtained the right of pension for social security service and age in the context of the Social Security Code;
- granting one-time financial aid for children of the Olympic medallists, who have ceased their active competition activity and whose right to receive lifetime monthly premium was terminated due to death.

232. The market for organization of gambling games is not monopolized by BST, and there are opportunities for entrance of other private companies such as Bulgarian commercial companies and commercial companies registered in a Member State of the EU as well as in another State – member of the European Economic Area

34. Article 14, para. 3 and para. 4 of the Law on Gambling of 1 Jul. 2012 in State Gazette issue No. 26 of 30 Mar. 2012. Article 57(b) of the Law on Sports also provides that the Minister of Youth and Sports in coordination with the Minister of Finance shall approve the scheme for allocation of the proceeds of BST.

(EEA) or in the Confederation Switzerland, provided that they meet the requirements of the Law on Gambling.

233. On 8 July 2005, the organization of only one toto-like game resembles those organized by BST and, therefore, in direct competition on the relevant market, has been licensed to the company Eurobet. However, this was enough to trigger the battle between the antagonistic interests of the State company and the representatives and lobbyists of the private businessmen on the arena of gambling. Representatives of BST and members of the Parliament raised their concerns that BST was placed in unequal position vis-à-vis the private companies due to its obligation to transfer 22% (at that time) of all proceeds of the gambling games to MYS in support of the Bulgarian sport, which obligation is not applicable with respect to the other participants on the market. The most pessimistic opinions even envisaged the bankrupt of BST and financial losses for the Bulgarian sport in the amount reaching 20 million, because that was the amount of the last at that time contribution of BST for the year 2005.

234. The BST representatives insisted on establishment of a State monopoly with respect to the organization of toto and loto games and periodic lotteries to be exercised by BST as a State company. In support of their claims, they maintained that such State monopoly exists in twenty-three countries in Europe regardless of whether explicitly provided for in the law or as a state of affairs.

235. The likely establishment of a State monopoly over the toto and loto games and periodic lotteries, however, would contradict the Constitution. Indeed, the supreme legislative Act allows the establishment of a State monopoly over certain economic activities, which may be entrusted to State companies or other legal entities by virtue of the law. The list of said activities is exhaustive because the State monopoly may exist only by way of exception and, therefore, this list cannot be amended or supplemented by the legislator on the latter's discretion.[35] As far as the organization of toto and loto games and periodic lotteries is not specifically mentioned in Article 18, paragraph 4 of the Constitution, the establishment of such a monopoly will definitely conflict the supreme legislative Act.

236. BST, in fact, has enjoyed a monopolistic position for years. This position was not provided for in the law but was successfully maintained by the rigid licensing requirements to the potential new participants on the relevant market. This way, their entrance was rendered practically impossible. However, in 2005 Eurobet took the advantage of the political situation characterized with lack of clear vision for the BST future just before the new Parliament elections, and succeeded in meeting the requirements, which at that time were either weakened or some of them even abolished.

237. The newly formed government after the elections in 2005 also rejected the claims for establishment of a State monopoly as well as the claim for extension of BGN 20 million for modernization of the facilities managed by BST for the purpose of placing the State company on equal footing with its competitors. In order to outweigh the negative in terms of competitiveness effect of the BST obligation to finance the Bulgarian sport, it was suggested that the same obligation be extended also to the

35. In this respect, Decision No. 2 of 1996 under constitutional file No. 26 of 1995, Decision No. 33 of 1998 under constitutional file No. 30 of 1998 and Decision No. 6 of 2000 under constitutional file No. 8 of 2000.

competitors of the State totalizer. However, this revolutionary idea has not been accepted so far.

238. In 2012 the private company New Games became the second licensed operator of toto and loto games, however this company was linked to Eurobet through several subsidiaries, which provided grounds for some observers to call its entrance on the market as extension of the business of Eurobet and not as increase of the competition thereon. The first game, which New Games introduced was the so-called National Lottery, which had initially BGN 10 million for prizes. Later the company added to its portfolio also the loto game six of forty-seven, which entered into a direct competition with the most popular game of the BST '6 of 49'.

D. Conditions and Procedure for Financial Support of Sports Activities

239. The most recent act specifying the conditions and procedure for financial support to be granted to sports federations and sports clubs is Decree No 1 of 8 May 2014 issued by the Minister of Youth and Sport. The sports federations have to meet the following requirements:

- to be registered as non-profit legal entities for performance of activity in public benefit;
- to hold a sports licence;
- to have a valid membership with the respective international federation if such exists;
- to have no financial liabilities to the State and municipalities unless deferral or postponement of the payment has been admitted;
- to have fulfilled their obligations to the MYS arisen out of previous contracts; and
- to meet the conditions for application under the particular programme, under which the support will be granted.

240. Consequently, sports clubs in order to be eligible for financing by the MYS must:

- be registered as non-profit legal entities for performance of activities in public benefit and entered into the National Registry of the Sports Organizations kept by MYS;
- be members of the respective licensed sports federation.

241. The division between legal entities in public and private benefit is made by the Law on Non-Profit Legal Entities. What make the difference are the objectives of the particular non-profit legal entity, which is free to determine them as being in public benefit through its statute or founding Act. Legal entities in public benefit are subject to registration in a special registry kept with the Ministry of Justice and to some specific requirements listed in Chapter 3 of that law. Once having determined its activity as being in public benefit and registered it with the special registry, the non-profit legal entity is not allowed to change this circumstance neither could it transform itself into a non-profit legal entity in private benefit.

E. Financing Physical Education and Sport at Pre-school Institutions, Schools and Universities

242. Pursuant to Article 57, paragraph 1 of the Law on Sports, the State and municipal budgets shall provide funds for physical education and sport for children in the pre-school institutions and students in the primary, secondary and higher schools. The minimum amounts are determined by the Council of Ministers.

F. Financing Athletes by MYS

243. Sportsmen and sportswomen are entitled under Article 16, paragraph 3 of the Law on Sports to receive financial support from the State for their preparation and participation in the Olympic and the Paralympic Games. As already seen, athletes are also indicated as addressees of financial support from the MYS budget, which may be spent for provision of incentives and awards to the high-grade athletes, medallists and prize winners from European and World Championships, Olympic Games and analogous championships and games for disabled people as well as for social assistance of sportsmen, disabled sportsmen and sportsmen – veterans and coaches. Further, the funds generated from BST in support of the Bulgarian sport shall be granted, *inter alia*, for preparation and participation of Bulgarian sportsmen in European and World championships and Olympic Games and in similar championships and games for people with disabilities as well as for payment of monthly premiums to the Olympic medallists, who have ended their sport careers.

244. The resources granted for payment of monthly premium for winning one medal at Olympic Games shall be determined as follows:

- gold medal at Olympic Games – three minimum labour salaries fixed for the country;
- silver medal at Olympic Games – 90% from three minimum labour salaries fixed for the country; and
- bronze medal at Olympic Games – 80% from three minimum labour salaries fixed for the country.

245. The minimum labour salary decreed for the country as of 1 January 2016 amounts to BGN 460 (approximately EUR 230).[36] Therefore, the amount of the premium reaches EUR 690 for gold, EUR 621 for silver and EUR 552 for bronze. Said premiums shall become due upon the date of winning the medal and are not in any way dependent on fulfilling certain age.

246. It is further possible in case of lack of funds in the MYS budget that funds from the central budget intended for expedient expenses be directed to the MYS and

36. Decree of the Council of Ministers No. 22 of 26 Jan. 2017 for determination of new amount of the minimum labour salary for the country.

ultimately granted to sportsmen.[37] This happened in 2006 with the preparation and participation of the Bulgarian chess player and at that time world champion in chess Vesselin Topalov, who had to defend his title in Elista – the capital of the Russian Republic of Kalmikia – in a tournament lasting from 20 September until 12 October 2006 against then pretender and ultimately the new world champion Vladimir Kramnik from Russia.

247. The amount of BGN 100,000 (approximately EUR 50,000) was granted not personally to Topalov but to 'the Bulgarian delegation' by virtue of a Decree of the Council of Ministers.[38] Said amount covered the expenditures spent for the preparatory camp of Topalov and his supporting team, remuneration of coaches, seconds, doctors, psychologists and rehabilitation therapist, provision of material and technical support, purchase of medicines for recovery and maintenance of good sports shape, advertisement materials in Bulgarian and Russian languages (colour brochures, albums, T-shirts, etc.), business trip expenses of the Bulgarian delegation for transport, visas, medical insurances, daily expenses and accommodation, equipment, press conferences, official meetings, telephone conversations and the like.

G. *Latest Developments*

248. The role of the State in supporting financially the sports activities is deemed to be marginal due to the shortage of the funds in the State budget. The current policy of MYS is directed to disclosing and promoting alternatives of the State financing to the sports organizations such as the financial options under the EU funds, which may be used in result of sport-related projects, strategies for lure of private investors and sponsors and the like in order to allow the managers of sports organization to run their activity as a normal business operating under the market conditions.

249. However, all other stakeholders in sport continue insisting on bigger involvement of the State in the field of sport, partly driven probably by the habit for relying on the State as part of the socialist behavioural heritage. This trend together with the uncertainty of the funds to be granted by BST under the new market conditions as well as the lack of tax and other incentives for the potential investors in sport provided for in the law motivated a proposal for designation of 0.5%[39] of the Gross National Product (GNP) of the country for sport. Said proposal was reproduced in the

37. Article 58, s. 7 of the Law on Sports allows certain activities in the field of sport, designated by law or Act of the Council of Ministers to be financed by the State budget.
38. Decree of the Council of Ministers No. 255 of 15 Sep. 2006 for granting additional funds to the budget of SAYS for 2006.
39. Some of the members of the Children, Youth and Sports Affairs Committee have calculated that the resources so far provided by the State budget for sports amounted to 0.02% of the GNP per annum. The fixation of the percentage was based on the similar practice in some municipalities to allocate 0.5% of their budget for sports activities. Also, 0.5% of the GNP per annum has been already employed as a criterion for fixation of the funds to be allocated in support for the Bulgarian agriculture provided for in the respective law. However, due to force majeure and needs for reallocation of State resources to other fields having priority, the entrance into effect of said provision has been constantly postponed for the next budgetary year. This was one of the main arguments of the Ministry of Finance for avoidance of the fixation of percentage in the case of sports.

draft for the amendment of the Law on Sports exactly in result of the firm and unanimous insistence of the stakeholders during the preliminary discussions organized by the Children, Youth and Sports Affairs Committee with the Bulgarian Parliament.

250. The idea for allocation of resources from the State budget in support of the Bulgarian sport was generally upheld by the Ministry of Finance but fixing a percentage instead of a concrete amount was not accepted as a budgetary techniques, because its potential implementation would be unique for the sports sector and this way would likely entail claims for similar financing of other sectors of the economy. The same cons exposed by the Ministry of Finance were further articulated in the Parliament by the opposition during the first discussion of the draft.

XXIII. Supervision over the Activity of the Sports Organizations

251. Pursuant to the consistent practice of the Constitutional Court of the Republic of Bulgaria in cases concerning delegation of public powers to non-profit organizations existing under private law, the provision of legal mechanisms for control of such organizations shall be a mandatory requirement for the validity of the powers' transfer. In line with this practice, the Law on Sports devoted its Chapter 12 to the supervision over the activity of the sports organizations. This supervision was also necessary with a view to the use of public funds by such organizations.

252. Article 64(a) of the Law on Sports provides for the establishment of an inspectorate, which is directly subordinated to the Minister of Youth and Sports has the main function to exercise supervision over the activity of the sports organizations and the persons who offer publicly sports services as well as current and follow up control over the activities of the sports and youth organizations financed by the MYS.

253. The employees of the inspectorate are authorized to require all necessary documents related to the activities subject to control, to obtain information and to carry out inspections on the spot. In case of auditing sports organizations, the inspectorate is specifically authorized to require documents and collect information in order to fulfil the tasks entrusted thereto, to propose to the Minister of Youth and Sports the commencement of proceedings for imposition of conservative measures with respect to the property of the persons inflicted damages and to initiate court proceedings against them, to attend the meetings of the management and control bodies of the audited sport organizations or to receive their decisions.

254. In case of breaches of the Law on Sports acknowledged by the employees of the inspectorate, the latter can propose to the Minister of Youth and Sports the notification of the respective competent State bodies. The specialized State control bodies can require information and other assistance from MYS in exercising control over the sport organizations and their activity.

255. The sports federations are also granted the power to exercise control with respect to their members for the observance of the Law on Sports in compliance with the federations' statutes. The sports federations may further require from MYS to carry out inspections with respect to their members.

256. The sports organizations that have received resources from the State or the municipal budget shall account and prove to the relevant financing authority the expediency of the spent resources. The inspectorate of MYS shall carry out current inspections of the sports organizations for the expedient and lawful spending of the resources.

257. The Minister of Youth and Sports is entitled to request the district court in whose region the headquarters of the sports organization is located, to revoke the decisions of the general meeting of the sports organizations that contradict their statutes or a legislative Act.

§3. Sport and Tort Law

I. Introduction

258. The Bulgarian case law does not reveal any examples of court proceedings having as a cause of action tort liability in contact sport. Therefore, the Bulgarian courts have not been able so far to rule on and construe this issue, which in other countries proved to be specific with a view to its peculiar sporting circumstances. Likewise, the possible defences against such claims for tort in sport have not still come under the courts' scrutiny.

II. Assaults on Other Players

259. Notwithstanding the absence of court practice in sporting cases, actions based on tort can be indisputably tried pursuant to Article 45 of the Law on Obligations and Contracts (LOC)[40] setting the general liability of every person to redress the damage he has faultily caused to another person.

260. It is settled case law in Bulgaria[41] that this general rule would be inapplicable if a special law governs the issue of tort liability in the particular relationship. However, such special law to govern relationships based on tort in sports cases does not exist and claims for damages arising from infliction of injuries in the course of sports games would fall within the general rule.

261. Tort liability under the Bulgarian law shall be enforced through court proceedings and depends on the intention of the injured person to sue the person causing the injury. There are four mandatory conditions precedent, which have to be established in the course of the court proceedings in order to trigger the tort liability.

262. The first one is the unlawfulness of the act causing the injury, that is, the act must infringe an effective legal rule. Unlawfulness will be present whenever certain conduct contradicts the general obligation under Article 45 LOC.

263. Second, the defendant must be found guilty for inflicting the injury. The guilt in cases of tort may take the forms of intention and negligence. Usually, sporting cases in negligence are the most common. The burden of proof lies with the defendant

40. LOC of 22 Nov. 1950 in the State Gazette issue No. 275 of 22 Nov. 1950.
41. Decision No. 1064 of 21 Mar. 1983 of the Supreme Court of Cassations under civil case No. 4082 of 1982.

because pursuant to the second indent of Article 45 in all cases of tort, guilt is presumed unless proven otherwise. The reverse burden of proof in comparison with the penal law could become significant for disputes arisen of injuries caused in result of sports tackles. This would be the defendant and not the plaintiff injured, who should prove that he did not inflict the injury either deliberately and intentionally or without laying the due and reasonable care for avoidance of the injury in case of a negligent tackle.

264. The third condition precedent for establishing tort liability is the damage suffered in result of the injury, which may comprise the actual loss and the loss of profit to the extent they are direct and immediate result of the injury and could have been anticipated as of the time of its infliction.

265. The fourth condition precedent to be evidenced in the court proceedings is the cause-consequence connection between the action and the injury allegedly caused by that action.

266. Further to the tort liability born by the wrongdoer, in certain cases the person, who has assigned a work to the latter, will be vicariously liable on the ground of Article 49 of LOC. The vicarious liability is not predetermined by any culpability on the part of that person and has the function to guarantee that the injured will be effectively compensated for all the damage he/she suffered.

267. Although LOC utilizes the concept assignment of a work instead of merely referring to employment, in fact its drafters meant exactly a work exercised under relationship of employment. Pursuant to the case law, in exceptional cases the vicarious liability may be extended to a work performed under a service contract as far as the particular case either reveals all necessary elements of employment relationship, that is, the service contract amounts to a disguised employment contract, or the principal has such powers under the service contract to organize and manage the work so it would be justifiable, with a view to the particular circumstances of the case, to be held liable for the damage caused by the contractor.

268. Consequently, sports clubs can be vicariously liable with respect to the damages caused in result of the intentional or negligent actions of their employees-athletes on the sports field. As a rule, status of employees is enjoyed by all participants in collective sports. However, in some individual sports where relations are deemed to be other than employment and established by way of a service contract, the issue of the vicarious liability of the organizer of the sport event will be judged on a case-by-case basis.

269. Furthermore, under Article 49 of LOC, in order to trigger the vicarious liability of the employer the injury has to be caused in, or in connection with, the performance of the work assigned. Therefore, accidents where one player hits another 'off-the-ball' will not meet the above requirement.

270. The athlete caused the injury and his/her employer-club will be jointly and severally liable before the athlete injured. However, the employer being vicariously liable is entitled to claim back from the employee who has culpably caused the injury the whole amount of the compensation paid by the former on the ground of Article 54 of LOC. Similar stepping into the rights of an injured athlete against the wrongdoer could be exercised also by any insurance company who has paid compensation to said athlete pursuant to Article 213 of the Insurance Code.[42]

42. Insurance Code of 1 Jan. 2006 in the State Gazette, issue No. 103 of 23 Dec. 2005.

III. Hooliganism

271. In the words of the former Head of the Operations of the State Agency for Youth and Sports Ms Vessela Lecheva, hooliganism is not a Bulgarian phenomenon, but rather transplanted in the Bulgarian society by certain members thereof who try to follow the model developed in Western Europe. This explanation might seem quite oversimplified, one-sided and ultimately reveals only a very small part of the truth, but in fact it is quite natural explanation with a view to the total overall absence of any kind of sociological and anthropological research on the topic of sports fans behaviour during the socialist period and the current transitional period.[43]

272. Several reasons could be stated why hooliganism as a phenomenon was not presented or at least its presence was not disclosed in the communist society.

273. Taylor attributed the origin and genesis of hooliganism to the English working class, which has been subject to a process of rapid economic and social differentiation resulted in unemployment and isolation of numerous young people. Football hooliganism was deemed to be the reaction of the members of such marginalized groups.[44]

274. Further, the observed subculture of the working class members such as the superiority of men over women, the formation of segregated groups according to age, sex and sense of belonging to particular districts contributed to the acceptance and even desire for fighting and 'men-like' behaviour including demonstration of superiority in the society through acts of aggression and violence.[45] Notwithstanding the critique against this theory in England itself, it obviously would have been absolutely inapplicable in a homogeneous, in terms of class differentiation, society formed solely by members of the working class like the Bulgarian society in the communist years, further characterized with 0% unemployment. Moreover, the official policy tolerated the sexual equality although perceived as a kind of fellowship between men and women, who together, hand by hand, must build up the new life.

275. Any social tensions provoked by religious differences, as in the case of Rangers and Celtics fans in Glasgow, are unthinkable in a communist society where the church was controlled by the State and religion was considered a threat for the promotion of the communist dogmas. Therefore, religious differences could not serve as a source of antisocial behaviour and, hence, for rise of hooliganism.

276. As a rule, the totalitarian State maintains the level of crimes including antisocial conducts to a minimum, however, by means of interference in and control over all spheres of life as well as human rights infringements. This way, hooliganism was lacking its suitable environment for development.

---

43. One comprehensive study on hooliganism and related issues is M. Iliycheva, *Faithful Until Death: Sport Fans and Nationalist Discourse in Bulgarian Internet Forums* (Ctrl. European U. Press 2004).
44. T. Taylor quoted by E. Archetti & A. Romero, *Death and Violence in Argentinean Football*, in *Football, Violence and Social Identity* 40 (R. Giulianotti, N. Bonney & M. Hepworth eds, Routledge 1994).
45. E. Archetti & A. Romero, *Death and Violence in Argentinean Football*, in *Football, Violence and Social Identity* 42 (R. Giulianotti, N. Bonney & M. Hepworth eds., Routledge 1994).

277. Hooliganism further contrasted the image of sport, which was closely related to the image of the entire regime and sort of a showroom for its achievements. With a view to the style of the whole sports literature produced in Bulgaria prior to 1989 where the praise of the communism dominated the purely sporting and scientific issues, hooliganism, even if present in some forms and even as a research topic, was politically and doctrinally incompatible.

278. Nevertheless, the roots of today's hooliganism, which constitutes one very serious social problem, may be traced back to certain extent to the years of communism. Stadiums at that time were used as arenas for first exhibition of dislike to the regime under the form of irony and also a place where spectators and not the official authority chose which persons (in this case sportsmen) to idealize and make them heroes, thus neglecting the heroes imposed by the communist party.

279. In this respect, the most noteworthy example is the FC Levski Sofia and its most famous player in the 1960s, Georgi Asparouhov – Gundi. Gundi was probably the first real hero heralded as such by the people and after his death in a car accident in 1971, he became a legend. The mourning made thousands of people (according to unofficial information, the number reached 500,000) to attend the funeral.

280. The club Levski Sofia was historically predetermined to become an antipode of what the communist regime wanted to achieve. The club was founded in 1914, that is, after the Balkan wars, which caused a national catastrophe for Bulgaria and was called upon to revive the patriotic feelings of Bulgarians and motivate them to continue struggling for the fulfilment of the national ideal.

281. The role of FC Levski Sofia in preservation and defence of the national ideal normally was found to be in conflict with the ideas for internationalism imposed by the communist regime. The club was named after the greatest Bulgarian revolutionist Vassil Levski, which further associated the club with the general idea for support of Bulgaria and the Bulgaria-ness. The regime tried several times to change the name of the club including by imposition of the name Dynamo, which was popular name for a FC from the former socialists countries, but faced the strong opposition of the fans, which ended up with the arrests of the most active opponents.

282. The confrontation with the government formed the ideological basis for the big rivalry between Levski (considered by its fans as the team of the people) and FC CSKA Sofia, which was perceived as the team of the communist party. After the changes in 1989, this rivalry led to the most extreme and shocking examples of football hooliganism and the first death caused after the match between the two teams in November 2000.

283. In 1969, the regime changed the strategy and united FC Levski Sofia with Spartak Sofia, which at that time was the team of the militia (the then police). The unification was painful for the real fans of Levski, who severely opposed any connections with the Ministry of Interior. This historical confrontation later served as a source of motivation of the fans of the club for their scrimmages with the police, which in the recent years significantly increased in number and scale.

284. Certainly, the years of communism created some historically motivated behavioural patterns, which found a suitable environment for transformation into acts of hooliganism after the collapse of the regime. However, even if certain seeds were planted during these years, the real conditions and soil for the growth of the thorn-apple hooliganism came into existence upon the changes in 1989.

285. The fall of the restrictions for the freedom of speech caused radicalization of football fans' language, which shortened the way from words to deeds. The sudden withdrawal of the total control from the totalitarian State and the values it had imposed on the society resulted in situation where no values existed in practice. The process of degradation of the moral value system marked the whole transitional period and affected many segments of the society transforming from homogeneous to class society. This way, the conditions under which hooliganism arose and developed in other countries such as England appeared in Bulgaria as well.

286. Along with the mentioned and certainly other reasons, which remained beyond the scope of this monograph, the influence of the English football 'culture' was also part of the whole picture of this phenomenon in Bulgaria.

IV. Vandalism and Public Order

287. During socialism, hooliganism, in general, was prosecuted on the ground of the Criminal Code,[46] in the cases where it constituted a crime, and a special decree issued by the State Council in the cases of misdemeanour. The two pieces of legislation continued being enforceable with respect to sport hooligans after the changes. In the end of 2004 due to the compelling need for addressing the problem with the football hooliganism, in particular, the Law on Public Order Protection at Conduction of Sports Events (LPOPCSE)[47] was enacted, which excluded the application of the State Council Decree in the cases of sports hooliganism.

288. Sports hooliganism was defined under Article 21 of the new law as:

> in-decent behaviour, manifested by swearing or other disgraceful expressions and gestures which are of especially cynical nature, by provoking or participation in fighting, by penetration onto the sport field, by extermination or damaging of some-body else's property, by using of prohibited objects, by refusal to execute orders of the persons in charge of the sports event or of the police authorities, or by other similar action offending the public order, which action cannot be qualified as a crime in the meaning of the Criminal Code and which action is committed in connection to the sports event with malice intention in the area of the sports site or the zone surrounding it, before, during or immediately after the sports event, as well as on the way to and on the way back from the sports site.

46. Criminal Code of 1 May 1968, promulgated in the State Gazette, issue No. 26 of 2 Apr. 1968. Pursuant to the Criminal Code: '[W]ho commits an indecent act, grossly violating the public order and expressing obvious disrespect of the society, shall be punished for hooliganism by imprisonment of up to two years or by corrective labour, as well as by public reprobation. If the act is accompanied by a resistance against a body of the authority or a representative of the public carrying out an obligation of protecting the public order, or it is distinguished, by its contents, by an exceptional cynicism or impertinence the punishment shall be imprisonment of up to five years.'
47. The LPOPCSE of 30 Nov. 2004 in the State Gazette, issue No. 96 of 29 Oct. 2004.

The punishments imposed on sports hooligans include arrest in a local structure of the Ministry of Interior, fine and unpaid labour of public benefit.

289. LPOPCSE allegedly followed its English counterpart. However, the former General Secretary of the Ministry of Interior on duty at the time of the enactment of the law alleged that the latter departed from the English model by amounting swearing to hooliganism. According to him, the presence of such text would result in the right of the police to arrest almost the whole audience of the football matches.

290. LPOPCSE provides for the establishment of National Information Centre to assist the bodies and persons having activities related to organization and conduct of sports events, public order protection and guaranteeing the security of the sports sites as well as Unified Automatic Registry where certain data regarding sports hooligans and their behaviour are kept.

V. Owners/Users of Sports Sites and Organizers of Sports Events

291. Article 7 of LPOPCSE sets the liabilities of the owners/users of sports sites and the organizers of sports events. They are obliged to undertake all necessary measures in order to guarantee the order and security during the organized sports events and to interact with the respective State and municipal bodies for prevention of sport hooliganism.

292. The organizers are further obliged under Article 8 to postpone the event in case of direct danger for the life and health of the citizens where suitable measures for its prevention or elimination cannot be undertaken.

293. The owners or the users of sports sites shall appoint a person in charge for the security of the sports site and the professional sports clubs shall appoint a club security coordinator trained in the field of protection of public order in case of holding of sports events.

294. Various measures concerning the right of access to the sports sites (requirements for entrance tickets, official passes and invitations; protection against forgery or repeated use of the documents evidencing the right of access; designation of sporting zone; organization of sale of tickets to the fans of the rival teams at separate ticket offices; placing the fans of the rival teams in different sectors or blocks with leaving between them blank buffer zones, denial of access to certain persons who refuse to be checked, bring in forbidden objects, are in non-sober status, minors without a grown-up to accompany them or persons with imposed mandatory administrative measure prohibition to visit sports events in the country and abroad), supply of alcoholic beverages (prohibited on the area of the sporting zone at the day of the sport event and three hours after its finish) are provided for in LPOPCSE.

295. The organizers of sports events have further obligations under Articles 16 and 17 of LPOPCSE with respect to the security of the event such as notifying the citizens by information boards stated at visible places or by loudspeaker equipment that that video cameras are used for the purposes of the security of the site, without clarification of their exact location. Before a sports event is conducted, the organizers of sports events shall arrange meeting between representatives of the fans of the sport teams. The organizers of sports events and representatives of the fans of the sport team shall appoint as accompanying persons of the fans and persons in charge of fans such persons who command respect among fans.

296. The accompanying persons are obliged to undertake measures for blocking the actions of fans that are dangerous for the order and the security in the relevant sector; and identification and notifying of persons who prepare for or commit acts of brutality or abet for such acts. Said persons shall further inform the fans about the rules of order in the sports site and in the area of the sporting zone, take care for the order in the relevant sector and in the cases where necessary shall notify the police authorities, accompany the fans during the sports events in the country and abroad, popularize sports ideals and fair play concept among the fans.

297. The heads of the clubs of supporters shall appoint a contact person who shall carry out the coordination between the organizers of sports events, the manager of the sports event, the person in charge for the security of the sports site, the club security coordinator and the authorities of the respective regional directorate of the Ministry of Interior; and encourage the fans to observe the established standards of decent behaviour while the sports event is taking place. The contact person shall further collect and provide information to the bodies of the respective regional directorate of the Ministry of Interior about scheduled tours of fans to the locations where sport events shall take place, persons who tend to perform actions that threaten the sports event order and safety or such persons who have performed, preparing to commit or committing acts of brutality or abet for such acts.

VI. Spectators of Sports Events

298. Spectators of sports events are also made subject to obligations set out in Articles 18, 19 and 20 of LPOPCSE. They shall stay at the places marked at their access certification except in cases where for sake of security they are removed to other places. During the sports events, each spectator is obliged not to endanger or harm the near-standing spectators.

299. Spectators are prohibited from bringing in certain objects, devices and substances as well as from committing certain actions such as coming over constructions, facilities, fencing devices placed in the area of the sports site or the sporting zone, entering zones forbidden for spectators, candling flames, firing and shooting signal rockets, writing, claying or drawing on the sports sites and constructions or on the buildings and roads leading thereto, using alcoholic beverages, narcotic or other opiate substances, polluting the sporting zone and using camouflage, which impedes their identification. The breaches of the above obligations result in expulsion of the breaching fans from the sports site.

VII. Security in Sports Venues

300. A ministerial decree of 8 September 2000[48] adopted in implementation of Articles 2 and 4 of the European Convention on Spectator Violence and Misbehaviour

48. Ministerial Decree of 8 Sep. 2000 in State Gazette, issue No. 74 of 8 Sep. 2000.

at Sports Events and in particular at Football Matches regulates the engineering and technical requirements to the sports sites in order to guarantee the security in sports venues. Sports sites may be allowed for use only if it meets the safety requirements in construction and technical respect as determined by the relevant legislative rules.

301. Section 2 of the decree further specifies the requirements for:

- *the sporting zone* and its accessibility for the individual and public transport;
- *the parking lots* for automobiles and buses located near the sporting zone, which is to have enough place for manoeuvres and be lighted in case of use in the evenings;
- *the streets and roads* leading to the sporting zone (to ensure free access for the anti-fire automobiles);
- *the external fence of the sports site* (at least 2.2 m height, not allowing jumping over, unauthorized entering, undermining and removal and allowing video surveillance);
- *the entrances and the exits of the sports sites* (to be located in a way allowing the movement of specialized motor vehicles and citizens without disturbance, to be in number corresponding to the maximum capacity of spectators, but not exceeding 2,500 spectator per entrance);
- *the sports sites*, which must have emergency exits with doors, opening towards the pitch and meet other requirements for width, way of construction and control on the opening of the doors for emergency exits (distance and manual or only manual control);
- *the internal fence*, which divides the pitch from the sectors for spectators;
- *the seats for spectators* at open sports facilities (to be individual, steadily fixed, made of shock-proof materials, having certified origin and quality, number of rows);
- *the safe parapets* constructed behind the sectors for spectators (at least 1.5 m height); and
- *the premises* for the police, medical office and fire-safety bodies.

As well as requirements for video surveillance and video connection, lighting, loudspeaker facilities for informing the audience, phone connections, water supply in case of fire, other fire precaution measures, etc.

302. It shall be noted that most of the requirements although drafted as mandatory rules to date have in practical terms only the nature of recommendations. FCs are not willing to invest in improvement of the security through installation of facilities and provision of video surveillance and any other equipment under the pretext that they are not owners of the sports sites. They pretend that such investments will be made once the long lasting problem with the ownership and usage of sports sites and facilities is solved.

303. It is further not clarified in the law and the decree who, among the owners, users of sports sites, organizers of sports events or the police is liable for installation of video equipment and the conduct of video surveillance. LPOPCSE confers to the organizers of sports events the obligation to notify the citizens about the use of such equipment without specifying its particular location and to the person in charge of the security for the destruction of the video records within the statutory time limits. The decree also provides for video surveillance of the spectators without specifying the particular addressee thereof.

304. However, provision of video surveillance under the decree falls within the engineering and technical requirements, which should be definitely met by the owners of the sites.

305. Failure to meet some of the technical and engineering requirements may result in negative evaluation made by the respective municipal commission in charge for the inspection and control of sports sites with respect to their security pursuant to Articles 45 and 46 of the decree and hence to refusal of the Minister of Youth and Sports to permit the use of the particular sports site. Such refusal has been issued with respect to the stadiums used by PFC Lokomotiv Sofia (stadium Lokomotiv) and FC CSKA (stadium Bulgarian Army) as a result of the inspection of the stadia made by the municipal commission in Sofia in the spring of 2010.

306. Pursuant to Article 26, paragraph 4 of the decree the physical security in sports venues shall be provided by the police on contractual basis. In 2006, the president of the Professional Football League (PFL), which was organizing the final match from the Cup of Bulgaria tournament, decided to avail himself of the provision in the Law on Private Guarding Activity[49] effective as of 2004 entitling also private companies after obtaining licence to provide security to sports events and to conclude a contract with such a company for the security of the final match. The experiment had a negative outcome since the private guards did not manage to prevent the severe fighting between the fans of the two teams, many people were injured, including children, and ultimately, the police had to intervene.

§4. Dispute Settlements

I. Sports Adjudication and Sports Arbitration

307. The Law on Sports empowers the sports federations to exercise sports adjudication as well as sports arbitration with respect to their members, thus resolving all disputes arisen within the particular sport involving the federation and its members without necessity for recourse to the general court system. The key issues are how to determine the scope of the sports adjudication and which disputes would qualify as sports disputes capable of being resolved by the sports federations by virtue of the transfer of said adjudication power under the Law on Sports.

308. Various kinds of disputes may arise from the activity of the sports federations such as:

- technical disputes (regarding purely sporting rules and their application by the competent bodies and persons);

49. The Law on Private Guarding Activity of 24 Feb. 2004 in State Gazette issue No. 15 of 24 Feb. 2004.

- administrative disputes (against the regulations adopted by the sports federations in exercise of their power to adopt specific normative, methodological and administrative regulations for managing their respective sports as well as the power to grant, terminate and revoke the competition rights of athletes);
- disciplinary disputes (against the sanctions imposed by the sports federations on athletes and officials, who have admitted use of doping and application of doping methods in the training and competition activity); and
- financial disputes (arising out of the contracts between players and their clubs as well as between the federation and athletes, who are paid for their participation in the national teams, for instance).

309. The term sports adjudication is lacking definition in Bulgarian legislation. The issue on the scope of the sports adjudication power conferred to the sports federations has not been, as such, interpreted by court decisions or by works of legal authors for a long time. In two recent court decisions, however, this concept has been construed by the respective courts. According to the Sofia Regional Court in the case *Lipenski v. CSKA* [50] sports adjudication is adjudication of disputes related to organizing and administering of sports events including sanctioning of athletes and sports officials, who have admitted violations of the sports regulations and the statutes of the respective sports federation. According to the Administrative Court of the City of Sofia in the case *CSKA v. BFU,* [51] this is adjudication of each dispute, which arises between athletes, their representatives and/or their organizations on the occasion of the sport practised.

310. In a ruling of 30 August 2011,[52] for the first time the Supreme Court of Cassations commented on the concept of sports adjudication by comparing the arbitration provided for in Article 19, paragraph 1, section 10 of the Law on Sports, exercised in the particular case by BFU, with the arbitration for private civil financial disputes in the context of Article 4 of the Law on the International Commercial Arbitration. The Supreme Court of Cassations concluded the following:

> It is obvious that the case at hand concerns the creation of one specific voluntary football arbitration, envisaged by the legislator, which arbitration in the view of its scope and function is different than the arbitration for private civil financial disputes and shall embrace only disputes of non-financial nature between parties, who are members of the BFU.

By the said ruling for first the time in Bulgarian court practice, such conclusion has been reached that sports adjudication and sports arbitration may include only disputes of non-financial nature. Up to that moment, sports federations have allowed themselves to resolve disputes of financial nature and even such of significant material value.

---

50. Decision of the Sofia Regional Court under civil case No. 32356/2009.
51. Ruling of the Administrative Court of the City of Sofia of 18 Feb. 2010 under administrative case No. 9167/2010.
52. Ruling No. 682 of the Supreme Court of Cassations of 30 Aug. 2011 under private commercial case No. 756/2010.

II. Judicial Review of the Acts of the Sports Federations Adopted in Exercise of Their Adjudication Power

311. The first case, reported in the computer-based legal information systems in Bulgaria, where the issue about the possibility for judicial review of the acts of the sports federations adopted in exercise of their adjudication power was discussed, happened in the year 2000.

312. The court proceedings commenced on the occasion of appeal against a decision of the Regional Council of the BFU revoking the decision of its Sport and Technical Commission, whereby the competition rights of the player Radev had been temporarily suspended and his team had been punished with administrative loss of certain number of games.

313. The District Court of Plovdiv, as a Court of First Instance, construed the provision on transfer of adjudication power under the Law on Sports as such excluding the judicial review regarding the acts of the sports federations. According to the court analysis, the decision in question was adopted within the adjudication power of the BFU and the latter's internal regulations specifying the procedure for implementation of this power has been validly accepted by the member clubs on the ground of their membership. Hence, the court concluded that there was voluntary sports (football) arbitration, excluding the decisions adopted in conformity with the respective procedure from judicial review.

314. On the appeal of the decision before the Supreme Administrative Court (SAC), the latter disagreed with the finding of the District Court of Plovdiv. The SAC defined the acts of the sports federations as individual administrative acts since such acts may be issued also by non-governmental organizations authorized to do so by virtue of the law.[53]

315. Consequently, the same judicial review available for the individual administrative acts in general, was further applicable to the acts of the sports federations. Any finality of the judgment of the sports body resolving the dispute mentioned in the respective internal regulations of the sports federation could refer only to the review made by other appellate bodies within the dispute resolution system of that federation or within the particular sport. However, such a provision cannot exclude the judicial review under the Code on the Administrative Procedure since it was not provided for in the law.

316. SAC perceived the adjudication power of the sports federations as part of the whole process of administration of sport, for which sports federations are responsible under the Law on Sports and, therefore, the acts issued in exercise of that power constitute administrative acts. However, SAC explicitly emphasized the need for the court, which is supposed to rule on the merits of the case, to judge also whether the decision rendered by the sports federation corresponds to the scope of its competence under Article 19 of the Law on Sports. To put it differently, the issue whether a decision falls within the competence of the sports federation to exercise sports adjudication and sports and technical arbitration will be posed with respect to every individual case.

317. In this respect, some types of sports disputes appear to be problematic. These are disputes that have largely economic repercussions, for instance all kinds of

53. Resolution No. 5068 of 2000 of the SAC.

financial disputes. Further, a ban for competition activity imposed as a punishment for use of doping would deprive the athlete of the funds necessary for his/her living. Can the decisions of sports bodies resolving such disputes be covered by the concepts of 'sports adjudication' and 'sports and technical arbitration'? This is a question, which in my opinion is to be answered in negative.

318. The court practice in the years 2010, 2011 and 2012 overruled the conclusion made in the SAC ruling of 2000 that the acts of the sports federations adopted in exercise of their adjudication power were individual administrative acts and, this way, denied the possibility for judicial review by the administrative courts. In a court ruling in 2010,[54] in the Administrative Court of the City of Sofia the court held that the Arbitration Committee of the BFU acted as special jurisdiction and its acts cannot be appealed within administrative procedure. This finding was subsequently confirmed by the SAC upon the appeal. Likewise, in another ruling[55] of the same Court of First Instance, the latter found that there was explicit will of the legislator to leave adjudication of sports disputes to the sports federations themselves. The issue whether this legislative decision was in line with the Constitution was, according to the legal analysis of the court in the cited ruling, for the Constitutional Court to decide and until such decision of the Constitutional Court is rendered the courts are obliged to apply the laws as they are.

319. The acknowledgment of the fact that sports federations act as special jurisdictions and the exclusion of the acts adopted in exercise of their adjudication power from judicial review via administrative court proceedings is troublesome, to say the least. In Bulgaria special jurisdictions, i.e. bodies exercising adjudication powers which fall outside judicial system, are prohibited by Article 119 of the Constitution of the country. Nevertheless, existence of such jurisdictions is allowed by virtue of the Law on Protection against Discrimination and The Law on Patents and the Registration of Utility Models, for instance. However, the acts of adjudications of the Commission on Protection against Discrimination and the Dispute Resolution Unit at the Patent Office are subject to appeal before the administrative courts. Pursuant to Decision of the Constitutional Court No. 6 of 11 November 2008, the possibility for appeal of the acts of special jurisdictions, which have been allowed by virtue of individual laws, before a body having status of court is a mandatory condition for compliance of the adjudication activity of such jurisdictions with the Constitution. Therefore, if the firm conclusion of the courts in Bulgaria is that the arbitration bodies of the sports federations act as special jurisdictions, it would be the single logical solution that the appeal against their acts rendered in exercise of their adjudication power is allowed on the basis of the analogical right of appeal against the acts of all other existing special jurisdictions in Bulgaria. The absence of explicit legal provision providing for such appeal in the Law on Sports must be, in the author's opinion, considered as *lacuna* and the Law on Sports should be considered as incomplete regarding that matter and not as expressly providing for non-appeal of the decisions.

54. Ruling No. 1 of 1 Feb. 2010 of the Administrative Court of the City of Sofia under administrative Case No. 6403/2009.
55. Ruling No. 1 of 18 Feb. 2010 of the Administrative Court of the City of Sofia under administrative Case No. 9167/2010.

III. Arbitration

320. In football, all disputes arising out of the contract or the annexes thereto between the football player and his club used to be resolved by the arbitration commission and the appellate commission established with BFU pursuant to Article 16(2) of the effective in 2006 Regulations on the Status and Transfer of Football Players. The respective commissions of the football union were entitled to adopt procedural and mediation rules for settlement of the disputes referred to them pursuant to Article 13 of the Appendix to the Regulations on the Status and Transfer of Football Players[56] issued by BFU. In 2008, the arbitration commission was replaced by the Court of Arbitration with BFU (CABFU). The said arbitration court has almost the same functions – it shall resolve disputes arising of the contracts between football players or coaches and their clubs; or between FCs. It has to be mentioned that such disputes may invoke financial interests at stake, such as a dispute for unpaid salaries under the football contract. Consequently, the decision of the CABFU could fall within the scrutiny of the court for compliance with the scope of the power of BFU to exercise sports adjudication and sports and technical arbitration in case of challenge.

321. The CABFU in its statutes is declared to be competent for resolving disputes between:

- football players, coaches, officials, players' agents and FCs members of the BFU arisen from their interrelations within the system of the BFU;
- between FCs and football players or coaches – regarding performance, non-performance or termination of contracts concluded; regarding the ground for, the kind and the amount of compensations for terminated or non-performed contracts; the existence, amendment or termination of competition rights; the existence, amendment or termination of licensing agreements concluded with coaches; and
- between FCs regarding performance, non-performance or termination of transfer agreements, contracts for loan of players, disputes concerning the kind and the amount of training compensations for players.

322. As a court of second instance, the CABFU is competent to hear:

- disputes between football players or clubs and players' agents regarding performance or non-performance of contracts concluded. In such cases, subject of appeal is the decision of the Commission for Licensing of Players' Agents; and
- disputes concerning the decisions of the Sports and Technical Commission of the BFU, which expressly provide for such appeal before the CABFU.

323. The latter statutes specify which disputes are excluded from the CABFU jurisdiction, namely the following:

56. The Regulations on the Status and Transfer of Football Players and the Appendix thereto were revoked in 2008. At the time of writing, the legal basis is laid down by the Regulations on the Status and Transfer of Football Players adopted by the Executive Committee of BFU on 4 Nov. 2009.

- those falling within the exclusive jurisdiction of the Disciplinary or Appeals Commission of the BFU;
- those falling within the exclusive jurisdiction of the Licensing Commission or the Appeals Licensing Commission; and
- having as cause of action appeal of the decisions of the Executive Committee of the BFU, the Managing Board of the PFL and the Managing Board of the Amateur Football League (AFL).

324. The statutes of the CABFU point out that during the performance of their functions, arbitrators shall be independent and impartial and shall be subordinated only to the law, the statutes and the other normative documents of the BFU, UEFA and FIFA.

325. To make the situation even more complicated and legally uncertain, financial disputes concerning rights under employment relationship are expressly prohibited from being resolved by way of arbitration pursuant to Article 19, paragraph 1 of the Code on Civil Procedure.[57] Football players as well as all athletes engaged in collective sports are deemed to be employees as a rule. Therefore, the disputes between football players and their clubs regarding their contracts are prohibited from being resolved by way of arbitration although the statutes of the CABFU provides exactly for such dispute settlement. Several court decisions proved the illegality of the arbitration as a dispute settlement mechanism with respect to labour law disputes. This triggered amendment in the Law on Sports regarding the sports adjudication and the sports and technical arbitration power of the sports federations. Under the new paragraph in force since 2010, sports federations carry out sports adjudication and sports arbitration as well as adopt rules for the activity of an arbitral body therewith, which shall rule on the emergence, temporary suspension and termination of competition rights and with respect to other disputes designated in the respective regulations of sports federations.

326. The 2010 Amendment was obviously an attempt for circumvention of the prohibition for resolution of labour law disputes by way of arbitration by introducing the idea that actually sports arbitration bodies rule on issues that stem from the athletes' competition rights thus implying that such disputes do not concern employment relationships. However, the very concept of competition rights appears to be problematic because it has been abandoned in the other EU Member States.[58] Also, pursuant to the Implementing Regulations competition rights may be terminated by the mere wish of the registered player expressed in writing. If termination is left on the will of the player no further considerations regarding the validity of termination will be relevant, provided that such will be evidenced in a written document.

327. The non-arbitrability of employment disputes questions further the legitimacy of the international dispute resolution system in football from the point of view of the Bulgarian law.

328. In 2006, the Nigerian player of FC Beroe Dino Eze referred the dispute between him and the club as regards unpaid salaries to the FIFA Dispute Resolution Chamber. The international element of the case due to the Nigerian nationality of Eze

57. Code of Civil Procedure to become effective as of 1 Mar. 2008 in: the State Gazette issue No. 59 of 20 Jul. 2007.
58. *See* more about the concept of competition rights in Part II, Ch. I, §4 *infra.*

opened the way to the FIFA body. The Chamber declared the employment contract terminated and ordered FC Beroe to pay him BGN 4,381.50 and USD 9,180. The decision was subject to appeal before the CAS in Louzanne; however, regardless of the claims of Beroe for lack of competence on the part of the FIFA Chamber, the club did not avail of the option to appeal. Nevertheless, the hypothesis of a potential arbitral award issued by the CAS and its enforcement in Bulgaria is worth to be examined.

329. The CAS would have resolved a dispute, which is not arbitrable according to the Bulgarian law and, therefore, the award rendered might have been set aside by the Supreme Court of Cassations pursuant to Article 47, section 3 of the Law on the International Commercial Arbitration.[59] The similar effect would have been reached also by triggering Article 5, paragraph 2 of the UN Convention on the Recognition and Enforcement of Foreign Arbitral Awards saying that recognition and enforcement of an arbitral award may be refused if the competent authority in the country where recognition and enforcement is sought finds that the subject matter of the difference is not capable of settlement by arbitration under the law of that country.

330. In practice, in football there is no need for resort to any governmental authorities for the purpose of enforcement of the arbitral awards rendered by its international dispute settlement bodies. Enforcement is reached by the threat of disciplinary sanctions to the persons contesting the awards imposed by the disciplinary commissions of the international football governing bodies.

331. This happened also in the case of Beroe and Dino Eze. However, this method of enforcement does not alter the acknowledgement that certain types of disputes, which the Bulgarian State has explicitly reserved for settlement by the national court system, have been taken from its domain in contradiction with the national law. The arbitral awards of CAS are similarly enforced at the places where recognition is sought. They are effective in Switzerland at the seat of arbitration and cannot be rendered ineffective on the ground of the applicable Swiss law. There is no rule precluding the arbitration of employment disputes in Switzerland, and rulings given by the CAS are only open to appeal before the Swiss Federal Court.

332. The circumvention of the rule for non-arbitrability of employment disputes poses very significant issues.

The reason for many national laws to preclude labour disputes from being resolved by way of arbitration is that employees as the weaker party would not be at equal footing with the other party to the arbitration. This dispute resolution method is suitable in disputes between independent and equal positioned litigants such as independent merchants. If the present state of affairs is acknowledged as part of *lex sportiva*, the latter would be probably the first law of transnational origin trying to withdraw one typical relationship of subordination from the jurisdiction of the national State and regulate it differently. This would result in undermining the principle of legal protection, which is one of the fundamental principles inherent to all national legislations.

333. Arbitration is a dispute resolution method available only for financial disputes, that is, disputes related to rights having monetary equivalence pursuant to Article 19, paragraph 1 of the Code on Civil Procedure. The said article lays down the general principle for arbitrability of all private law financial disputes and further

59. Law on International Commercial Arbitration of 5 Aug. 1988 in: the State Gazette issue No. 60 of 5 Aug. 1988.

enumerates a few exceptions. Along with the already discussed exception in case of a dispute having as subject matter, a right under employment relationship disputes concerning property rights or possession of a piece of real estate and alimony or child maintenance are also not arbitrable.

IV. Sports Arbitration Court with the BOC

334. The Sports Arbitration Court with BOC was established in Bulgaria in 1999. Till date, seventeen sports disputes have been tried before it. In line with the policy of the IOC to require from the member-countries to provide conditions and mechanisms for settlement of all disputes related to sport by way of arbitration, there have been recently attempts for increase of the role of this court and, consequently, its workload.

335. Pursuant to Article 58 of the Statute of BOC, the decisions of the appellate commissions of the national sports federations and national sports organizations may be appealed before the Bulgarian Sports Arbitration Court. Any decision adopted by the Bulgarian Sports Arbitration Court may be appealed before the CAS in Lausanne which is the final instance for the settlement of the dispute within twenty-one days from the receipt of the decision as provided for in Article 59.

336. The legal ground for the existence of the arbitration court with BOC is contained in the Law on the International Commercial Arbitration and more specifically Article 4, which sets the option for establishment of arbitration institutions without any restrictions for their number. The Bulgarian legal literature also confirms the possibility for establishment of arbitration institutions to organizations other than chambers of commerce, which most frequently establish such arbitration institutions.[60]

337. Notwithstanding the title of the Law on the International Commercial Arbitration, it will be applicable also in cases of domestic arbitration, that is, both parties thereto have their seats or reside in Bulgaria, subject only to the restriction of the application of just a few provisions specific for the international arbitration. According to Professor Zhivko Stalev and again in contrast with its title, the Law on the International Commercial Arbitration would further apply with respect to disputes on non-commercial matters, which would mean also in sports disputes. The provision of Article 1, paragraph 2 thereof authorizing the international commercial arbitration to resolve civil financial disputes arising from external economic relations is still present in result of the omission to be deleted during the reform of the law according to Stalev.

V. Mediation

338. Mediation is a voluntary and confidential procedure for out-of-court settlement of disputes whereas a third-party mediator assists the disputing parties to settle their dispute regulated by the Law on Mediation.[61]

60. Z. Stalev, *Bulgarian Civil Procedural Law* 628 (Ciela 2001).
61. Law on Mediation of 17 Dec. 2004 in the State Gazette issue No. 110 of 17 Dec. 2004.

339. Unlike the arbitration, mediation may be used with respect to employment disputes and generally to all kinds of disputes that may arise in sport pursuant to Article 3, paragraph 1 of the Law on Mediation. Mediation shall be performed by natural persons, who may unite themselves in order to perform the mediation activities as stipulated in Article 4. Mediation ends up with the conclusion of an agreement for settlement of the dispute, which is binding for the parties to the dispute but cannot be enforced vis-à-vis third parties. The agreement binds the parties only with respect to what have been explicitly agreed therein as stated in Article 17 of the Law on Mediation.

VI. Conciliation

340. Conciliation is not a special procedure as mediation and is not regulated by special law accordingly. LOC contains a provision for a settlement agreement, whereby the parties may settle one existing dispute or avoid one potential dispute by providing mutual concessions to each other. The negotiations between the parties may be facilitated by a mediator or conciliator. The role of the conciliator is perceived by legal authors as more active than the role of the mediator. The conciliator is expected to propose drafts of settlement agreement and even to certain extent to exercise some pressure on the parties.

§5. Taxation

I. Introduction

341. The objective of this chapter is to outline the main types of taxation applicable in the Bulgarian sports sector.[62] When we talk about taxation in sport, we have two main groups that are subject to taxation – individual athletes and sports clubs. Individual athletes could be amateurs or professionals, but in any case, they due taxes under the Law on Individuals Income Taxation of 1 January 2007.[63] Sports clubs are also two types – amateur sports clubs registered as sports associations under the Law on Non-Profit Legal Entities and professional sports clubs registered either as sports associations or as companies limited by shares (sports companies established in accordance with the Law on Commerce). Sports clubs owe direct taxes under the Law on Corporate Income Taxation;[64] however, they also could be subject of taxation with Value Added Tax (VAT).

62. For a detailed analysis of the Bulgarian Tax Law applicable to the sports sector, *see* T. Simov & B. Kolev, *Bulgaria*, in *International Guide to the Taxation of Sportsmen and Sportswomen* (R. Betten ed., NOLOT BV 2007).

63. Law on Individuals Income Taxation of 1 Jan. 2007 in the State Gazette issue No. 95 of 24 Nov. 2006.

64. Law on Corporate Income Taxation of 1 Jan. 2007 in State Gazette issue No. 105 of 22 Dec. 2006.

II. Direct Tax of Individual Athletes

342. The incomes of individual athletes are taxable in accordance with the Law on Individuals Income Taxation. Since 1 January 2008, an entirely new system of taxation under the Law on Individuals Income Taxation has become effective. The new approach envisages the introduction of a flat rate of taxation of the income of all individuals amounting to 10%. This new system is named proportional and is deemed to replace the old system where the taxes due were determined by using a formula approach, under which the particular amounts of the tax rates have been calculated on the basis of a progressive table providing for increase of the rate to apply upon the increase of the level of income. This tax regime with 10% flat rate for personal income is a great advantage for Bulgarian sportsmen in comparison to their colleagues in the EU.

343. The legal regime of social and health contributions is provided in the Social Security Code. We give a brief explanation of the said contributions in this part, because their amount is of relevance for determination of the tax base for individuals' personal income. There are two main specifics of the social and health contributions. The first one is that the maximum security base is limited to BGN 2,600 or EUR 1,329.36. The second one is that the social and health contributions are shared between the employer and the employee. The figures for social contributions under employment activity are 13.16% of the security base for the employer and 10.14% of the security base for the employee. Altogether for social contributions are due 23.30% over the security base till the limit of BGN 2,600. Health contributions are 8% of the security base and are divided between the employer and the employee in ratio 60:40 or, meaning that health contributions for the employer are 4.80% of the security base and health contributions for the employee are 3.20% of the security base.

344. In case of an employment activity of a sportsman, the income is reduced with the personal share of social and health contributions and the residual amount is subject to taxation with 10%. In practice, the employment activity is the main form for engaging athletes and their main channel of incomes.

345. In case of business activity of a sportsman performed under private law contract, the income for tax purposes shall be reduced with 25%, which are recognized by virtue of law as expenditures necessary for the performance of said activity.

346. In case of a business activity, the security base constitutes the income reduced with 25%, which are presumed to cover the above-mentioned expenditures recognized as necessary for the performance of the said activity. The figures of social and health contributions under private law contract are as follows: social contributions – 10.46% of the security base for the sports club and 8.34% of the security base for the individual and health contributions – 4.8% of the security base for the sports club and 3.2% of the security base for the individual athlete, respectively.

347. For private law contracts, the income that is reduced first with 25% expenditures necessary for the performance of said activity and, second, with the personal share of social and health contributions on that decreased base, is subject to taxation with 10%.

348. From taxation point of view, there is no difference between amateur or professional athletes since in both cases they would be taxed as far as they generate income from the income categories subject to taxation. Consequently, taxation of athletes shall be made in accordance with the general rules of the applicable tax laws under the respective tax regime.

III. Sources of Income for Individual Athletes

349. In accordance with their source, the types of income for athletes pursuant to the Law on Individuals Income Taxation are grouped as follows:

- income from employment;
- income from other business activity;
- income from rent or other granting of rights or property for use against consideration;
- income from transfer of rights and property; and
- income from other sources as well as income taxed with final taxes on income originating from a source in Bulgaria or abroad under Chapter 6 of the law on the individual's income taxation.

350. Athletes usually derive income from employment or other business activity performed under private law contracts.

351. Pursuant to Article 29 of the Law on Individuals Income Taxation, the income that is subject to taxation is reduced as follows:

- in case of business activity of an athlete performed under a private law contract, the income for tax purposes shall be reduced by 25%, which are recognized by virtue of law as expenditures necessary for the performance of said activity;
- in case of transfer of rights, the derived income shall be reduced by 40%.

352. Pursuant to Article 31 of the Law on Individuals Income Taxation, the income from rent or other granting of rights or property for use against consideration shall be reduced by 10%.

IV. Sports Clubs

353. As we already mentioned above, sports clubs may be registered either as non-profit associations or as companies limited by shares. As regards sports companies, it is relevant from taxation perspective whether they qualify as resident companies or as non-resident companies. In order to be considered, resident companies have to meet the following requirements:

- to be legal entities established in accordance with the Bulgarian law; and
- to be companies registered pursuant to Regulation (EC) No. 2157/2001 of the Council and the cooperatives registered pursuant to Regulation (EC) No. 1435/2003 of the Council where their seat is located in the country or they are registered in Bulgarian registry.

354. Non-resident companies shall be those that are not resident.

355. The Law on Corporate Income Taxation regulates the taxation of legal entities including sports clubs.

V. Direct Tax of Sports Companies

356. The possible income sources for sports companies are not statutorily enumerated. Therefore, sports clubs are entitled to generate income as every commercial company only subject to the special provisions regarding the particular type of sports organizations as provided for in the Law on Sports.

357. For sports clubs, registered as non-profit associations, we may have several channels of funding their activity – member fees, State subsidies and other incomes that have type of business activities. The funding of member fees is not subject of taxation under the Law on Corporate Income Taxation as well as the subsidies. Only profits derived from business activities of the sports clubs, reduced with the relevant expenditures are subject to taxation under the Law on Corporate Income Taxation.

358. Profits of the sports companies are taxed under the regime of the Law on Corporate Income Taxation. The taxable profit shall be the positive value, determined on the basis of the financial result (accountancy profit/loss), which is established as a difference between the income and the expenses, not including the taxes on account of the profits, and adjusted in accordance with the provisions of the Law on Corporate Income Taxation. The tax rate since the beginning of 2007 amounts to 10%. In the said law, there is a strict regulation about the acceptable expenses the companies are able to accrue while forming their financial result. The main rule applicable is that expenses must be related to the business activities. Also, if a sports company incurs some expenses enumerated in the law that are not directly connected with its activities, for example expenditures for maintaining vehicles for the administration of the sports club, such company shall be obliged to pay one-off tax on these expenses in the amount of 10%.

359. Resident companies limited by shares, as well as resident non-profit associations are subject to corporate income tax on their worldwide income, on the income generated from sources located in Bulgaria as well as on the income from sources from abroad.

360. Non-resident companies shall be taxed under the Law on Corporate Income Taxation for their income realized through a place of business located in the Republic of Bulgaria as well as with respect to income specified in the Law on Corporate Income Taxation having a source of income in the Republic of Bulgaria.

361. In case of distribution of the profit in favour of the owners of the registered capital of a company, we have two main cases:

(1) The owners of the capital (shares) are private persons – then the tax due amounts to 5% of the undistributed profit. For instance, if a company has a profit of BGN 100, there will be 10% corporate tax, and the undistributed profit would amount to BGN 90. If the latter BGN 90 is distributed to the owners of the capital, there will be additional charge of 5% one-off tax. So, we may assume that the complete

taxation rate under the Law on Corporate Income Taxation will reach 14.50% in case of such distribution.

(2) The owners of the capital (shares) are companies. If these companies are resident in countries members of the EU – then the distribution of the profit will generate revenues for them and will not be taxed with 5% one-off tax here in Bulgaria. If the companies are not resident in countries members of the EU – then generally 5% one-off tax is retained. If there is a double tax treaty agreement available between the countries, then the regime of distribution of the profit should be considered under this treaty.

VI. Sports Activities under the Law on VAT

362. The Law on VAT defines the term 'service' as everything of value, which is different from a good, the money in circulation and the foreign currency used as an instrument for payment. Every physical and intellectual activity, including sports activity, qualifies as a provision of service pursuant to the Law on VAT.[65]

363. It is settled case law in Bulgaria[66] that a transfer of a sportsman from one club to another for the purpose of taxation with VAT is equated to a provision of service. Sports services as well as services in general are deemed to have their place of provision at the place where they are actually rendered.

364. There is a special regime for services provided by legal entities registered for VAT, which entities reside in a Member State of the EU. The tax in case of transactions involving sports services within the EU shall be due by the person who is the beneficiary of the service. For instance, if a player is transferred from a Bulgarian club to a club from Germany under a transfer contract, the tax treatment will be as follows:

> For the Bulgarian club said transaction shall be taxable with VAT at a rate of zero, the so called regime – reverse charge and the tax shall be due by the German club in accordance with the applicable German tax laws and regulations.

365. In the reverse situation if a player is transferred to a Bulgarian club from a German one, the tax exposure shall be the same whereas the tax due shall amount to 20% of the amount of the transaction pursuant to the Bulgarian Law on VAT.

366. However, VAT shall not be due in cases where sports services are rendered by sports organizations, which are registered as non-profit legal entities for performance of activity in public benefit. For example, such service may be the provision of a skating-rink for children, which shall be exempted from VAT if the provider is registered as a non-profit entity. Otherwise, all activities, which do not fall within the concept of public benefit, shall be taxable under VAT, like for instance, catering, snack bar, etc.

65. Law on Value Added Tax of 1 Jan. 2007 in the State Gazette issue No. 63 of 4 Aug. 2006.
66. Decision of SAC No. 1282 of 3 Feb. 2006 under administrative case No. 7270/2005, *see* Part II, Ch. 1, §4, *supra* .

Chapter 2. Private Regulations

§1. The BOC

I. Nature and Functioning of BOC

367. BOC was established on 30 March 1923. In 1924 it was acknowledged as a member of the IOC. BOC was registered with the Sofia District Court as a non-profit association on 17 April 1952.

368. The Law on Sports contains a few provisions concerning BOC. It is a non-profit legal entity, which shall exercise the powers and competences related to the development of the Olympic movement and popularization of the Olympic ideas within the country. BOC is governed in its activity by the provisions of Bulgarian legislation and the rules of the Charter of IOC as stated in Article 16, paragraph 2 of the Law on Sports. BOC is the single institution that may authorize the use of the Olympic symbols and signs.

369. BOC is a non-profit legal entity established for carrying out activity in public benefit under Chapter 3 of the Law on Non-Profit Legal Entities.

370. Detailed and elaborated provisions on the membership with BOC, its functions, governing bodies, etc. are included in the BOC Statute. BOC unites Bulgarian sports federations, national sports organizations registered as legal entities and natural persons. Among the individual members of BOC may be persons having special merits for the development of the Olympic movement, active athletes or former athletes who participated in the Olympic Games.

371. Currently BOC comprises eighty-four members (the chairman, thirty-nine sports federations managing Olympic sports, twelve public organizations and unions and thirty-two individuals).

372. BOC is obliged to participate on the Olympic Games by seconding athletes. It is held liable for the conduct of the Bulgarian delegation during the Olympics. BOC adopts the final decision for participation of athletes who are proposed by the national Olympic federations.

373. One of the peculiar provisions in the BOC Statute is Article 11, paragraph 6, which determines the function of BOC to grant, temporarily suspend and revoke the licence of the national Olympic federations. This function of BOC resembles the competence of MYS to license the sports federations. However, in this case the licence means the official acknowledgement of a federation for a given sport by BOC for the purpose of its compliance with the requirements for joining the Olympic movement. This conclusion is confirmed by Article 11, paragraph 7, which restates the general principle laid down in the Olympic Charter that only one single federation may be acknowledged for a given sport. Instead of acknowledgement, however, the BOC statute speaks about licensing of a single national federation for a sport managed by the respective international federation.

374. In order to be acknowledged and accepted as a member of BOC, a given sports federation must exercise concrete and real sports activity, to be affiliated to an international federation acknowledged by IOC and perform its activity in compliance with the Olympic Charter.

II. Bodies and Functions

375. The supreme body of BOC is the General Meeting of the BOC members. The General Meeting elects the President of BOC for a four-year term of office by a simple majority of the members attended the respective session.

376. The President manages the whole activity of BOC and represents BOC before the State and municipal bodies as well as before other legal entities and individuals in the country and abroad in accordance with the scope of his representative power as granted by the Executive Bureau. The President is responsible for chairing the sessions of the General Meeting, appoints the administration and the auxiliary personnel and is held accountable before the General Meeting.

377. The Executive Bureau of BOC functions as a managing body and has the legal nature of management board within the meaning of the Law on Non-Profit Legal Entities. It consists of seven to twenty-one persons and includes the President, the first deputy president, deputy presidents, members as well as the members of IOC for Bulgaria. The Executive Bureau elects the General Secretary who manages the administration of BOC in implementation of the decisions of the General Meeting, the Executive Bureau and the President.

378. The Supervisory Board consists of three to six members and performs controlling functions through inspections of the implementation of the programmes, the annual agendas, the documents and the expedient and lawful adoption of the decisions and their fulfilment.

379. BOC may also establish auxiliary bodies – commissions designated by the Executive Bureau, and in case of necessity also temporary working groups following a decision of the Executive Bureau.

III. Financing of BOC Activities

380. The BOC Statute determines in its Article 49 the sources of financing of its activities:

- membership fees;
- expedient subsidies provided by the competent State body in the field of sport (MYS);
- special funds and subsidies provided by IOC;
- royalties from licensing the Olympic symbols and signs in compliance with the Olympic Charter;
- revenues from the additional commercial activity;

- income from advertisement, TV and radio broadcasts of sports events organized by BOC;
- donations and sponsorships; and
- other sources not forbidden by the law.

381. There are several purposes under Article 38, paragraph 1 of the Law on Non-Profit Legal Entities, for which non-profit legal entities designated for carrying out activity in public benefit (such as BOC) shall spend their property:

- development and strengthening of moral values, the civil society, health care, education, science, culture, techniques, technologies or the physical culture;
- support of the socially weak, of the disabled or the persons needing care;
- support of the social integration and individual self-promotion; and
- human rights and environment protection.

382. According to Article 51, paragraph 1 of its Statute, BOC may perform additional commercial activity such as construction and exploitation of sports sites and facilities, training, education and specialization of athletes, coaches and sports administrators, advertising and publishing activity, distribution of published works, issuance of licences for use of the Olympic symbols and BOC signs as well as other activities necessary for achievement of the objectives specified in the BOC Statute.

383. The general rule under the Law on Non-profit Legal Entities is that non-profit legal entities may carry out additional commercial activity only if it is related to the main registered scope of activity and if the generated revenues are used for achievement of the objectives laid down in their statutes. The fact that said activity is additional prevents BOC from advertising itself as provider of certain commercial services because such advertising would be in collision with the promotion of the social objectives of BOC. This triggered the decision of the Executive Board for establishment of a commercial company named Bulgarian Olympic Pool to perform advertising activity upon assignment by BOC. In 2008, the company was registered in the commercial register kept by the Registry Agency. Later BOC renamed the company to BG Sport Pool.

IV. Control of the Activity of BOC

384. BOC being a non-profit legal entity for carrying out activity in public benefit is obliged to report annually information about its activity for the previous year before the central registry with the Ministry of Justice. Said information includes, *inter alia*, the objectives of the spent financial resources with a view to their compliance with Article 38 of the Law on Non-Profit Legal Entities.

385. The Minister of Justice is entitled to exercise ongoing control by requesting information about circumstances subject to registration. In case of breaches of the law acknowledged during the control, the Minister of Justice is obliged to notify the respective competent authorities.

§2. Internal Regulations of the Sports Federations

I. Introduction

386. As already clarified, the main specification of the Bulgarian sports legislation is the mixed legal nature of the sports federations. Although registered and operating as non-profit legal entities under the private law, they also have obligations for carrying out public functions transferred to them by the State by virtue of the Law on Sports. Furthermore, the Law on Sports has explicitly authorized the sports federations to regulate certain matters through their internal regulations. The particular matters left to be regulated that way as well as the particular scope of the legal authorization will be addressed below.

II. Status and Definition of Sportsman and Team

387. The status of the amateur and professional athletes and sports referees is left by virtue of the Law on Sports to be determined by the internal regulations of the Bulgarian sports federations. In turn, said regulations have to be approved by the Minister of Youth and Sports as required by Article 35, paragraph 3 of the Law on Sports.

388. Sports federations are obliged under Article 8 of the Implementing Regulations within six months from obtaining their licences to submit draft regulations on the status of the amateur and professional players, governing the granting, termination and revocation of the athletes competition rights to the Minister of Youth and Sports for approval.

389. The Implementing Regulations contain a definition of 'professional team', which is 'a group of persons registered as professional sportsmen who perform training activity on a regular basis and play a given kind of sport in organized manner on the behalf of one sports club'.

III. Amateur and Professional Athletes

390. The Law on Sports provides definitions of the terms 'amateur athletes' and 'professional athletes'. Amateur athletes would qualify as those persons, who conduct an activity of training and participation in competitions on a regular basis but said activity does not constitute a main profession for them. On the contrary, persons for whom the activity of training and participation in competitions constitutes a main profession qualify as professional athletes.

391. Amateur athletes may receive awards for the achieved top sport results and are entitled to funds covering their expenses incurred in result of their participation in the training and competition while maintaining their amateur status pursuant to Article 16 of the Implementing Regulations.

IV. Sports Referees

392. Sports referee is defined as a person with special qualification and right to manage sports competitions in a particular kind of sport, to control the observance of the rules for their conduct and to register the achieved sports results. Said qualification and right shall be acquired through education according to methods approved by the Expert Council on Physical Education and Sports and passing examination before the respective Bulgarian sports federation which shall determine the status of the sports referees independently in compliance with the requirements of the respective international sports federation. The referees who have obtained such a status with respect to particular kind of sport are subject to registration in a separate registry kept by the respective sports federation.

V. Status of Amateur and Professional Athletes and Sports Referees Pursuant to the Regulations of the Sports Federations

393. As mentioned above, the Law on Sports delegates to the sports federations the power to determine further the status of the amateur and professional athletes and sports referees involved in the particular sports they are managing. Those internal regulations of the sports federations that determine the status of the amateur and professional athletes are subject to approval by the Minister of Youth and Sports and this way certain status of public regulators is attributed to them. On the other hand, the regulations concerning the status of the referees shall comply with the acts of the respective international sports federation. Therefore, the part of the monograph dealing with the internal regulations of particular sports federations would necessary examine the provisions of sports federations regarding the status of amateur and professional athletes, which have been approved by the Minister of Youth and Sports, as well as the provisions regarding the status of the referees.

VI. Scope of the Delegation for the Sports Federations to Determine the Status of Athletes

394. The Law on Sports and the Implementing Regulations do not provide clear-cut answer of the question about the precise scope of the discretion of the sports federations to determine the status of the amateur and professional athletes and sports referees. As a clue, for the possible ambit of the delegated powers by virtue of the Law on Sports to sports federations may serve the previous version of Article 35 of the Law on Sports, which authorized the predecessor of MYS and SAYS, the Committee on Youth, Physical Education and Sports, to issue a decree clarifying the status of amateur and professional sportsmen, which status had to include:

- the conditions and procedure for granting and termination of competition rights;
- the conditions and the rights of sportsmen in case of a transfer;

- the main and supplementary social insurance of sportsmen, the medical supervision and cares, the control and insurance policies against traumatic and other injuries;
- the conditions and procedure for negotiations, professional qualification and requalification of athletes;
- the obligations for respect of the international legislative acts for participation in training and competition activity at all levels; and
- the right of forming professional associations.

§3. The Bulgarian Football Union

I. Introduction

395. The first FC in Bulgaria was founded in Sofia in 1909. Nevertheless, the real beginning of the organized football in Bulgaria took place in 1923 when the Bulgarian National Sports Federation (BNSF) came into existence and football constituted the main sport therein. The football department with BNSF organized the first football championship in 1924. Said department existed up to 1944 when the Central Football Committee was established, transformed in 1948 to Republican Football Section and ultimately in Bulgarian Football Federation in 1962.

396. The current governing body in football is the BFU, established on 27 June 1985, and it is a legal successor of the Bulgarian Football Federation.

II. Structure

397. BFU has its seat in Sofia and its bodies are the following:

- The Congress acting as a General Assembly of the member clubs consisting of delegates that are nominated by the affiliated FCs according to the procedure specified in the Statute.
- Executive Committee, which is the governing body of BFU. It is organizing the operation of BFU in the period between two congresses and consists of fifteen persons: the President, the first Vice President, two deputy Vice Presidents and eleven members. The term of office of Executive Committee's members is four years. They can be re-elected without limitation of the number of terms of office.
- The President is elected by the Congress for the term of four years. He cannot be elected for more than two consecutive terms of office. The President represents BFU before the State authorities, local self-government authorities, legal entities and physical persons in the country and abroad. A Congress for electing President and members of the Executive Committee is held every four years.

398. When exercising their authority provided by the legislation, the Statute and the internal regulations of BFU the governing bodies are assisted by the standing and the temporary committees and BFU Secretary's Office. The names and the operation of the standing committees are stipulated by the Statute and the internal regulations of the BFU.[67]

399. Arbitration bodies in the BFU system are the Disciplinary Committee, the Appeals Committee, the Licensing Committee and the Appeals on Licensing Committee.

400. The Secretary's Office provides assistance for the organization and the operation of other BFU bodies, as well as for the interaction between them. The Secretary's Office is organizing the implementation of the decision of the Executive Committee by other auxiliary bodies and BFU's administration. The Secretary's Office includes the Executive Director and the directors of departments in BFU's administration. The operation of the Secretary's Office is managed by the Executive Director.

401. The Executive Director is responsible for the whole administrative, organizational, sporting and technical activity of the BFU and in organizing the implementation of the decisions of the BFU's Congress and the Executive Committee.

402. If required temporary committees and other auxiliary bodies can be established with decision of the Executive Committee.

III. Objectives

403. Pursuant to Article 13 of its Statute, BFU has the following objectives:

- promoting football as sports and facilitating its distribution at the territory of the Republic of Bulgaria by implementing youth and other programmes in order to recognize its integrating, educational, cultural and humanitarian characteristics;
- developing the organizational, administrative, sporting and technical regulations for football, as well as managing their application and controlling their observance;
- organizing and implementing the national calendar of sports;
- managing and controlling other football games played on country's territory;
- protecting the interest of union's members before State authorities, local self-government authorities and other non-profit legal entities;
- providing control of the introduction and application of FIFA and UEFA regulations, as well as controlling their observance by union's members;
- limiting and preventing actions that infringe the honesty of football games or a misuse the game;
- establishing international sports relations regarding football in all aspects of this game;
- organizing and playing games between the national football teams and the representative teams of other national football federations;
- recognizing the national and international prestige of the Bulgarian football;

67. The standing committees are the following: Financial Committee; Ethics and Fair Play Committee; Media Committee; Women's Football Committee; Futsal Committee; Sporting and Medical Committee; Beach Football Committee; Licensing and Players' Agents Affairs Committee; Juniors and Youth Football Committee; Legal Committee; Sporting and Technical Committee; Referees Committee; Disciplinary Committee; Appeals Committee, Licensing Committee; Appeals on Licensing Committee; Grassroots Committee; Veteran Affairs Committee.

- assisting the development of junior and youth football, women's football, futsal and beach football; and
- combating against the use of doping and violence in football.

IV. Leagues

404. The PFL is an association of the FCs affiliated to BFU. PFL unites FCs that develop and perform football at professional level. PFL protects the interest of its member clubs and the professional footballers before BFU's bodies.

405. PFL is entitled to receive part of the income from the football competitions held in the system of BFU, from advertising and TV programmes, as well as from other sources. The procedure for spending and the accounting of the funds shall be stipulated by the Executive Committee. PFL cooperates in terms of organization and personnel with the bodies of BFU. It participates with own representatives in the standing committees. The statute, the regulations and the decisions of the PFL bodies shall not contradict the BFU's Statute and internal regulations.

406. The AFL unites FCs with amateur teams in order to protect their interest before BFU's bodies. AFL assists BFU's bodies in the management and control of the championships and tournament for amateurs. AFL is entitled to receive funds from BFU for the development of AFL. The procedure for spending and the accounting of the funds shall be stipulated by the Executive Committee.

407. In Bulgaria, there is one 'A' professional football group consisting of fourteen teams having professional status and two professional 'B' groups of fourteen to eighteen teams (Western and Eastern) also enjoying the status of professional teams. Four amateur leagues called 'C' groups exist where the teams are amateur.

408. The youth teams' senior age are organized in four zone groups consisting of eight to sixteen teams. Twenty-eight regional 'A' groups and twenty-eight regional 'B' groups for amateur men are organized in accordance with the regional boards of BFU. The same structure is also applicable with respect to the youth teams' junior age and children. The organization of the women's football championships is made through issuance of special regulations or instructions to that purpose.

409. The administration and organization of the State championships in 'A' and 'B' professional groups as well as the tournament for the Cup of Bulgaria is entrusted to PFL, which has the status of a non-profit legal entity established for performance of activity in public benefit and it is independent in terms of structure and legal organization from BFU. The other State championships are administered and organized by the respective zonal or regional councils of BFU or AFL. The zonal and regional councils are territorial bodies of BFU and operate in the respective zone or region.

V. Football Clubs

410. According to Article 18, paragraph 1 of the BFU Statute, members of BFU can be FCs that are registered as legal entities according to the Law on Non-profit

Legal Entities or the Law on Commerce and comply with the requirements for sports clubs stipulated in the Law on Sports.

411. FCs are accepted as members based on a decision of the BFU Congress. No club can be member if later it takes a name similar to the name of a club that is already a regular member of BFU, unless the second club grants its permission.

412. A FC can be suspended for breaching BFU's Statute and internal regulations, the statutes, regulations and the decisions of FIFA or UEFA or for any other conduct of club's members or officials, which makes further membership incompatible.

413. A FC which does not pay the due fees for membership and licence and/or does not participate in BFU's championships and other sports events for one sporting year shall be disqualified from the union.

414. BFU has adopted special Regulations on the Status of the FCs – Members of BFU. The regulations govern the rights and obligations of the clubs, the conditions and procedure for their participation in the football competitions held in the BFU system and the relationship between the clubs and BFU as well as among the clubs themselves.

415. BFU introduced a system for licensing with respect to the member clubs. The licensing is to be made in accordance with the status of the club and following the procedures set forth in the Law on Sports and the internal BFU Acts. The Law on Sports does not provide for mandatory licensing of sports clubs, however, the respective federations may opt for such licensing system. In order to obtain licence, clubs must meet all the requirements under the regulations including sports and technical requirements, financial requirements, requirements to sports sites and facilities, etc. License will not be issued or will be withdrawn if one individual or legal entity has the control over one or more FCs participating in the same national division championship.

416. Professional clubs are obliged to set a benefits quota of no less than 10% for maintenance of their schools for sport training of children and young people. The quota is 20% in case of amateur FCs.

VI. Players

417. Pursuant to Article 90, paragraph 1 of the BFU Statute, the players in the system of BFU are professional and amateur footballers.

418. 'Professional footballer' as defined in the Additional Provisions of the BFU Statute is a footballer who plays in a team of a licensed professional FC and receives remuneration based on a labour contract.

419. 'Amateur footballer' is respectively defined therein as a person who conducts an activity of training and participates in football competitions on a regular basis but the said activity does not constitute a main profession for him.

420. Players' status, sporting and transfer rights are stipulated by internal regulations endorsed by the Executive Committee pursuant to Article 90, paragraph 2 of the BFU Statute.

421. The BFU Regulations on the Status of Football Players list by way of example the compensatory payments of any source payable to an amateur player for the purpose of supporting his activity, which payments shall not affect his amateur status. Such expenditures could be associated with, travel costs, hotel, accommodation, equipment, preparation, health insurance and the like.

422. Pursuant to Article 27 of the BFU Regulations on the Status of Players, the basic requirement for a football player to obtain competitions rights and acquire status of professional athlete, respectively is the presence of a contract with a FC. The other requirements that the BFU used to apply in the past (the licence agreement with BFU and the certificate for registration by the Association of Bulgarian Professional Football Players) do not find place in the provisions of today's effective Regulations. The BFU Regulations on the Contracts and Transfers of Players implement a mandatory form and content of the contract, which the parties shall comply with. The content of the contract is specified in sections 1–9 of Article 3, paragraph 1 thereof where the clauses that have to be included in the contract between the athlete and the FC are strictly determined. The contract shall include:

- date of execution and the beginning of performance;
- its term of validity;
- the amount of the remuneration of the football player and the terms for its payment;
- the rights and the obligations of the club and the player;
- provisions for the insurance, as well as the health, medical and social insurance of the player;
- the conditions and the procedure for terminating the contract including in case of a transfer;
- the compensations due by the breaching party;
- an arbitration clause by virtue of which all disputes between the parties shall be within the jurisdiction of the Court of Arbitration with the BFU, unless the law provides differently; and
- information about player's agent name when he/she introduces the football player or the club.

423. Paragraph 67 of the same article goes even further – it provides the imperative rule by virtue of which the Executive Committee issues a model contract that is obligatory for the FCs and the football players. The contract is for a fixed-term, which shall not exceed three years. The minimum period of the contract is until the end of the sporting season. The professional football player acquires competition rights after registration with the BFU. Pursuant to Article 35(a), paragraph 4 of the Law on Sports, the application for registration shall be made by the club to which the athlete has provided his/her competition rights. With the act of the registration, the football player agrees to observe the statutes and the regulations of BFU, UEFA and FIFA.

VII. Status of Professional Football Players under the BFU Regulations

424. The Regulations on the Contracts and Transfers of Players issued by the BFU have only one provision related to the social and health insurance of professional football players – the explicit clauses for the insurance that shall be included in the contract between the club and the player. However, in 2006 there was an interesting case regarding the status of the football players and the applicable regime for their insurance, which deserves a special note. That is why, in the following paragraphs, the articles of the then BFU Regulations on the Status and Transfer of Players for the season 2006/2007 will be examined and interpreted.

425. Article 5 of the BFU Regulations on the Status and Transfer of Players[68] declared that the professional football players exercise the game of football as a liberal profession at their risk and on their account. Article 6(6) went even so far as to provide that all issues related to the mandatory social and health insurance of professional footballers shall be governed by a normative Act of BFU[69] coordinated with the National Social Security Institute (NSSI), National Revenue Agency and the Association of Bulgarian Football Players.[70]

426. The issue is whether the status of sportsmen for tax and social security treatment could be left to the sports federations to decide upon. The version of Article 35 as of 1996 explicitly delegated to the Head of the then Committee on Youth, Physical Education and Sports the power to determine the main and supplementary social

68. Revoked in 2008.

69. Although the term 'normative Act' is used, BFU as a sports federation does not qualify as a body empowered to adopt normative Acts under the Law on Normative Acts.

70. In reply to the request of the football officials to the NSSI regarding the possibilities for treatment of football as a liberal profession, NSSI delivered an official opinion. NSSI did not explicitly answer the question whether football as professional activity constitutes an employment or a liberal profession but rather commented the weight of the characteristics in support of employment vis-à-vis the weight of the characteristics showing that liberal profession is present.

Pro liberal profession arguments: – Special kind of preliminary registration of football players with their federations similar to the registration of the individuals pursuing liberal professions. – The activity is performed under a contract which type is not determined by the law and which content resembles the content of private law agreements. – Professional footballer is a person who performs training and competition activity and exercises the game of football as profession, that is, there are elements of exercise of liberal profession. NSSI relied on the definition of 'professional team' under the Implementing Regulations and Art. 6 of the Regulations on the status and transfer of footballers issued by BFU; however, it is not clear why NSSI considered said provisions as argument that football may be a liberal profession.

Pro employment arguments: – The activity is not exercised at own risk and account as required by the Decree on Social Security Aspects of self-employment. – The opinion further outlines the elements of the relationships in football that are at odds with the employment relationship and may question the existence of the latter. – Written form of the agreement under the sample approved by BFU with notary certification of each page. – Disputes arising out of the agreements shall be tried before and resolved by the Arbitration Commission with BFU (today by the CABFU) and not before the competent national court as provided for in the Labour Code. – Agreements may be terminated only by virtue of decision of the Arbitration Commission with BFU (the CABFU) under conditions significantly different than the ones stated in the Labour Code. – Remuneration due to football players for playing football as profession is set not with respect to a particular work, but at an amount 'exceeding the expenditures incurred for the performance of the activity'. The overall opinion of NSSI is that professional football players shall be treated as employees unless they are included in the list of persons pursuing a liberal profession by means of an amendment to the Decree of the Council of Ministers on the Social Security of Self-Employed Persons and all provisions of the internal regulations of BFU on the status and transfers of footballers, which provides for application of provisions of the Labour Code are deleted or replaced in a way not referring to the Labour Code in any manner.

insurance of sportsmen as a part of their status. This specification is missing from the current version of the article but may provide some clues regarding the precise scope of the delegation in support of the understanding that sports federations are entitled to determine the status of sportsmen for social security purposes in conformity with the law if they receive an approval of the Minister of Physical Education and Sports. In result, sportsmen would be treated for the purpose of their social insurance according to the particular status granted to them by their respective federations. Furthermore, the social security treatment would also affect the taxation as far as the decision about the applicable tax regime is partly dependent on the status of sportsmen as self-insuring individuals.

427. This approach, however, is quite formalistic and apparently does not take into consideration the substance of the relations in football and those in any other collective sport. Such treatment of footballers can be legally challenged with enormous chances for success.[71] The reasoning of the court in similar cases is quite predictable. This treatment of football players would infringe the principles of totality and equality of the insured individuals. By the same token as applied in the case at hand, football officials may generally exempt football players from any social security obligations.

428. Further, it is settled case law[72] that the obligation for self-insurance must be explicitly stated in the law and must specify what kinds of risks shall be covered by the social insurance and the amount of the income for social security purposes. Such obligation for self-insurance of sportsmen is neither specifically stated in the Law on Sports nor specifically delegated to the sports federations, which questions the lawfulness of the equation of football players to the individuals pursuing a liberal profession in accordance with the Social Security Code.

429. Finally, all other sports federations would be able to apply the same strategy, and this way all sportsmen in Bulgaria would be treated as self-employed individuals exercising liberal professions similarly to artistes.[73]

430. Therefore, tax and social security authorities in Bulgaria cannot derive the status of football players or any other sportsmen for the purpose of tax and social security treatment solely on the ground of provisions included in the internal regulations of the sports federations.

431. The options for treatment of football players as persons exercising liberal profession are inevitably connected with legislative amendments through listing football players among the 'individuals exercising liberal profession' under the Law on the Individuals Income Taxation, which would trigger also their status of self-insured individuals under the Social Security Code[74] since the latter refers to the tax laws.

432. However, it would be quite unlikely and unreasonable to expect, in authors' opinion, that the Bulgarian Parliament would vote in favour of an amendment to the

71. The range of the persons who would have standing in a potential legal proceedings against a legislative Act on the ground of contradiction with laws of a higher rank Act is quite broad since the subjective judgment of a person for being affected by the challenged Act would suffice.
72. Court Decision of the SAC No. 8525 of 29 Dec. 2000 rendered under administrative case No. 3261 of 2000.
73. Pursuant to the Law on Protection and Development of Culture, the profession of the persons exercising an activity in the field of culture independently is a liberal profession.
74. Social Security Code of 1 Jan. 2000 in the State Gazette issue No. 110 of 17 Dec. 1999.

Law on Individuals Income Taxation listing only professional football players without any considerations to be given regarding other collective sports such as basketball, volleyball, handball, etc. which sports could put forward the very same arguments in order to claim preferred status for players of these sports and, moreover, without taking into account the legal substance of the relations in the collective sports, which are of employment nature.

433. In absence of such amendment in the Law on the Individuals Income Taxation, specific provisions in the Law on Sports or in another legislative Act could be adopted laying down the obligation of sportsmen for self-insurance and the amount of the income for social security purposes and referring to the procedure for self-insurance as provided for in the Decree on Social Security Aspects of Self-employment.[75]

434. The idea of the football officials to equate football players to individuals exercising liberal profession and self-insured individuals is further in contradiction with the BFU statute saying that professional football players receive remuneration based on a labour contract. 'Internal regulations' are defined in the Additional Provisions of the BFU Statute as the regulations, decrees, statutes and decisions endorsed by the Congress, the Executive Committee or committees authorized by it, and other auxiliary bodies of BFU with regard to the application of the Statute or any of it provisions. Obviously, the internal regulations may not contradict the Statute, on the ground of which they are adopted.

435. Furthermore, the above idea is in conflict with many other provisions of the internal BFU regulations, which explicitly determine the contracts in football as labour law contracts. The biggest paradox is that even the second indent of the Article 5 specifying the practising of the game of football as a liberal profession used to set the rule that the professional player shall respect his obligations to the club until the termination of his employment contract by the BFU competent bodies.

VIII. Player Membership

436. No individual membership of physical persons is allowed pursuant to Article 18, paragraph 2 of the BFU Statute. This means that football players being individuals are not considered BFU members. The BFU regulations do not become mandatory for the players on the ground of the latter's membership with BFU but on the ground of the authorization provided for in the Law on Sports allowing sports federations to adopt regulations in order to determine the status of professional and amateur players.

437. However, any provisions that may fall outside the scope of the legal authorization under the Law on Sports would not be applicable to football players on the ground of the principle of freedom of association since they are not members of BFU. This would be practically important with respect to any possible insertion of arbitration clauses. Such clause, as was mentioned above, is inserted in the model contract, which is obligatory for the FCs and the players by virtue of the latest adopted Regulations on the Status and Transfer of Players. Usually in sport, the arbitration

75. Decree on Social Security Aspects of Self-Employment and the Bulgarian Citizens Working Abroad of 1 Jan. 2000 in the State Gazette issue No. 21 of 17 Mar. 2000.

clauses laid down in the regulations of the international and national sports federations are considered accepted by the players due to their membership with the respective federation.

438. It is, therefore recommendable that BFU Statute provides for membership of football players therewith. Similarly to Italian footballers, they may become members of BFU by making a request submitted through the club prior to certain deadline.[76]

439. Pursuant to the BFU Regulations on the FCs, members of BFU professional football players cannot be members of their clubs either. Membership with their clubs is allowed only with respect to players having status of amateurs.

Membership is possible only with respect to clubs registered as non-profit legal entities.

IX. Football Coaches

440. Pursuant to the Law on Sports, 'coach' is a sports pedagogue in a kind of sport who organizes and carries out training and activity of sportsmen having different qualification.

441. A special BFU Regulations on the Status of Coaches determine the system of positions attributed to the football coaches: senior coach in football (manager), football coach and teacher – football coach. In order to train players or a team or manage the latter during friendly and official matches, a person must hold valid licence issued by the Coach Commission of BFU or by Coach Commission acknowledged by FIFA and UEFA by virtue of the UEFA Convention on the Mutual Recognition of Coaching; otherwise, the person must have begun educational course for coaches of the respective level. The person eligible for teaching or training players or teams obtains a diploma and a license evidencing his competence to practise the profession of a coach. Such persons are further registered with the Technical Committee of BFU to obtain the so-called licence for work.

442. The regulations on the status of coaches confirm that they are employees of their clubs and enter into a fixed-term employment contracts accordingly. The regulations indicate two legal options for termination of a contract: by mutual agreement of the parties at any time of the sporting year or on grounds stipulated by the contract or by the effective legislation. The mutual agreement of the parties shall be expressed in written form and presented to the Technical Committee of BFU. Pursuant to Article 325 of the Labour Code, the party to which the proposal for termination of the contract is addressed shall inform the other party of its position within seven days following the receipt of the proposal. Failure to do so shall be deemed as refusal to accept the proposal. All disputes related to the existence and the performance of the contract shall be within the jurisdiction of the Arbitration Court with BFU. In case the club has faultily terminated the contract, the coach has the right to conclude a contract with another club during the same sporting year. In the reverse case of termination with fault made by the coach, the latter would be sanctioned with withdrawal of the licence

76. M. Colucci, *Italy*, in *International Encyclopaedia of Laws: Sports Law* (R. Blanpain & F. Hendrickx ed., Kluwer Law International 2004).

for one year. The coach is further obliged to inform the Technical Committee within seven days for the conclusion or the premature termination of the contracts.

443. It shall be noted that the 2009 regulations overcame the contradiction between the procedure for termination of coaches' contracts, provided for in the previous redaction of the BFU's Act and the procedure for termination under the Labour Code. According to the regulations of 2006, the single competent body to rule on the termination of those contracts was the, acting at that time, Arbitration Commission which had the powers to indicate the cause for termination and to establish whether the contract has been performed or not. The grounds for termination are listed in the Labour Code and every party could avail of those, for which it is entitled under the code. The single body that may intervene in a procedure for termination is the Labour Inspection in certain cases where its permission for termination of the employment contract is required pursuant to the Labour Code. Authorization of any other bodies especially established by virtue of internal regulations of non-profit legal entities would definitely contradict the Labour Code.

444. Nevertheless, there are certain deficiencies in the new internal regulation on the status of coaches – it empowers the Court of Arbitration of BFU to settle disputes related to the existence and the performance of the contract between the coach and his club. The Civil Procedure Code explicitly prevents disputes concerning rights under employment relationship from being referred for settlement by courts of arbitration. The juridical relation between the coach and the FC clearly has an employment nature and shall not be resolved by way of arbitration.

445. An interesting issue was raised upon the termination of the employment contract of the coach of CSKA Sofia Plamen Markov unilaterally by the club in the beginning of the spring football season in 2007. The coach had a clause in his contract for payment of compensation at certain amount in case of unilateral termination by the club. CSKA maintains that pursuant to the Labour Code the club was entitled to terminate the agreement and in such cases the compensations due could be only provided for in that code.

446. The single ground for termination of the employment agreement that could have been applicable in the case at hand and used by CSKA is the one set in Article 328, paragraph 1, section 5 of the Labour Code – absence of qualities of the employee for effective performance of the work. Certainly, the legality of the termination based on this ground could be challenged before the court, and the club would have the burden to prove its existence in the particular case.

447. If, presumably, this ground for termination was available the club claimed that the compensation due in such case could be only the one specified in the Labour Code – the compensation for breached period of notice required by the code. In case of a fixed-term agreement, this period amounts to three months and the employer has the option to pay three times the gross labour remuneration of the employee instead of waiting for the expiry of the period of the prior notice. Exactly this compensation CSKA offered to Plamen Markov claiming that it is the single one due under the Labour Code, and that the compensations set therein are mandatory and cannot be derogated by way of provisions in the individual contracts.

448. This understanding cannot be shared. The Labour Code was enacted during socialism, and its provisions are largely made in favour of the employees. One of the main principles of the Bulgarian labour law is the protection of the employees whereby all provisions of the code must be construed in a way to better off the position of the employees. Consequently, a provision in an individual contract allowing the employee to receive a larger amount of compensation would be undoubtedly valid.

449. Furthermore, Article 331 of the Labour Code provides the option for the employer to terminate the employment contract of his employee upon the former's initiative against compensation agreed between the parties. The amount of this compensation cannot be less than four times of the most recently received monthly gross remuneration by the employee. The absence of a statutory stated maximum of the compensation means that the parties may agree on significantly higher compensation. Therefore, no obstacles exist for the parties to stipulate in advance the amount which would be due by the employer in case it decides to terminate the agreement on its own initiative.

450. However, the arguments of CSKA could be meaningful if the club would oppose any possible sanctions imposed by the, acting at that time, BFU Arbitration Commission for the unilateral breach of the employment contract of the coach. Such imposition would lack any legal basis in the Labour Code and the Law on Sports.

451. The case with CSKA and its former coach Plamen Markov reveals a very small part of the complex relations between the legal regulation of sport under the association law of the international and national sports federations and the Bulgarian labour law. Sometimes the results from the interaction of such norms originating from different levels of governance are quite unpredictable and undesired. Other examples and elaboration of this matter would be provided in the Part II of the monograph dealing with Sport and Employment.

§4. Bulgarian Volleyball Federation

I. Introduction

452. In accordance with Article 1, paragraph 1 of its Statute, the Bulgarian Volleyball Federation is a non-profit legal entity designated for performance of activity in public benefit and constituting a union of sports clubs in volleyball and beach volleyball as well as a union of school, university, militarized workers and village sports clubs registered as non-profit legal entities.

II. Component Parts and Objectives of the Bulgarian Volleyball Federation

453. The supreme body of the Bulgarian Volleyball Federation is the General Meeting of the federation consisting of all sports member clubs. The Management Board of the federation consists of five to twenty-five members elected for a term of four years. The General Meeting elects the President of the Management Board.

454. The objectives of the Bulgarian Volleyball Federation are set forth in Article 4 of its Statute and contain the following:

- development, improvement and popularization of volleyball in Bulgaria in compliance with the main directions of the national policy in the field of physical education and sport and in accordance with the adopted national programmes;
- coordination of the development, practice and administration of volleyball on the territory of Bulgaria;
- creation of conditions and assistance to the volleyball clubs in Bulgaria for development of high sporting quality of the players and teams in volleyball and beach volleyball with a view to adequate expression of the sports and technical talents of the sportsmen and achievement of prestigious positions for the Bulgarian volleyball at the international field;
- organization of a system for provision of professional realization as well as for acquisition and maintenance of the qualifications of the sports specialists in the field of volleyball;
- assistance, coordination, promotion, regulation, organization, control, guiding and management of volleyball within the country;
- permanent control with respect to the conditions for acquisition and holding of sports licence from the sports clubs as well as with respect to the observation of the rules for handling the training and competition activity on the part of the leadership of the various volleyball clubs, coaches and sportsmen; and
- protection of the ethical and moral fundaments of the Bulgarian volleyball.

III. Regulations on the Status of Volleyball Players

455. Pursuant to Article 10 of the Regulations of the Bulgarian Volleyball Federation on the Competition Rights and the Status of the Amateur and Professional Volleyball Players amateur sportsmen are persons who practice training and competition activity on regular basis but it is not main profession for them.

456. The amateur volleyball player is not entitled to receive remuneration apart from the funds necessary for covering the expenditures for the training and competition activity carried out by that amateur player. However, amateur athletes are entitled to receive awards for the achieved top sporting results.

457. Pursuant to Article 13 of the regulations, a professional volleyball player carries out training and competition activity under employment contract against remuneration.

458. Therefore, with a view to the relations between players and clubs in volleyball, the contracts undoubtedly qualify as employment contracts. Only in the cases where players represent the national team the contracts may be of different nature – service contracts governed by civil law.

459. The regulations specify the requisites of the contracts between professional volleyball players and their clubs, which are stated in the Implementing Regulations and shall be discussed *infra* in Part II Sport and Employment.

460. The regulations contain a special ground for termination of the contract by the player – in case of failure of the club to make the mandatory social security and health contributions in accordance with the Bulgarian law for a period exceeding three months. In such cases, the Bulgarian Volleyball Federation is obliged to carry out inspection.

461. The grounds for termination of an employment agreement are enumerated in an exhaustive list in the Labour Code. Additional grounds cannot be established in other Acts that are subordinated to the Labour Code in the hierarchy of the legal instruments. Pursuant to Article 327, section 2, the employee is entitled to terminate his employment agreement without prior notice in case the employer has delayed the payment of compensation due under the social security system. This case, however, is different than the case of non-payment of social security contributions by the employer and, therefore, there is no a valid ground for termination in accordance with the Labour Code.

462. The reason for the insertion of such a ground for termination of the agreements in volleyball is the necessity available also in all collective sports for responding to the problems concerning payment of players' social security contributions due by their clubs.

463. Similar problems frequently happen in football as well. For instance, at the end of the 2004–2005 season even the Bulgarian football champion at that time CSKA Sofia had unpaid debts to the National Social Security. However, in football the problems are solved through the licensing system by threatening the clubs having such unpaid debts with losing their licences. Every FC is obliged to prove its economic stability by presenting, *inter alia*, a declaration and evidence for paid obligations to the State social insurance, the mandatory and the additional voluntary pension insurance, health insurance, occupational accidents and the taxable income under the Law on Individuals Income Taxation.

464. It is recommendable that volleyball officials would deal with the problems concerning unpaid social security contributions by means that do not contradict the Labour Code.

§5. Bulgarian Basketball Federation

I. Introduction

465. The Bulgarian Basketball Federation (BBF) is determined in Article 1 of its Statute as an independent voluntary union of basketball clubs and associations in the Republic of Bulgaria exercising activities pertaining to the development of basketball in the officially recognized by the International Basketball Federation (FIBA) disciplines – standard basketball, 3x3, basketball in wheelchairs and basketball for veterans. The BBF is a non-profit legal entity for exercise of activities in public benefit.

II. Component Parts and Objectives of the BBF

466. The General Assembly is the supreme body of the federation, which shall be convened at least once a year. It consists of one authorized representative of each club participating in the State championships for adolescents not in all age categories, two authorized representatives of the clubs participating with a team in the State championship for men and/or women or in the State championships for adolescents of all ages for one g sex, three authorized representatives of the clubs participating with a team in the State championship for men and/or women and in the State championships for adolescents of all ages for one of the sexes and four authorized representatives of the clubs participating with a team in the State championship for men and women and in the State championships for adolescents of all ages and of both sexes, the members of the Management Board, the honoured Chairman of BBF, the Chairman of the Supervisory Board, the Chairman of the Arbitration Commission, the chairman of the other permanent commissions established with the federation, the members of the bureau and the permanent commissions of FIBA and FIBA Europe, honoured members of FIBA or FIBA Europe,. The General Assembly elects the President of the federation for a term of five years.

467. The President of the federation is entitled to appoint the Executive Vice President among the Management Board members. He approves the head coaches of the national basketball teams upon proposal made by the Management Board.

468. The Management Board is a collective body of BBF and shall be consisted of the BBF President eight to fourteen members. The Management Board members shall be elected for a period of five years and may be re-elected. The powers of the Management Board are listed in Article 19 of the BBF Statutes.

469. The Supervisory Board exercise overall control with respect to the funds of the federation as well as the way and procedure for accumulation and spending of said funds. It has the right to check the documents of the Federation including the performance of the decisions of the General Assembly and the Management Board. It consists of one chairman and two members elected by the General Assembly for a term of five years.

470. The Arbitration Commission is the body in charge for hearing, resolving and interpreting disputes and objections in relation to decisions and normative Acts of the BBF and all its bodies other than the Management Board and the General Assembly. Before 18. September 2014 the decisions of the Arbitration Commission could be appealed before the Bulgarian Sports Arbitration Court in the cases where they fall within the competence of the latter and provided that the two parties to the dispute have agreed to refer it to arbitration before that institution. However, following the amendment on the above-mentioned date the decisions of the Arbitration Commission were declared to be final. Likewise, the previous text of Article 23, paragraph 7 of the Statute of the Federation explicitly stating that the decisions of the Arbitration Commission are subject to judicial review was abandoned. The Arbitration Commission consists of a chairman and four members elected by the General Assembly for a term of five years.

471. The Referee Commission and the Coach Commission are permanent bodies of the Federation, which members are designated by the general meetings of the licensed referees and officials as well as coaches, respectively. Further to the above-listed auxiliary bodies, other permanent bodies and commissions may be established for support of the BBF activity by way of decisions of the Management Board of the Federation.

472. The objectives of the BBF are stated in Article 2 of its Statute:

- developing and promoting basketball in Bulgaria;
- development of directions, the main methodical requirements and documents for practising of the basketball game in Bulgaria in compliance with the national policy and the national programme in the field of physical education and sport and observance of their fulfilment;
- functioning and development of the game of basketball in Bulgaria in full compliance with the established national and international standards and requirements for that sport;
- promotion of basketball to a level of widely spread and socially significant sport;
- promoting basketball as a sport that helps for the education, the social communication and the formation of behaviour culture and ethics among youngsters;
- increase of the level of the sports proficiency;
- increase of the national and the international significance of basketball; and
- luring highly qualified experts and improvement of the qualification of the specialists involved in basketball.

III. Regulations of the BBF on the Competition Rights and the Status of Basketball Players

473. The Regulations on the Competition Rights and the Status of the Basketball Players issued by the BBF define the professional basketball player as an athlete who has been registered with a basketball club for participation in a State championship for men or women and who has concluded a contract, under which he receives a pay. The amateur basketball player is defined in two ways: as an athlete, who has completed his secondary education or has turned age of 19, who has been registered with a basketball club for participation in a State championship for men or women, who does not have a contract with a basketball club or as an athlete who has not completed his secondary education and has not turned the age of 19, with or without a contract for sports preparation and development. A basketball club may pay to an amateur athlete only the funds necessary for covering the expenditures for his/her participation in that activity. The expenditures, with respect to which the athlete is permitted to receive reimbursement without changing his/her amateur status, are enumerated by way of example – transport, daily payments, rents, sports equipment, medical services, medicaments, insurances, etc.

474. The Regulations on the Competition Rights and the Status of Basketball Players further defines the professional athlete as one who performs the training and competition activity against remuneration and for that purpose concludes a contract in writing with a basketball club, where he/she wants to be registered.

§6. Bulgarian Swimming Federation

I. Introduction

475. The Bulgarian Swimming Federation is a non-profit legal entity exercising activity for public benefit and uniting sports clubs running swimming sports (swimming, diving, synchronized swimming and free-water swimming). Water polo is governed by a separate Water Polo Federation. The Bulgarian Swimming Federation is a member of the International Amateur Swimming Federation (FINA) and a member of the European Swimming League, which is the counterpart of FINA at European level. The main scope of activity of the federation embraces coordinating the development, exercise, regulation and administration of the swimming sports at national level and their representation before the State and the international sports organizations.

II. Component Parts and Objectives of the Bulgarian Swimming Federation

476. According to Article 47 of the Statute, the General Assembly is the collective supreme governing body of the Bulgarian Swimming Federation. The Management Board is the managing body of the federation having a mandate of five years and thirteen members. The President of the federation can be also elected for a term of five years, and his duties include operational management of the whole activity of the federation and representation before State and local authorities as well as natural and legal persons within and outside the country. The President of the Federation is also a president of the Management Board pursuant to Article 48 of the Statute.

477. The organizational structure of the Bulgarian Swimming Federation further includes a general secretary, permanent committees, permanent commissions – referee commissions in the three types of sport, disciplinary and arbitration commissions,. In case of necessity, the Management Board may adopt decision for establishment of other commissions for particular issues and tasks.

478. The Statute of the Federation provides for internal system for maintaining sports justice. According to Articles 78 and 79, all disputes within the system of the Federation shall be resolved in accordance with the provisions of the Statute and the internal regulations by the committees and commissions of the Bulgarian Swimming Federation, whose decisions are subject to appeal before the arbitration commission. The decisions of the arbitration commission may be appealed before the Management Board for the cases of disqualification of a team from a competition and athlete's suspension for more than a year.

479. Pursuant to Article 80, all decisions of bodies of the Bulgarian Swimming Federation that might conflict the laws, the Statute or previous decisions of the General Assembly may be contested before the General Assembly by all members or bodies of the federation. The Statute provides also that any recourse to the general court system prior to availing of the sports justice mechanisms and procedures shall be considered as a conduct of disrespect to the Statute.

480. The objectives of the Bulgarian Swimming federation stated in Article 10 of the Statute are promotion and preservation of the national and international prestige of the Bulgarian swimming as well as increase of the social importance and enlargement of the international prestige of swimming sports through working in collaboration with the State, municipalities and other organizations.

III. Regulations for the Granting, Termination and Withdrawal of Competition Rights and the Status of Sportsmen Participating in the Training and Competition Activity of the Bulgarian Swimming Federation

481. Article 5, paragraph 1 of the internal regulations of the Federation dealing with the status of sportsmen in swimming sport define the amateur athlete as the one who practises a given type of swimming sport with a swimming club member of the Bulgarian Swimming Federation and who has been registered in line with the said regulations, but this is not a main profession for him and he is not bound with the club through a contract whether employment or otherwise under which he is to receive a regular remuneration against systematic exercise of the respective swimming sport and against participation in the competition and training process. Pursuant to Article 7 thereof the amateur sportsman may be supported financially with funds by the swimming club or the Bulgarian Swimming Federation under terms and conditions specified by the Management Board for covering the expenses for the participation in the training and competition activity and such covering will not trigger any change in his amateur status.

482. In order for a swimmer to qualify as professional, he/she must exercise training and competition activity as a main profession against pay and as for that purpose has to have concluded a contract whether employment or otherwise as a swimming club member of the Bulgarian Swimming Federation.

Part II. Sport and Employment

Chapter 1. Sports Regulation

§1. The Labour Code of 1987

I. Introduction

483. Bulgaria does not have a special law dealing with the employment relations between professional athletes and their clubs. Therefore, the provisions of the general Labour Code would apply to sportsmen whenever their relationship is deemed to reveal the necessary key elements of the employment relationship.

II. Definition of Employment Relationship

484. The Labour Code[77] lacks an explicit legal definition of the employment relationship. Pursuant to Article 1 thereof, the Labour Code shall govern the employment relations between the employee and the employer as well as other relations related thereto. On the basis of this provision, employment is defined by the legal theory as a relation regulated by the labour law rules. This means that formation, content, termination and legal consequences of employment are provided for in said rules.[78] Consequently, administrative and judicial bodies while dealing with relations in sport are supposed to examine whether and to what extent the rules of the Labour Code are present in order to qualify the particular relationship as employment.

485. Despite the lack of a clear-cut definition of employment in the law, it may be concluded that Bulgarian labour law scholars do not depart in their interpretation of the key elements of the employment from the conventional concept of employment as developed in most of the contemporary national legislations. Under Bulgarian legal theory, employment shall be similarly present in the cases where for a certain period of time a person provides labour for and under the direction of another person in return for pay.

77. Labour Code of 1 Jan. 1987 in the State Gazette issue No. 26 of 1 Apr. 1986.
78. V. Mrachkov, *Labour Law* (SIBI Press 2004).

486. Provision of labour constitutes the subject matter of the employment relationship. In legal theory, it is also called a rent of labour, which assumes certain dependence of the employee and superiority of the employer, respectively. The reason for this assumption is the impossibility for the employer to dispose effectively of the labour inherent to the personality of the employee without having certain power with respect to that personality. Therefore, although not specifically stated as an element of the employment relationship in the Labour Code, dependence constitutes a necessary consequence from the provision of labour as subject matter of the employment relationship.

487. Dependence amounts to a legal bond and results in the fact that the employer is obliged to respect, comply with and follow the orders of the employer and, therefore, be dependent on said orders.[79] The element dependence is crucial for the demarcation of employment from the independent work of the self-employed individuals.

III. Definition of Self-Employment

488. Self-employment is present where a person exercises his/her profession at his/her risk and account. Self-employed individuals independently organize their work process and are subject solely to the orders they themselves are giving to them. Such persons in accordance with the Bulgarian jurisprudence are those who exercise liberal professions or independent craft or who are entrepreneurs. They enter into private law contracts and owe as consideration certain results agreed between the parties, unlike employees, whose main obligation is to provide labour to their employers.

489. The difference between employment and self-employment entails different tax and social security regimes. In social security, context demarcation of the concepts of employment and self-employment is significant also due to the fact that the level of protection for both is different. For instance, self-employed persons are not entitled to unemployment benefits, which they will have if they enjoy a status of employees.

490. The presence of the third element – pay – is particularly important in sport context since it concerns the difference between amateur and professional sportsmen.

491. In practice, the majority of the athletes even those practising individual sports such as light athletics, weightlifting, wrestling, judo, boxing, swimming, etc. conclude employment contracts with their clubs. In most of the cases, the individual sports are run by clubs, which pay wages to their athletes and the latter represents the clubs in the competitions in consideration for the wages so received.

492. However, the option for the individual athletes to be considered self-employed persons pursuing a liberal profession on the basis of the specifics of their activity is available. In such cases, the individual athlete would be an independent member of the respective federation without belonging to any particular club.

493. For instance, Bulgarian sprinter Ivet Lalova, who in Bulgaria was practising her sport under an employment contract with Levski Sofia, took part in a competition in Greece on behalf of the Greek club Panionis. At the end of the competition, that is, upon the fulfilment of the duties for which she had been contracted and for which she

79. *Id.*, 145.

had received remuneration, which was to run the 100 m once or twice (depending on the number of participants) the contract expired automatically.

494. Likewise, the young Bulgarian tennis player Cesil Karatancheva participated in a tournament in France on behalf of the tennis club Tcherno More Elit Varna and in the German Tennis Bundesliga for the German tennis club Moerns 08 besides participating individually in tournaments of the World Tennis Association.

495. Furthermore, the club of the athlete in light athletics Petar Datchev wanted to terminate his employment contract due to the fact that he participated in just two competitions for the whole year and wanted to pay the athlete fees in consideration for his services with respect to said competitions. It was not justifiable from club's point of view to pay a wage each month in the course of the year.

496. In the particular examples of Lalova and Karatancheva provided above, the risk for the performance of the sports activity is vested in the athlete unless born by a third-party insurer. The two athletes are themselves accountable for preparing for the particular competitions and owe to the club result, that is, participation in the particular tournament and not provision of labour. Therefore, those athletes who organize their sport activity in the above-described way would clearly qualify as self-employed individuals pursuing liberal profession at their risk and account.

§2. Sports Contracts

497. The Law on Sports lays down the obligation of the professional sports clubs to have concluded contracts with their professional athletes in accordance with the status of the athletes as conferred to them. The nature of these contracts is not specified. The language of the provision is further ambiguous with respect to which body was meant to have conferred that status – the sports federation, which is authorized by virtue of Article 35 of the Law on Sports to determine the status of the professional athletes or the status determined by the tax and social security authorities for the purpose of the respective treatment.

498. Pursuant to Article 17 of the Implementing Regulations, professional athletes perform training and competition activity under agreement against payment. Said agreement shall be concluded between the professional athlete and the sports club, be in writing and have mandatory content consisted of provisions regarding the term of agreement, the amount of the remuneration of the athlete, insurance and medical insurance of the athlete, the conditions and procedure for termination of the agreement including in case of a transfer, and the compensations due by the breaching party.

499. The agreement indicated in the Implementing Regulations cannot be construed to be a special sports contract other than employment contract, having specific legal regulation and capable to derogate the applicability of the general provisions of the Labour Code. Pursuant to Article 1, paragraph 2 of the Labour Code all contracts concerning the provision of labour must be concluded in the mandatory form of an employment contract. Consequently, regardless of what the parties call their contract, it will be considered an employment contract if it concerns the provision of labour or contains the necessary elements of an employment contract. This provision is intended to prevent employers from circumventing their obligations under the Labour

Code to the detriment of their employees and to deprive them from their labour law, social and other rights inherent to the status of employees.

500. In case the relationship between the club and the player is found to be employment, the contract must further contain the minimum mandatory content of the employment agreements as specified in Article 66, paragraph 1 of the Labour Code.

This means that the following requisites must be included in the contract:

- the title of the position;
- the date of the contract's execution;
- the date on which the employee is to commence work;
- the duration of the contract;
- the duration of basic paid annual leave and additional annual paid leave;
- the notification period for termination of the employment relationship, which must be the same for both parties;
- the basic and additional remuneration of a permanent nature and the terms of payment; and
- the duration of the working day or week.

501. An employment agreement shall be concluded in writing and notified to the National Revenue Agency.

§3. Players' Obligations

502. Players' obligations are not regulated specifically by the law. They are specified in the respective regulations of the sports federations and become mandatory for the players on the basis of their membership with the sports federations since said membership is considered to be voluntary, that is, on the basis of the freedom of association. Further, the obligations of the players are integral part of the individual contracts which players sign with their clubs. They constitute contractual obligations and, therefore, are also based on the principle of freedom of contracts.

503. However, in case the sports relationship amounts to employment, the Labour Code would make numerous other obligations applicable to sportsmen who are employees such as the obligation of the employee to perform the work agreed, the obligation to comply with the labour discipline and the others enumerated in Article 124 of the Labour Code.

§4. The Concept of Competition Rights

504. The Law on Sports has introduced the term 'competition rights'. Its definition is contained in Article 35(b), paragraph 1 of the law and Article 11, paragraph 5 of the Implementing Regulations, according to which the competition rights are a combination of the right of the athlete to participate in the training and competition activity of a sports club including the material and the moral rights related thereto. The athlete is obliged to compete only on behalf of the club, which he has been registered to.

505. The amendments in the Law on Sports in 2008 extended the legal regulation of the competition rights by inserting provisions regarding the registration of sportsmen, which, up to that moment, was entirely governed by provisions set in the Implementing Regulations. Registration is an act, through which competition rights are created with respect to particular individual who obtains a status of sportsman. Registration is made only following the wish of such individual willing to be registered expressed in writing. The amateur and professional sportsmen are granted competition rights after registration with the licensed federation organizing the respective sport. The application for registration is made by the club, to which the player has given his/her competition rights. The latter wording confirms the conclusion that sports clubs are holders of competition rights. The act of registration by the sports federation provides validity to the competition rights given by the particular sportsman to his/her club, that is, the sports federation acknowledges the status of sportsman of such individual and the right of his/her club to hold his/her competition rights.

506. The Implementing Regulations continue containing more detailed provisions regarding competition rights in comparison to the Law on Sports. They confirm that competition rights arise upon registration of the player. The licensed sports federations may independently determine the conditions and procedure for registration of professional and amateur athletes. The registration is valid for one sporting year, that is, for one sporting season. The registration is made by the federation only after the athlete has expressed in writing his/her wish to be registered established in concluded contract for sport preparation and development and upon proposal of a member-club. The sports federation enters the data of the proposed athlete in a separate registry and issue an official document – a player's card. The player's card is the evidence and the embodiment of the right of a player to compete in a competition.

507. The competition rights of the professional athletes shall be exercised for the period of the contract and those of the amateur athletes – for the term of registration. An athlete whose contract has been terminated or whose registration has been expired is entitled to choose independently which sports club will register him.

508. The sports federations grant, terminate and revoke the competition rights. They exercise this power either independently or upon proposal of the sports clubs. The existence of such a power of the sports federations does not mean that the competition rights belong to the federation. Competition rights are granted upon registration to the club and belong to the latter. In addition to the explicit provision in the Law on Sports, this is also confirmed by Article 14 of the Implementing Regulations stating that a sports federation may revoke the competition rights of an athlete registered thereby for a certain period of time or completely acting on its own initiative or following a motivated proposal of the sports club holding the competition rights.

509. The Implementing Regulations specify the ways for termination of the competition rights arising from the registration, which are the following:

- mutual consent of the parties;
- the wish of the registered person expressed in writing;
- expiry of the term of registration;
- death or imposition of full judicial disability of the registered person; and
- deregistration of the sports club.

510. Competition rights may be called also federative rights since they very much resemble (despite the possible nuances) the meaning of the federative rights described by FIFA in the following way:

> Federative rights can be defined as a juridical link existing between a club and a player, which began with the registration of the player for that specific club at an Association. This link ended with a new registration of the player for another club. This juridical link was separate and independent from the link created by the employment contract signed by the player and the aforementioned club.[80]

511. It is particularly noteworthy that FIFA currently denies the existence of federative rights as such. The example of Bulgaria, however, proves that federative rights are still used in the EU.

512. This inevitably poses the question whether third parties – agents, companies or even investment funds may acquire competition rights and, hence, the right to register the player with a club. Such a practice may entail a serious infringement of the free movement of workers.

513. The SAC in its decision of 3 February 2006 construing the transfer of sportsmen for the purposes of taxation with VAT has come in its own words to the 'single correct conclusion' that the transfer of sportsmen does not constitute a transaction with merchandise but rather a provision of the service 'transfer of the intangible assets what competition rights are'. SAC had to classify the subject matter of the transaction 'transfer of sportsmen' under the effective tax legislation either as a sale of a product or as a provision of service and naturally found in favour of the latter since 'football players are not products and their competition rights do not constitute ownership or other property right within the meaning of the Law on VAT'. According to SAC, the service, which is rendered with the transfer of a sportsman amounts to 'provision of personnel', regardless of whether employment, civil law or other relations shall arise between the club and the sportsman or another provision of service having the same subject matter would immediately follow with respect to another sports club.[81] This point of view is also shared in other decisions of SAC.[82]

514. The equation of competition rights to intangible assets, however, opens principally the way for them to serve as subject of various transactions including acquisition by third parties. Whether this principal possibility may be used in practice is a question, which may be answered after careful examination of the concepts of 'transfer of sportsmen' and 'transfer rights' under the Bulgarian law.

80. Fax received from the FIFA Director of the Legal Division and Omar Ongano, Head of Player Status on 27 Feb. 2006 as cited by R. Martins, *Freedom of Movement in Relation to Sport*, 1–2 Intl. Sports L.J. 104 (2007).
81. Decision of SAC No. 1282 of 3 Feb. 2006 under administrative case No. 7270/2005.
82. For instance Decision of SAC No. 5451 of 13 May 2008 under administrative case No. 572/2008.

§5. The Concepts of Transfer of Sportsmen and Transfer Rights

515. Paragraph 5 of the Additional Provisions of the Law on Sports defines the transfer of sportsmen as 'a normatively regulated act for a change in the club belonging as well as in the competition rights of sportsmen'. Transfer is, therefore, governed by a legislative Act and not a matter for the parties to a contract to freely decide on its content. This definition reveals two aspects of the transfer of sportsmen – first, it concerns change of clubs, and second, it entails transfer of the competition rights of the sportsmen.

516. Article 13 of the Law on Sports empowers only the sports clubs to carry out transfer of sportsmen, which is further enumerated among the financial sources for the sports organizations registered as non-profit legal entities.

517. Provisions on the transfer of the competition rights of sportsmen are mainly contained in the Implementing Regulations. This is obviously the legislative Act that should govern the transfer of sportsmen referred to by the Law on Sports.[83]

518. The competition rights of a sportsman are transferred from the club, where that sportsman is registered, through a transfer contract for pay, in result of which the sportsman changes his/her club's belonging. The use of the competition rights may be transferred for a limited period of time from one club to another club within the sporting year. The written consent of the player in advance is required in both cases of transfer of competition rights and transfer of the use thereof.

519. The written form of the contracts for transfer of sportsmen is mandatory and further a notary certification of the signatures of the parties thereto is required for their validity. The contracts are subject to registration in a special transfer registry kept with the respective sports federation.

520. The price of the transfer is freely negotiable between the parties. Article 20, paragraph 3 of the Implementing Regulations authorizes sports federations to adopt regulations specifying the conditions and procedure for transfer of competition rights of amateur sportsmen and professional sportsmen. The regulations shall be approved by the Minister of Physical Education and Sports and shall comply with the Law on Sports.

521. The fact that competition rights belong to the sports club and that they may be transferred from one club to another on the basis of legislative Act means that

83. Court decisions are still relying on the Decree No. 3 on the Status of the Persons participating in Training and Competition Activity and Transfer of Competition Rights. The said decree is still presented in Bulgarian legal information systems as a part of the currently effective Bulgarian legislation. However, its validity in its part dealing with the status of sportsmen might be questionable due to the fact that although not officially revoked, Art. 35 of the Law on Sports which was relied on for the issuance of the Decree No. 3 was amended in a way withdrawing the right of the Head of the Committee on Youth, Physical Education and Sports to regulate the status of sportsmen by virtue of a decree. The decree was considered effective with regard to the transfer of competition rights and that is why it was relied in number of decisions of the SAC for the purpose of clarifying the legal nature of the transfer of sportsmen. However, most of the provisions of the decree on the transfer of competition rights are reproduced in the Implementing Regulations and in author's opinion, the Implementing Regulations should be considered the single normative Act regulating the transfer of sportsmen thus implicitly revoking also this part of the decree.

competition rights although defined by the Bulgarian court as intangible assets cannot be freely acquired by third parties other than sports clubs whether commercial companies, individuals or investment funds.

522. In 2008, a new Article 35c has been inserted in the Law on Sports providing definition of the concept of transfer rights. The latter are the combination of the right to negotiate change of clubs for a sportsman and the right to receive the transfer price. The said article expressly provides that transfer rights shall belong to the club, for which a person has been registered as a sportsman. A person who does not have a valid contract with a sports club and such person is not registered, he/she may independently negotiate the conditions for acquisition of competition rights with a given sports club.

§6. Termination of Contracts in Sport

523. Pursuant to the Implementing Regulations, the contracts concluded by professional sportsmen must specify the conditions and procedure for termination of the agreement including in case of a transfer. Usually sports federations also regulate this matter in their internal regulations considering it as a part of the status of sportsmen, which they are authorized to determine under the Law on Sports. Termination of contract in case of a transfer of a sportsman is also dealt with in this way by the sports federations on the basis of their power to determine the conditions and the procedure for transfer of the competition rights of professional and amateur sportsmen conferred to them pursuant to the Law on Sports.

524. Presence of employment agreement, however, would mean that parties may terminate the agreement only on the grounds and by the methods provided for in the Labour Code without being able to depart from these rules at their discretion. The same is further valid for the legal consequences of the employment termination.[84]

525. The existence to some extent of a kind of authorization link among the Law on Sports, the Implementing Regulations and the regulations of the sports federations cannot justify any derogation of the mandatory provisions of such fundamental legislative Act as the Labour Code especially if made by private bodies such as sports federations regardless of the public functions that might have been transferred to them. This way, the overall legitimacy of the conditions and procedure for termination of contracts in sport in the cases where they are deemed to be of employment nature is at stake as far as they contradict provisions of the Labour Code.

526. One of the most noteworthy examples of the incompatibility of the methods for termination of individual employment contract in sport context under the Bulgarian law is the provision of Article 326, paragraph 2 of the Labour Code permitting a unilateral termination of a fixed-term contract by the employee who may give three months' notice or a notice the term of which equals the remaining time until the expiry of the term of the agreement, whichever is shorter.

527. Players' contracts with their clubs are as a rule fixed-term contracts, which would mean that a football or other team sports player considered an employee would be entitled to leave his club at his own discretion without even having completed a single full season with the team and even without owing any compensation to the club.

84. Individual employment agreements may be validly terminated by the employer only on those grounds explicitly stated in the Labour Code and strictly following the procedure set out therein. On the contrary, termination by an employee need not be made on particular grounds, as long as the employee observes the term of prior notification to the employer, or is prepared to pay the compensation due to the employer in the event of failure to comply with this term. Employment agreements may be terminated by mutual agreement upon either party's initiative or upon employer's initiative against payment of compensation. Legal grounds for termination of an employment agreement upon prior notice by the employer without employee's default are enumerated in Art. 328 of the Labour Code and are the following: (i) closing the enterprise, in which the individual is employed, or of a part of the enterprise; (ii) reduction of the number of working positions; (iii) decrease of work volume; (iv) discontinuation of work by the employing enterprise for more than fifteen business days; (v) lack of capacity of the employee for effective performance of his/her labour duties; (vi) lack of professional qualification or required educational background, necessary for effective performance of the labour duties; (vii) refusal of the employee to relocate to another town or location together with the enterprise, in which the employee works; (viii) change of the requirements for performance of the labour duties inherent to the position, provided that the employee fails to meet these requirements; (ix) the employee acquiring the right to retire on old age pension; (x) objective impossibility for performance by the employee; (xi) if the position has to be vacated for an employee who was reinstated in the position after having been illegally dismissed or for an employee who is released from his military service prior to the expiry of its regular term, or whose military service was postponed; (xii) execution of an agreement for assignment of management with members of the managing bodies of the employing entity (in the latter case an employer is entitled to terminate employment agreements only with managerial personnel; this right lapses upon the expiry of nine months from the commencement of the agreement for assignment of management).

Article 330 sets out the valid grounds for termination of an employment agreement by the employer without serving notice to the employee in case of grave breach of the employment contract or work discipline (i.e., disciplinary dismissal of an employee).

This is one very peculiar provision of the Bulgarian employment legislation that admits unilateral termination of a fixed-term employment contract on subjective grounds and in practice affects the very nature of the fixed-term employment contracts. The duration of such contract hardly could be defined as fixed and more correctly as uncertain.

528. This provision has not been ever used in practice by sportsmen, but its potential use threatens the stability of the contracts in sport. In football, for instance, the possible negative impact of this provision may be outweighed exactly through the concept of competition rights. The Regulations of the BFU on the Status and Transfer of Football Players set forth the grounds for termination of the football contract, which could be mutual agreement, just sporting or other cause and unjust sporting cause along with fault on the part of the football player. A potential termination of the contract by three months prior notice in line with the Labour Code would amount to termination for unjust cause and fault of the player, provided that the particular cause cannot be said to be just according to the practice of the FIFA Dispute Resolution Chamber which has developed the concept of just cause through a number of decisions. This termination would entail as consequence, first, automatic termination of the competition rights of the player with the club and, second, the necessity for obtaining competition rights after the expiration of the term of the terminated employment agreement.

529. This example also reveals big similarity of the competition rights as applied in football with the definition of federative rights used by FIFA. Although the contract is terminated, the player cannot register himself with and obtain competition rights for another club, which preserves the juridical link with his former club.

530. However, here we touch the issue about the relation between the FIFA dispute resolution mechanisms and the right of the national judges to rule on employment law disputes in sport. Article 64(2) of the FIFA Statutes lays down that proceedings to a normal court of law are forbidden unless otherwise established in the various FIFA rules. Article 22 of the FIFA Regulations for the Status and Transfer of Players on the FIFA competence in employment-related disputes explicitly indicates that any player or club is entitled to seek redress before a civil court for such disputes.

531. In FIFA Circular No. 769 entered into force on 1 September 2001, that is, on the same day as the 2001 FIFA Regulations and cited in the decision CAS 2006/A/1192 *Chelsea v. Mutu*, consideration 55 reads as follows:

> Players and clubs have the choice to submit the triggering, contract-related elements of their disputes to national courts or to football arbitration (see Article 42(1) of the Basic Regulations). Whatever the choice they make, the sportive sanctions envisaged in the present regulations can only be imposed by FIFA bodies, notably the [DRC]. Decisions of this Chamber are subject to appeal to [CAS].

532. Therefore, a national judge may rule on the 'triggering elements' of the dispute – that is, whether a contract was breached, with or without just cause or sporting just cause. In Bulgaria, it would mean that the judge would confirm the just cause for termination of the fixed-term agreement by the player by way of prior three months notice because this possibility is available for the player under the applicable national law. It is highly unlikely for the national judge to take into account any possibilities for avoidance of this outcome on the basis of the concept for the competition rights. Any neutralization of the negative effect of this particular provision of the Labour Code concerning the three months notices on the ground of the concept of the competition rights would deprive sportsmen from availing of a right that they have under the Labour Code, and this way the principle of freedom of employment could be violated.

533. The redress to the Bulgarian Labour Code if turned into practice threatens to undermine the very fundaments of the organization and regulation of the Bulgarian football at national level and would contradict the dynamic legal development of football at international level.

§7. Sports Contracts as Fixed-Term Contracts

534. Article 68 of the Labour Code sets out the cases where fixed-term contracts may be concluded. A fixed-term contract may be concluded for:

- the execution of temporary, seasonal or short-term works, as well as the ones performed by newly hired employees in the enterprises that are being declared bankrupt or in liquidation;
- until the completion of certain specified task;
- until an employee is being substituted;
- fulfilling the tasks of a position, for which a competitive examination must be taken, until such examination takes place; or
- for a certain mandate.

535. Article 68 of the Labour Code further provides for an exception that a fixed-term contract can be concluded for any type of work (even not temporary), if its duration is not shorter than one year. If there is a written request by an employee, such contract could be concluded for a non-temporary job for a shorter than one-year period. Anyhow, this cannot be used more than once a year. If the fixed-term contract is made in violation of the above rules, it will be re-qualified into an agreement for indefinite time.

536. In sport, fixed-term agreements may be concluded on the pretext that some kinds of sport may be practised only during certain time of the year (season). However, despite the possible breaks in the sports calendars, the exercise of sport as profession requires consistent sport and training activity and it would be difficult to prove that it constitutes a seasonal work.

537. Therefore, sportsmen may avail of the exception under Article 68 of the Labour Code that a fixed-term contract can be concluded also for any type of work if its duration is shorter than one year. This provision, however, seems to be contrary to the EC Directive 1999/70. First, there are not objective reasons, which would justify the conclusion and renewal of the fixed-term contracts. And second, the maximum total duration or the number of renewals is not restricted in any way.[85]

85. *See* , Robert Siekmann, *Promoting the Social Dialogue in European Professional Football – Candidate Member States* (TMC Asser Press 2004), http://www.sportslaw.nl/documents/cms_sports_49_1_Social%20Dialogue%20ed.pdf.

538. Furthermore, the Labour Code stated that fixed-term employment agreement shall not be concluded for a period exceeding three years unless a statute or an Act of the Council of Ministers provide for a longer period. Neither the Law on Sports, nor the Implementing Regulations as an Act of the Council of Ministers specify longer duration of sports contracts.

539. Nevertheless, contracts of such duration are largely used in sport. In football, for instance, after the European Court of Justice (ECJ) judgment in *Bosman*, clubs started to contract their best players for the maximum period allowed by the FIFA regulations, which is five years. The Regulations of the BFU State that the contract must be with minimum duration of one sporting year and maximum of three sporting years. As an exception, the length of the contract could be five years when the latter is concluded under the terms of the Law on Sports. The paradox is that compliance under the currently effective Bulgarian legislation would mean that contracts above three years infringe mandatory provisions of the Bulgarian labour legislation and, therefore, are void with respect to the period in excess.

540. This and other misfits of the general labour legislation with respect to sport[86] may be successfully eliminated only by enactment of a special law governing the employment relations in sport or by insertion of provisions into the Law on Sports allowing sportsmen to sign special sports contracts and making the Labour Code applicable only with respect to issues not specifically addressed by the Law on Sports. In absence of such a law or amendments in the Law on Sports, the situation of legal uncertainty and lack of coherence of the provisions applicable to sport as employment would continue to feature the legal regulation of sport in Bulgaria.

§8. Contract Stability and Release Clauses in Football

541. The applicable labour law provisions affecting the stability of employment contracts in sport apparently contradict the efforts of FIFA to promote and maintain the contractual stability in football. From the prospective of the national law and, more precisely, under the conventional theory for the hierarchy of legal instruments FIFA rules and regulations constitute an 'association law' which is subordinated to the national law.

542. Thus, very often conflicts between regulations of FIFA and national football associations, on the one hand, and provisions of the national law, on the other hand,

86. Other unsuited provisions of the Labour code with respect to sports may be found to be the lack of obligation for payment of compensation to the employer for expenses which the employer has incurred for the purpose of educating and training the player and for improving his skill. Such a provision is necessary to justify any claims for payment of a transfer fee in case the player wishes to change clubs before the age of 23 as for instance both FIFA and BFU Regulations provide; the fines as the most commonly used penalty in sport which are not listed as sanctions applicable to employees under the Labour Code and the disciplinary power of the club is based on its status of employer; the lack of any power of the employer to interfere in the private lives of its employees on the ground of the Labour Code, which in sport is very often required because of the need for athletes to observe a strict health and sporting regime. *See* further T. Simov & B. Kolev, *Players' Contracts in Bulgarian Football*, 1–2 Intl. Sports L.J. 110 (2006).

arise and the possibility for undesired outcome in case of their challenge before the national courts creates legal uncertainty and casts ambiguity with respect to the precise legal provisions applicable to athletes. Hence, the recognition by the states or incorporation in the national laws of the self-generated rules and regulations of football are indispensable for opening the way towards harmonization of the legal status of football players, in particular and athletes, in general.

543. The very interesting issue about the reconciliation of the so-called release clauses in the players' contracts and the new FIFA rules on contract stability in football arose out of the Angelov case. The player Stanislav Angelov had a valid employment agreement with his club Levski Sofia containing a clause in which it was laid down that he was free to go to any club that would pay EUR 180,000. The German club Energie Cottbus became aware of this clause, stated his consent to pay the amount, requested the bank account of Levski to transfer the money and contracted the player.

544. However, Levski alleges a breach of Article 18, paragraph 3 of the FIFA Regulations for the Status and Transfer of Players saying that:

> A club intending to conclude a contract with a Professional must inform his current club in writing before entering into negotiations with that Professional. A Professional shall only be free to conclude a contract with another club if his contract with his present club has expired or will expire within six months. Any breach of this provision shall be subject to appropriate sanctions. (Angelov has a contract with Levski expiring in the middle of 2008.)

545. In the official commentary to the FIFA Regulations, this provision is construed in the following way:

> The club with which the player is contracted needs to agree to the discussion between its player and the prospective new club. Without this agreement, the new club may be in a situation of inducing the player to breach his contract if it continues negotiations with the player.

The club maintained that neither negotiation between the clubs have ever taken place nor permission for negotiation between the player and Energie Cottbus has been given by Levski who asked the FIFA Dispute Resolution Chamber to rule on the dispute.

546. FIFA Regulations allow unilateral termination of contract only on the ground of 'just cause' as the meaning of this term is to be enlightened and elaborated in the course of the development of the jurisprudence of the FIFA Dispute Resolution Chamber. However, from the said jurisprudence, it appears that a similar case has not been brought before that Chamber. As an interim measure, the Chamber permitted the player to participate in the matches of his new team. The official decision and, which is more important, the reasoning of the Chamber have not been rendered and published on the FIFA website yet.

547. Said decision might be of significant importance with a view to the largely spread practice for utilization of release clauses in players contracts worldwide. The disclosure of such clauses to the potential new clubs by players having fixed amount for release in their contracts might constitute negotiations without the permission of the current employer of the player. On the other hand, the club may easily prevent the player from enforcing the release clause and leaving by simply refusing to give permission for the negotiations.

548. In case a player breaches his contract without a 'just cause', he can be ordered to pay compensation and a sporting sanction can be imposed on him (Article 17, paragraph 3). The new club of the player finds itself in a similar situation according to Article 17, paragraph 4. That situation is even worse for the new club because:

> [i]t shall be presumed, unless established to the contrary, that any club signing a Professional who has terminated his contract without just cause has induced that Professional to commit a breach.

§9. Injunction as a Remedy Against Prospective Breach of Contract

549. Possible remedy available for a FC in order to prevent unilateral termination of contract by its player is the injunction. Pursuant to the Code on Civil Procedure, national courts may be requested to impose conservatory measures prior to filing the statement of claim, which will bring about the court judgment. Further to the statutory determined conservatory measures, courts may designate other suitable measures for the purpose of securing the claim at its discretion upon request of the petitioner like for instance restraining orders. Such order may be addressed to an athlete preventing him from signing and playing with another club.

550. This remedy was used by FC Neftohimic in relation to its football player Stoiko Sakaliev in 2005. Sakaliev wanted to sign with CSKA Sofia alleging that his contract with FC Neftohimic had expired. The club maintained that the contract had been validly prolonged for another year and sought injunction before the court. A restraining order was issued prohibiting BFU from registering the player for a club other than Neftohimic because the court found that sufficient and convincing evidence existed to prove the club's allegation in the future litigation. The restraining order as a conservatory measure for securing the future claim further prevented BFU from performance of any acts of disposal with the international transfer certificate of the player.

551. At the end of the day, the dispute was resolved by the Appellate Commission of UEFA in line with the desire of the player to join CSKA Sofia and disregarding the decision of the Bulgarian court to impose injunction. From that point on, Neftohimic obviously gave up from using the law against the player if he was no longer willing to stay with the club. This outcome coincides with the conclusion of Andrew Caiger and John O'Leary in their Article 'The End of the Affair: The "Anelka Doctrine" – The Problem of Contract Stability in English Professional Football' that *it is very unlikely under English law that* FC*s to prevent a player jumping contract and playing for another club could use the law.*

552. The example of Anelka who wanted to leave Arsenal and join Real Madrid had demonstrated that Arsenal 'was ultimately unwilling to retain a player unwilling to play for it, nor did it want the court to pronounce on the law in this situation'.[87]

§10. Impact of the Bosman Judgment on the Bulgarian Sports Sector

553. As many authors have already observed, the judgment in *Bosman* was related to the application of Article 48 of the EU Treaty with respect to a cross-border transfer.[88] Consequently, purely domestic rules concerning transfer of sportsmen would remain unaffected by the *Bosman* ruling. Despite this option for departing from the ruling when a domestic transfer is concerned, the internal regulations of sports federations have largely introduced the out-of-contract rule laid down in *Bosman*. The reason was that internal transfer regulations very often reproduce the wording of those of the respective international umbrella federation, whose rules have been already reshaped in order to comply with the *Bosman* ruling.

554. For instance, the football governing body FIFA adopted its new Regulations for the Status and Transfer of Players in 2001 after consultations with the European Commission. In 2005, FIFA changed them again in order to further synchronize them with the EU law on freedom of persons and competition and avoid future contestation. The new transfer rules confirmed that transfer fees for the economic value of the player are not illegal, which, according to some authors, is a huge failure inviting *Bosman* 2. However, time will inevitably pass until the rules come to the scrutiny of the courts again and until the full liberalization of the players' market takes place.

555. The legality of a transfer system at national level allowing request for transfer sum even in case the player is out-of-contract seems to have been confirmed by the Implementing Regulations. Article 18, paragraph 2 of the latter states that a sportsman whose contract has been terminated or whose registration has expired may independently determine which club he wants to be registered with. Nothing in this wording indicates that payment of a transfer sum cannot be claimed by the former club.

556. The next Article 19 requires conclusion of a transfer contract against payment of a transfer sum in all cases of transfer of competition rights from the club where the player is registered to the new club. On the ground of the wording of that article, the right of the sportsman to move freely to another club without request for a transfer sum could be derived, provided that such player has no effective registration with any club. However, in case the player is simply out-of-contract but still registered with his last club, it is clear that a transfer sum may be successfully claimed. This demonstrates once again the incompatibility of the competition rights concept with the freedom of workers in general and the *Bosman* ruling in particular.

---

87. A. Caiger & J. O'Leary, *The End of the Affair: The "Anelka Doctrine" – The Problem of Contract Stability in English Professional Football*, in *Professional Sports in the EU: Regulation and Re-Regulation* 208 (A. Caiger & S. Gardiner eds., TMC Asser Press 2000).

88. *See* S. Weatherill, *European Sports Law, Collected Papers* 79 (TMC Asser Press 2007).

557. Article 20, paragraph 2 of the Implementing Regulations sets the principle for free negotiation of the transfer price, which, as already mentioned, is again in contrast with the *Bosman* ruling but nevertheless is still maintained even at European level.

558. The compliance of the Regulations of the Bulgarian Volleyball Federation for International Transfer used to be largely questioned and threatened with litigation. The particular provision that triggered the debate was the requirement to the players having status of free agents, that is, out-of-contract players, to pay to the Bulgarian Volleyball Federation a fee at the amount of EUR 10,000 in case they want to be transferred abroad. The provision was based on a similar provision in the Regulations of Federation Internationale de Volleyball (FIVB) stipulating the same amount. However, exactly due to the impact of the *Bosman* ruling, this requirement was waived with respect to the players from European countries, whose volleyball federations are members of Confederation Europeenne de Volleyball (CEV) under the latter's respective regulations specifying that in such cases of international transfer the requested amount shall not exceed EUR 500.

559. In case the matter is litigated, it would be a prima facie case of infringement of the freedom of workers as interpreted in *Bosman*. The requirement for payment would lay significant financial burden to the players, which indisputably constitutes an obstacle for free movement within the EU.

§11. Residence and Work Permits for Foreign Athletes

560. Under the provisions of the Law on Foreigners in the Republic of Bulgaria,[89] by foreigner it is understood a person who is not citizen of the Republic of Bulgaria. Any foreigner may legally reside in the country on the grounds of a validly issued visa, international treaty establishing a non-visa regime or permit issued by the authority in charge of administrative control over foreigners. The Law on Foreigners introduces basic types of residence:

- short-term residence (up to ninety days within each 180 days period from the date of entering the country);
- durable (up to one year);
- long-term residence (up to five years and option for renewal upon application); and
- permanent residence.

561. No permits are required for shortly residing foreigners, and they may reside in the country on the grounds of a valid visa or a treaty establishing a non-visa regime. Foreigners who are intending to reside in Bulgaria for periods longer than ninety days, including when intending to work in Bulgaria, should obtain a permit for long-term residence. Such permits are issued by the authority in charge for administrative control over foreigners (a division of the Ministry of Internal Affairs). The conditions and the

89. Law on Foreigners in the Republic of Bulgaria of 23 Dec. 1998 in the State Gazette issue No. 153 of 23 Dec. 1998.

procedure, under which citizens of EU Member States and the members of their families as well as the citizens of countries – parties to the Agreement of the EEA and Switzerland and the member of their families enter, stay and leave the Republic of Bulgaria are set in the Law on Entrance, Stay and Leaving the Republic of Bulgaria of the EU Citizens, who are not Bulgarian Citizens and the Members of their Families. The generally applicable regime for issuance of work permits for foreigners does not cover the above-mentioned persons, who exercise their right of free movement of workers.

562. In order to legally work in Bulgaria, foreigners have also to obtain a work permit. The issuance of work permit is among the grounds for granting a temporal residence permit. This is a separate procedure, which precedes the issuance of temporal residence permit. The legal framework is provided by the Law on Employment Promotion[90] and the Law on Labour Migration and Labour Mobility (the 'LLMLM').[91] One important restriction under the LLMLM is that access to the labour market may be allowed to third countries' citizens[92] for positions, which do not require Bulgarian citizenship, under the condition that for the preceding twelve months the total number of such third countries' citizens employed by a local employer shall not exceed 10% of the average listed number of employees on record, who are Bulgarian citizens or third countries' citizens belonging to the families of such Bulgarian citizens, citizens of other countries – members of the EU, of countries – parties to the Agreement on the EEA or of the Switzerland including members of the families of such citizens, third countries' citizens having long term or permanent permit for stay in the Republic of Bulgaria and the members of their families, third countries' citizens – members of the families of Bulgarian citizens, third countries' citizens having right of asylum or to whom international protections has been granted pursuant to the Law on the Asylum and the Refugees, and third countries' citizens, for whom work permit is not required on the ground of international treaty, to which the Republic of Bulgaria is a party.

563. Work permits are issued by the Executive Director of the National Employment Agency upon request of Bulgarian employer or of a local person, who is receiving a posted or seconded worker or employee from a third country, on which basis a long term stay permit is issued by the Ministry of Interior. The LLMLM provides also an option for uniform stay and work permit. Such is issued by the Ministry of Interior and contains the work permit by the Executive Director of the Employment Agency granted to third countries' citizens, who apply for residence for the purpose of seeking employment and who have a valid permit for reside on the territory of the Republic of Bulgaria for purposes other than employment.

564. Pursuant to Article 12, paragraph 1 of the Implementing Regulations right of registration with sports federations is conceded to individuals who are Bulgarian citizens, citizens of EU Member States, citizens of countries, which are parties to the Agreement on the EEA or Switzerland or to foreign citizens, to whom a long-term

90. Law on Employment Promotion of 1 Jan. 2002 in the State Gazette issue No. 112 of 29 Dec. 2001.
91. LLMLM of 21 May 2016 in the State Gazette issue No 33 of 26 April 2016.
92. The LLMLM introduces the term 'third countries citizens' instead of foreigners in order to demarcate those foreigners, who are not citizens of EU Member States, EEA countries or Switzerland from foreigners, who are such citizens.

residence permit in Bulgaria has been issued. The grounds for issuance of long-term residence permits are set out in the Law on Foreigners.

565. The most relevant and common ground for issuance of long-term residence permits to foreign sportsmen in Bulgaria, with a view to the general status of employees enjoyed by sportsmen under Bulgarian law in the majority of the cases, is their intention to work under employment relationship. Such work permit can be issued for a period up to one year pursuant to Article 41, paragraph 1 of the LLMLM.

566. Sportsmen willing to perform sports services as free-lancers are also subject to a procedure for issuance of a permit before the same government bodies. The practical difficulty for receiving a permit for performance of an activity as free-lancers stems from the fact that in the latter cases sportsmen would be required to attach along with the application a detailed plan for the activity with respect to the period of the permit. Issuance or extension of the period of validity of the permit may be refused if the plan for the activity or the report for its implementation is not grounded or the economic and/or public effect is not proved. The permit is issued for one year.

567. Long-term residence permit may be issued even in absence of the necessary conditions under the Law on Foreigners in favour of foreigners who proved their special merits towards Bulgaria in certain areas, among which sport is also included.

568. Work permits are not required with respect to participants in sports events who retain their habitual residence in case the duration of the activity of the athlete in Bulgaria does not exceed three months. For the purpose of participating in such sports events, foreign athletes may enter Bulgaria in compliance with the regime for short-term stay effective with regard to the nationals of their respective countries. The duration of short-term stay is set at ninety days within every 180 days period following the date of the entrance pursuant to the Article 23 of the Law on Foreigners.

569. In case of proven expedience, including for the purpose of encouraging investment in the Republic of Bulgaria, the Minister of Labour and Social Policy may allow access to the Bulgarian labour market to athletes and coaches after requesting opinions from the respective sports federations pursuant to Article 14 of the LLMLM. Another exception from the general requirements may be made with respect to athletes and coaches in sports clubs in case of interest in their employment confirmed by the BNSFs and unions due to the specific personal merits and high level of professional knowledge and skills of such athletes and coaches. Such athletes and coaches may receive uniform residence and work permit issued by the Ministry of Interior on the ground of Article 15, paragraph 4, section 5 of the LLMLM.

§12. Sport and Freedom of Association

570. Pursuant to Article 44, paragraph 1 of the Constitution, citizens shall be free to associate. Article 12, paragraph 1 states that associations of citizens shall serve to meet and safeguard the interests of their members and paragraph 2 that citizen's associations including trade unions shall not pursue any political objectives, nor shall they engage in any political activity which is in the domain of the political parties.

571. Workers and employees shall be free to form trade union organizations and alliances in defence of their interests related to work and social security pursuant to Article 49, paragraph 1 of the Constitution. Similarly, employers are also free to unite themselves in defence of their economic interests under the second paragraph of Article 49.

§13. The Social Dialogue in the Sports Sector

I. Legal Framework

572. The general framework for the establishment of social dialogue with respect to any type of labour relations is contained in the Labour Code. Article 2 thereof determines the role of the State to regulate the labour and the relations directly related thereto, the insurance relations and the issues of the living standard upon consultations and dialogue with the workers, employees, employers and their organizations in the spirit of cooperation, mutual concessions and respect of the interests of each of the parties.

573. Social dialogue under the Labour Code is a broad concept encompassing tripartite cooperation, collective bargaining, participation of workers and employees in the management and the formation of the respective management bodies, collective labour disputes settlement through negotiations, mediation, arbitration and other voluntary dispute settlement methods.

574. The clarification of the issues capable to be included in the social dialogue requires definition of the relations falling within its scope.

575. Labour relations are the relations connected with the provision of workforce and work under employment relationship, the rights and obligations of employers and employees (remuneration, working time, breaks and leaves, health and safety at work, social servicing).

576. Professional qualifications would be considered as part of the 'relations directly related to the labour relations'.

577. Insurance relations encompass categorization of labour for the purpose of retirement, range of socially insured persons, social risks covered, grounds and amounts of the compensations due to temporary disability, conditions for receiving, amounts and method of calculations of pensions, updating the amounts of the pensions and the insurance indemnifications.

578. The following would qualify as living standard issues: the ratio between the needs of the employees and the level of their income (prices-income), updating of the salaries, pensions and other insurance payments on the basis of inflation index and other similar issues.

II. Trade Unions and Employers' Organizations

579. Employees are entitled under Article 4, paragraph 1 of the Labour Code, with no prior permission, to freely form, by their own choice, trade union organizations; to join and leave them on a voluntary basis, showing consideration for their statutes only. Trade union organizations represent and protect employees' interests before government agencies and employers as regards the issues of labour and social security relations and living standards through collective bargaining, participation in the tripartite cooperation, organization of strikes and other actions, pursuant to the law.

580. Employers have absolutely reciprocal rights to form organizations and defend their interests under the Labour Code.

III. Collective Bargaining Agreements

581. The CBAs are the most frequently occurring materialization of the results achieved under the framework of social dialogue and are very significant in practice. Their introduction in the sports sector could contribute for the preservation of the specifics of sports by departing from the non-mandatory provisions of the labour law otherwise applicable to sportsmen.

582. In Bulgaria, CBAs may be concluded at four levels – enterprise, industry, branch and municipality. As enterprise would qualify any place whether office, organization, cooperative, establishment, project and the like, where work against payment is exercised. The term 'enterprise' should be understood broadly referring not only to economic activity related to the production and exchange of merchandise but including also management, social, cultural and sports activity.

583. The term 'industry' is determined by the Council of Ministers in compliance with the National Branch Classification. The term 'branch' within the meaning used in the Labour Code in the context of collective bargaining is narrower than the term referred to in the Branch Classification, that is, sub-branch thereunder. Prior to 2001, CBAs were concluded also at level profession; however, this option was revoked with the amendments in the Labour Code.

584. Only a trade union may be a party to CBA and not other bodies such as the general meeting of the employees, etc. At level industry and branch, only 'representative' trade unions and employers' organizations may be parties as the parties must be 'corresponding', that is, at one and the same organizational level of the industry or the branch.[93]

IV. Trade Unions and Employers' Organizations in the Sports Sector

585. National Sports Trade Union was registered with the Sofia City Court on 14 November 2005. No clearly established corresponding organization on employers' side currently exists in the sports sector.

586. Potential social partners are most visible in football where the Association of Professional Football Players and the PFL as organization of the professional clubs currently operate. However, while nothing seems to prevent the players' association from acting as a trade union in football, the same is not valid for the PFL. The latter's statute does not contain anything suggesting that this is an employers' organization and any mandate from the member clubs in this direction is, therefore, missing. Even if such a mandate is present, still conclusion of a CBA having binding effect with respect to all professional FCs and players would not be possible since the option for such a CBA at level profession does not exist any longer and football in economic terms is merely one profession.

587. Further, PFL is an association affiliated to BFU pursuant to section 8 of the latter's Statute. The PFL cooperates in terms of organization and personnel with the BFU bodies and participates with own representatives in the standing committees. The statute, the regulations and the decisions of the PFL bodies shall not contradict with the BFU's Statute and internal regulations. This way, PFL cannot be deemed to be an independent organization in order to be able to act as an employers' organization capable of representing its members in the social dialogue.

93. The criteria for an organization to be considered as representative at national level for trade unions are the following: – to have at least 50,000 members; – to have organizations of workers and employees in more than one quarter of the activities, determined with a code up to the second sign from the Classification of the Economic Activities approved by the National Statistical Institute with no less than 5% of the persons employed in each economic activity or at least fifty organizations having not less than five members in each economic activity; – to have local bodies in more than one quarter of the municipalities in the country and a national leadership body; and – to have obtained the capacity of a legal entity at least three years prior to submitting the request for recognition of the capacity to be representative.

The criteria for becoming representative at national level for employers' organizations are the following: – to have at least 1,500 members and not less than 50,000 workers in total in all members of the employers' organization,; or 100,000 workers and employees, hired under employment contract, in all members of the employers' organization; – to have organizations of the employers in more than one quarter of the activities determined with a code up to the second sign of the Classification of the Economic Activities approved by the National Statistical Institute with no less than 5% of the persons insured under employment agreement in each economic activity or ten members in each economic activity; – to have local bodies in more than one quarter of the municipalities in the country and a national leadership body; and – to have obtained the capacity of a legal entity acquired at least three years prior to submitting the request for recognition of the capacity to be representative.

588. The relevant levels, at which CBA may be concluded in the sports sector, are accordingly industry, branch or enterprise. Pursuant to the Branch Classification, where branch is understood as industry according to the Labour Code, sport falls within letter R – Culture, Sports and Entertainment. Within R are the following sub-branches (to be considered equal to a branch within the meaning conferred by the labour law), such as, R.90 – artistic and creative activities; R.91 – other activities in the field of culture; R.92 – organizing of gambling games; R.93 – sports and other activities related to entertainment and relaxation; R.93.1 – activities in the field of sports; R.93.11 – exploitation of sports sites and facilities; R.93.12 – activities of sports clubs; R.93.13 – activities of fitness centres; R.93.19 – other activities in the field of sports; R.93.2 – activities related to entertainment and relaxation; and R.93.29 – other activities related to entertainment and relaxation.

589. However, in order to conclude a CBA at level industry or branch, the social partners must be representative at national level and none of the existing organizations in the sports sector has obtained this quality. There is a possibility for employers' organizations in sport to benefit of the representative quality already conferred to existing employers' organizations if they become departments or administrative division units therein. According to the today's reality in the sports sector and the currently effective legislation, the single level for conclusion of a CBA is enterprise level, that is, at level professional club.

V. The Association of Professional Football Players

590. Unlike many of the 'old' Member States of the EU, where players' trade unions have been set up in the 1960s and 1970s of the twentieth century and, therefore, have already decades of experience, such trade unions in sports in Bulgaria have been very recently established. Interesting to mention in this respect is the fact that the players' union in football, that is, the Association of the Professional Football Players, was actually an offspring of PFL, which is the organization of the clubs from the two Bulgarian PFLs. The existing dependence of the players' union on PFL including financial dependence, questions the ability of this union to protect adequately the interests of the players.

591. The internal regulations of BFU for the season 2006/2007 provided for compulsory membership of each professional football player with the Association of the Professional Football Players. Moreover, in order to obtain status of professional any footballer had to hold a certificate for registration with the association. The contracts concluded between players and clubs had to be deposited with the association of the professional football players. The membership with the association was further announced as *a conditio sine qua non* for the players in order to obtain competition rights.

592. This compulsory membership obviously departed from the principle of freedom of association laid down in the Constitution. Workers and employees shall be free to form trade union organizations and alliances in defence of their interests related to work and social security, but they cannot be obliged to do so. It is true that compulsory membership with specifically designated organization sometimes constitutes condition precedent for obtaining right to practise certain profession. However, such a requirement must be provided for in the law and have some constitutional justification.

593. For instance, attorneys at law are obliged to participate in attorneys college by virtue of the Law on Bar.[94] The exercising of the profession of attorney at law is activity, provided in the Constitution, for legal assistance and protection of freedoms, rights and lawful interests of individuals and corporate bodies. It is implemented in compliance with the principles of independence, exclusivity, self-management and self-financing as stated in Article 2 of the Law on Bar in connection with Article 134 of the Constitution. Taking into account the important role and specificity of this profession Article 134, paragraph 2 of the Constitution provides for regulation of the organization and the procedure of the Bar through enactment of a special law.

594. Similar situation cannot be said to exist in football in order to justify such deviation from the fundamental principle of freedom of association.

595. Consequently, the respective BFU regulations from the season 2010/2011 provide only the option for players to become members of the Association of the Professional Football Players. The other questionable requirements have been deleted from the BFU regulations.

§14. Right to Strike

596. The right to strike is of minor practical significance in the field of sport since it has never been used so far in the sports sector. The right to strike is in general a new right, which had not existed during the socialist period and even before that. Professor Vassil Mrachkov characterizes that right as 'the most significant novelty in the Bulgarian legislation' since the changes in 1990.[95]

597. The right to strike is recognized in Article 50 of the Constitution of Bulgaria in favour of the workers and employees for protection of their collective economic and social interests. The Constitution specifies that the conditions and procedures for the exercise of the right of strike are to be determined in a law. Such a law is the Law on Collective Labour Disputes Settlement.[96]

598. The right to strike is an instrument available only for employees. That means that similarly to collective bargaining and generally social dialogue only athletes enjoying such a status may avail thereof. On the basis of the provisions of Article 50 of the Constitution and Article 11 of the Law on Collective Labour Disputes Settlement, the right to strike has been defined by Professor Vassil Mrachkov as the possibility provided and guaranteed by the law for a worker or an employee to suspend temporarily the fulfilment of his/her labour duties in order to protect his/ her collective economic and social interests.[97]

94. Law on Bar of 25 Jun. 2004 in the State Gazette issue No. 55 of 25 Jun. 2004.
95. V. Mrachkov, *Labour Law* 842 (SIBI Press 2004).
96. Law on the Collective Disputes Settlement of 13 Mar. 1990 in the State Gazette, issue No. 21 of 13 Mar. 1990.
97. V. Mrachkov, *Labour Law* 843 (SIBI Press 2004).

Chapter 2. Personality Rights

§1. Protection of Privacy

599. The general personality rights for the protection of privacy of citizens including sportsmen are set forth in the Constitution. In the chapter dealing with the fundamental rights of the citizens, it is proclaimed that:

> [T]he privacy of citizens shall be inviolable. Everyone shall be entitled to protection against any illegal interference in his private or family affairs and against encroachments on his honour, dignity and reputation. No one shall be followed, photographed, filmed, recorded or subjected to any other similar activity without his knowledge or despite his express disapproval, except when such actions are permitted by law.

The right of any citizen to refuse to be filmed and photographed in certain cases not falling within the permissible exceptions may serve as a ground for athletes to commercially exploit their general personality rights by agreeing to be photographed and filmed against a fee.

§2. Personal Data Protection

600. The Law on Personal Data Protection (LPDP)[98] was enacted in 2002. Since then, the definition of 'personal data' has encountered several amendments. According to Article 2, paragraph 1 of LPDP, personal data shall be any information related to a natural person, who is identified or may be identified directly or indirectly by an identification number or through one or more specific indices.

601. Pursuant to the LPDP for personal data processing will qualify any action or set of actions which may be carried out with respect to personal data by automatic or other means such as collecting, recording, organizing, storing, adapting or modifying, restoring, consulting, using, disclosing through delivery, disseminating, submitting, updating and combining, blocking, erasing or destroying.

602. Athletes' image expressed under the form of a photograph indisputably would qualify as personal data under LPDP. Consequently, the use, dissemination and otherwise disclosing of such photographs or other holders of the athletes' images would amount to processing of personal data pursuant to paragraph 1 of the Additional Provisions of LPDP. The processing of personal data would be admissible in certain cases listed in Article 4 of LPDP, among which the case where the natural person to whom the data refers has given explicitly his/her consent as well as in the cases where it is performed only for the purposes of journalistic, literature or artistic expression,

98. LPDP of 1 Jan. 2002 in the State Gazette issue No. 1 of 4 Jan. 2002.

as far as the procession does not violate the right of private life of the person whom the data refers to.

§3. Limitation of the Right of Privacy

603. Right of privacy inevitably collides with the freedom of expression and, therefore, the borderline between the two must be clearly marked.

604. The issue about the limitation of the right of privacy has been discussed by the Constitutional Court in a decision rendered on the occasion of alleged lack of proportionality between the significance of the freedom of expression and the imprisonment as a sanction against violation of the right of privacy committed through insult and slander.[99] The Constitutional Court emphasizes that the freedom of expression as proclaimed in Article 10 of the European Convention on Human Rights is not absolute since pursuant to paragraph 2 of said Article 10 is subject to such formalities, conditions, restrictions or penalties as are prescribed by law and are necessary in a democratic society, in the interests of certain values including the protection of the reputation or the rights of others. Similarly, the Constitution indicates the rights and good name of the other citizens among the values, which protection justifies the limitation of the freedom of expression.

605. The Constitutional Court found that the criminal liability resulted in alternative penalties imprisonment and fine was not disproportionate because the protected value was so significant to require the most rigid intervention in the freedom of expression. The Court furthermore noted that said penalties were among the lowest for a personality crime, and that many other European countries such as Germany, France, Holland, Austria and Denmark also introduced the imprisonment as an appropriate sanction for this kind of crimes.

§4. Right of Portrait

606. A work of art or photography constitutes a portrait of a person other than the author of the work and is subject to copyright. In this case pursuant to Article 13 of the Law on Copyright and Neighbouring Rights,[100] the copyright shall belong to the author, but the use of the work may be subject to an agreement between the author and the portrayed person. The possibility for sportsmen to control the dissemination of their portraits and photographs by giving or not giving their consent opens commercial opportunities, of which the athletes could avail themselves.

---

99. Decision No. 20 of 14 Jul. 1998 of the Constitutional Court of the Republic of Bulgaria under constitutional file No. 16/98, State Gazette issue No. 83 of 1998.

100. Law on Copyright and Neighbouring Rights of 1 Aug. 1993 in the State Gazette issue No. 56 of 29 Jun. 1993.

§5. Right of Name

607. Right of name is a personal right that is imminent to every individual's personality. It is based on the legal principle for individualization of every member of the society through certain traits. However, the right of name may be invoked to address cases where the use of name is denied or risks exist for fraudulent impersonation. The use of trademark consisting of the name of famous athlete would neither constitute denial of name, nor fraudulent impersonation. Therefore, this ground might be called upon only if claiming that right of name is also part of the general personality right and such use of name could constitute encroachment on athlete's honour, dignity and reputation.

Chapter 3. Social Security

§1. Social Security Regime for Resident Athletes Working under Employment Relationship

608. Athletes, regardless of their particular nationality and citizenship, shall qualify as residents of Bulgaria under the Law on Individuals Income Taxation if one of the following requirements is present:

(1) Their permanent address is in Bulgaria.[101]
(2) They are physically present in Bulgaria for more than 183 days in any twelve-month period; in this case, the athlete shall be deemed to be a resident in Bulgaria with respect to the calendar year, in the course of which the presence of the athlete in Bulgaria has exceeded 183 days. For the purpose of calculation of the relevant period of presence, the day of leave and the day of entry shall be counted as two separate days of residence in Bulgaria. The period of stay in Bulgaria only for the purposes of education or medical treatment shall not be considered as residence in the country, which is an onerous provision of the Bulgarian tax legislation.
(3) They have been posted abroad by Bulgarian enterprises (in this case, sports clubs).
(4) Their vital interests are centred in Bulgaria. Vital interests centre shall be in Bulgaria, provided that the athlete's interests are strongly connected with Bulgaria. The following factors shall be taken into account for determining the vital interests centre:

    (a) the location of the family, and the properties of the athlete;
    (b) the location where the sportsman is playing as employed individual or otherwise in accordance with his/her status, and/or run other professional and business activities; and
    (c) the place wherefrom the sportsman is managing his properties. According to the law currently in operation, an athlete who has a permanent address in Bulgaria, but his vital interests centre is not located in Bulgaria, shall not qualify as a resident.

609. On the contrary, non-resident athlete shall be any sportsman who does not qualify as a resident person according to the above-stated requirements.

610. The monthly social security contribution rates depend on the particular category of work. 'Category' is a term used by Bulgarian labour law to denote the conditions, in which employees work, and in particular, the presence of factors harmful to the employees' health.

---

101. The definition of permanent address is contained in the §1, s. 3 from the Additional Provisions of the Law on the Bulgarian Identification Documents pursuant to which for permanent address is considered an address in a residential area in Bulgaria where a person (the athlete) has been registered in the registry of the population.

611. In view of the work conditions, employees in Bulgaria could belong to one of three categories, of which 'first category' implies extremely heavy work conditions, such as work underground, while 'third category' is the general term used for work conditions lacking significant harmful factors.

612. Athletes engaged under employment relationships shall belong to the third category. The category of the employee has an impact on the age at which he acquires the right to retire and receive a State pension, as well as on the amount of social security contributions and of additional payments, which is for employees belonging to third employment category and working under the conditions of normal working time, that is, eight hours a day, five days a week, are 23.30% of their gross monthly remuneration.

613. The two specifics of the social security and health security contributions under the currently effective regime in Bulgaria, namely the imposition of a threshold for the amount of the security base, which cannot exceed BGN 2,600 and the sharing of the contributions between the employer and the employee, have been already mentioned in the part of this monograph dealing with taxation of sportsmen. Since 1 January 2017, these contributions are distributed as follows:

- 13.80% (7.66% for the employer and 6.14% for the employee) to the State Pension Fund, for employees born after 31 December 1959, and 18.80% (10.46% for the employer and 8.34% for the employee) for employees born before 1 January 1960;
- additional obligatory social security contributions in the amount of 5% (2.80% for the employer and 2.20% for the employee) to the Private Pension Funds only for employees born after 31 December 1959;
- 3.5% (2.10% for the employer and 1.40% for the employee) to the Maternity Leave and General Disease Fund; and
- 1% (0.60% for the employer and 0.40% for the employee) to the Unemployment Benefit Fund.

614. The health security contributions amount to 8% of the employee's social security income. The levy for payment of health security contributions is distributed between the employer and the employee in ratio 60:40 or respectively 4.80% for the employer and 3.20% for the employee.

615. The obligatory additional social security is recognized with regard to all individuals born after 31 December 1959, provided that they are secured under the rules of the State basic social security. This type of security is designed to procure the so-called additional pension for the aforementioned individuals. No additional amounts are due by the employer for obligatory additional social security, but the 5% of the gross monthly remuneration shall be designated to the Private Pension Fund.

616. In practice, in terms of social security burden the two regimes for the individuals born before and after 31 December 1959 are equal. The single difference is exactly that the 5%, making the difference in the amounts due under the two regimes to the State Pension Fund, are designated to the Private Pension Fund in the case of individuals born after 31 December 1959. The payment obligation is distributed between the employer and the employee in the same way as the one for basic social security contributions.

617. It should be noted that the payment of the social security contributions due by the insurer shall be paid simultaneously with the payment of the remuneration of the insured person, thus making the receiving of the salary dependent on the payment of the social security contributions. The insurers are obliged to pay the social security contributions separately for each month by transfers from their respective accounts to the corresponding account of the State public insurance and the account of the additional obligatory pension insurance upon payment or accounting of the labour remuneration, including advance payments.

§2. Social Security Regime for Non-resident Athletes

618. The Law on Employment Promotion provides that employment and social security relations of non-resident persons employed on the territory of Republic of Bulgaria by local employers are governed by Bulgarian employment and social security law. Furthermore, Bulgarian employment and social security law will be deemed to apply in cases where the employer of a non-resident employee is a foreign individual or a foreign legal entity provided that the non-resident person is working on the territory of Bulgaria. Therefore, all provisions of Bulgarian law including those regarding rates of social security contributions as discussed above shall apply *mutatis mutandis* to non-resident athletes.

619. Non-resident athletes shall be obligatory secured against all secured social risks if employed for more than five working days or forty working hours in one calendar month notwithstanding the nature of the work, method of payment and source of financing.

620. Non-resident individuals employed by one or more employers for less than five working days (forty working hours) in one calendar month shall be obligatory secured against the social risks disability, old age and death, labour accident and occupational disease.

621. Health security contributions are payable to the National Health Security Fund with respect to persons residing in Bulgaria for a long term unless otherwise provided in international treaty to which Bulgaria is a contracting State, as well as with respect to persons to whom status of refugee or right of sanctuary has been granted. After the accession of Bulgaria to the EU on 1 January 2007 health security contributions are also due by persons, to whom the Bulgarian legislation applies under the Rules of Coordination of the Social Security Systems within the EU.

622. The amounts due as social and health security contributions are determined as a percentage of the total social and health security income as described above. In any event however, the amounts due as social and health security contributions shall be paid on a minimum amount of social and health security income per month as determined by the Law on the Budget of the State Social Security Fund,[102] which amount varies depending on the economic activity performed by the employer and the position of the employee. In other words, should the employee's remuneration be

102. Law on the Budget of the State Social Security Fund for the year 2007 in the State Gazette issue No. 105 of 22 Dec. 2006.

lower than the minimum amount of social and health security income specified by law, the contributions will, nevertheless, be paid on the (statutory) minimum amount.

623. As we mentioned above, the Law on the Budget of the State Social Security Fund also introduces a maximum amount of the social and health security income, which for the year 2014 is fixed to BGN 2,400 per month. Therefore, if an athlete's income exceeds the said amount, no social or health security contributions would be due in respect of the excess.

§3. Social Security Regime for Income Generated from Activities Other than Employment

624. Social security contributions with respect to income generated by activities other than employment are due, subject to deduction of the statutory recognized expenses necessary for the performance of such activities. The relevant statutory expenses for sportsmen are 25% for provision of independent services and 40% for licensing of copy and other rights such as image rights.

625. In case of a business activity under a private law contract, as mentioned already in Part I, Chapter I, §5 dealing with taxation of athletes' income the security base is formed after the income is reduced with 25%, which are deemed by the legislator to be enough to cover the expenditures necessary for the performance of the athletes' activity. The figures of social and health contributions under private law contract are as follows: social contributions – 9.90% of the security base for the sports club and 7.90% of the security base for the individual athlete and health contributions – 4.8% of the security base for the sports club and 3.2% of the security base for the individual.

626. Bulgarian labour law does recognize the principle of immediate benefits with respect to the health insurance. Pursuant to Article 109 of the Law on Health Insurance,[103] the failure for payment of contributions due to no fault of the insured individuals does not deprive them from their insurance rights. The amounts paid by such individuals for medical aid are subject to reimbursement.

627. There is an important issue to be addressed – the point about prioritization for social security purposes of incomes generated by individual in result of both employment and activities other than employment. Individuals who receive income from different activities representing separate grounds for social security obligations the payment of the contributions shall follow this order:

- income from employment and/or official legal relationship, management contracts and contracts for control and from activity as members of cooperatives;
- social security income as sole traders, owners or shareholders in commercial companies, liberal professions and or craft activity, registered agricultural producers and tobacco producers; and
- income from activities other than employment.

628. The various income categories qualify as different grounds for mandatory social insurance, subject to the aforementioned priority order. For instance, if an athlete

103. Law on Health Insurance of 19 Jun. 1998 in the State Gazette issue No. 70 of 19 Jun. 1998.

receives payments due on the ground of employment contract and under a private law contract, social contributions shall be due under both contracts observing the maximum of BGN 2,600. According to the priority rules, this means that if an athlete receives BGN 1,500 as a salary and BGN 1,500 as a payment for services rendered under a private law contract the final amount of social security contributions shall be due with respect to the whole amount of BGN 1,500 under the employment contract and for remaining BGN 1,100 till the social security maximum and part of the remaining BGN 1,125 of the income received as a freelancer (BGN 1,500 minus BGN 375 statutory expenses).

Part III. Doping in Sport

Chapter 1. Legal, Historical and Institutional Development of the Fight Against Doping in Sport at International and National Level

629. The first international legal document addressing the doping as the most serious problem of the contemporary sport was the Anti-doping Convention of the Council of Europe No. 135 issued on 16 November 1989 (the Anti-doping Convention). The Anti-doping Convention was ratified by the government of Bulgaria by way of enactment of a special law for that purpose on 22 April 1992 and promulgated in the State Gazette issue 50 of 24 June 1997. This way, the Anti-doping Convention has become an integral part of the Bulgarian legislation and, moreover, shall take supremacy over all provisions of the domestic law, which might be conflicting, pursuant to Article 5, paragraph 4 of the Constitution of Bulgaria. In line with Article 86, paragraph 2 of the Constitution, the laws and decisions of the Parliament shall be binding for all State bodies, organizations and citizens.[104]

630. Pursuant to Article 19, paragraph 1, section 9, sports federations are obliged to sanction athletes and officials for administration of doping and application of doping methods in the training and competition activity. The particular type and duration of the sanction as well as the procedure for their imposition are determined in the Decree on Doping Control of Competition and Training Activity No. 235 of 15 October 2010 adopted by the Council of Ministers.[105]

631. A protocol to the Anti-doping Convention was signed in Warsaw on 12 September 2002 with effect on 1 April 2004 providing for mutual recognition of the anti-doping control tests results and permitting anti-doping controls being performed by one State, signatory to the Convention, in another signatory State without prior notice. The law for ratification of the protocol was enacted by the Bulgarian Parliament on 9 February 2005 and promulgated in the State Gazette issue 17 of 22 February 2005.

632. Despite the significance of the Anti-doping Convention for drawing the attention and invoke the concerns for the future of sport threaten by the increasing use

104. The analysis of the Anti-doping Convention with respect to its incorporation in the Bulgarian legislation has been made by the SAC in its Decision No. 4889 of 24 Sep. 1999 under administrative file No. 2627 of 1999.
105. Decree on Doping Control of Competition and Training Activity No. 235 of 15 Oct. 2010 in the State Gazette issue No. 83 of 2010.

of doping, it did not provide effective measures needed for the successful fight against doping in sport.[106]

633. The fight against doping was significantly strengthened with the increase of the role of the EU in the process. The EU may intervene in doping affairs on the ground of its powers set forth in the EC Treaty regarding health protection policy, consumer protection, education and youth policy or workers protection. Some EU directives especially EEC Directive 65/65 amended by EEC Directive 89/341 prohibiting the taking of pharmaceuticals for achievement of purposes other than the intended ones would be applicable to athletes resorting to use of doping in order to improve their sporting achievements. Doping in sport may be also combated at EU level within the framework of the Third Pillar – Police and Judicial Cooperation in Criminal Matters.

634. The need for harmonization of the doping laws and for efficient coordination of the measures adopted by the various stakeholders at international and national level led to the establishment of a single body having the obligation to combat the illegal doping in sport. This body is the World Anti-doping Agency (WADA) constituted on 10 November 1999 and having as members representatives of the Olympic movement, the Council of Europe and government administrations as well as representatives of the EU in the person of the president of the European Council and members of the European Commission.

635. At its summit in Copenhagen in 2003, WADA adopted the World Anti-doping Code (WADC) aiming to harmonize the procedures and sanctions for using doping in sport. The WADC has been accepted by the BOC and the Bulgarian Anti-doping Centre as reported on the WADA website. Pursuant to Article 20(5)(1) thereof national anti-doping organizations are responsible for the adoption and implementation of anti-doping rules and policies at national level, which conform to WADC. In turn, the requirements of the Anti-doping Centre as well as those of WADA become binding for the Bulgarian athletes by virtue of the special provision to that end of Article 45, paragraph 4 of the Law on Sports.

636. Nevertheless, at international level, the proper mechanism for enforcement of the provisions of WADC was found to be their reflection in the adopted on 19 October 2005 World Anti-doping Convention by United Nations Educational, Social and Cultural Organization (UNESCO) (the UNESCO Convention) thus triggering the respective international public law enforcement instruments.

637. Consequently, the Bulgarian Parliament passed the Law for Ratification of the UNESCO Convention on 13 December 2006. It was promulgated in the State Gazette issue No. 105 of 2006 and became fully effective as of 1 March 2007.

638. The dynamic and important legal development of the fight against doping in sport in the years following the enactment in Bulgaria of the Decree on Doping Control of Sport, Competition and Training activity in 1995 necessitated the drafting of an entirely new decree. The Council of Ministers completed that task by adopting a new Decree on Doping Control of Competition and Training activity in 2008.[107] However, the structural changes made in the system of the State bodies managing the

106. *See* M. Kedzior, *Effects of the EU Anti-doping Laws and Politics for the International and Domestic Sports Law in Member States*, 1–2 Intl. Sports L.J. 111 (2007).

107. Decree on Doping Control of Competition and Training Activity No. 128 of 4 Jun. 2008 in the State Gazette issue No. 54 of 2008 (revoked).

physical education and sports brought along the enactment of a new decree that revoked the previous one. The provisions on organization, disciplinary measures and procedures for doping control in Bulgaria will be presented below with a view to the new decree (the Decree).

Chapter 2. The Decree on Doping Control of Training and Competition Activity in Force as of 9 January 2015

639. Article 45, paragraph 3 of the Law on Sports serves as a legal basis for adoption of a decree regulating doping control. Said article authorizes the Council of Ministers to determine the conditions and procedures for doping control, prevention and the combat against doping in sport. Article 1, paragraph 1 of the Decree on Doping Control of Training and Competition Activity in force as of 3 May 2011 specifies the scope of the decree as including the organization and the control for prevention of the use of prohibited substances and prohibited methods by sportsmen and official persons,[108] establishment of the doping offences and the sanctions imposed.

640. The Decree uses the same definition of doping as present in WADC and the UNESCO Convention, namely the occurrence of anti-doping rules violations. It further utilizes the term 'prohibited substance or method', which is defined as a substance or a class of substances or method indicated as such in the Prohibited List adopted by WADA. This is absolutely in line with the definitions of the terms 'prohibited method' and 'prohibited substance' provided for in WADC where all methods and substances described in the Prohibited List adopted by WADA would be prohibited. The UNESCO Convention further provides for the right of WADA to update the Prohibited List.

641. The anti-doping rules violations as described in the Decree are corresponding to those described in the UNESCO Convention and WADC.

108. Official persons are defined in the additional provisions of the decree as each coach, instructor, manager, agent, member of the team's entourage, sports and technical or medical person, a parent as well as any other person who provides treatment, give assistance or work with a sportsman who participates or prepares to participate in a sports competition.

Chapter 3. The Strict Liability Principle

642. Specifically noteworthy in this respect are the Article 2(1)(1) and 2(1)(2) of WADC establishing the principle of strict liability of the athlete in case of presence of a prohibited substance or its metabolites or markers in an athlete's bodily specimen. As explained in the commentary of WADC under the rule of strict liability violation occurs whether or not the athlete intentionally or unintentionally used a prohibited substance or was negligent or otherwise at fault.

643. The UNESCO Convention is also missing a clearly stated principle of strict liability, that is, liability without fault, in order to make it applicable on the ground of its incorporation in the Bulgarian legislation following the ratification and entering into force of the UNESCO Convention in Bulgaria. Notwithstanding the presence of the text in the Law on Sports making the Acts adopted by WADA, as WADC is, binding with respect to all sportsmen in Bulgaria, the application of the principle of strict liability would inevitably pose some constitutional concerns.

644. It might be argued, for instance, that the strict liability rule contradicts the presumption of innocence stated in Article 31, paragraph 3 of the Constitution. The same would be valid with respect to the European Convention on Human Rights, where Article 6(2) states that everyone charged with a criminal offence shall be presumed innocent until proved guilty according to the law. In a legal opinion on the conformity of certain provisions of the draft WADC with commonly accepted principles of international law, G. Kaufmann, Kohler and G. Malinverni, relying on the outcome of the case *Salabiaku v. France* decided by the European Court of Human Rights, opined that 'if one assumes that the criminal law principles of Article 6(2) are applicable to doping offences, this provision does not prohibit offences of strict liability'.[109]

645. However, the outcome of a potential challenge before the Constitutional Court of the principle of strict liability provided that it is applied by the Anti-doping Centre on the ground of its subordination to WADA and due to the obligation to respect its WADC accordingly, cannot be predicted.

646. Furthermore, the fact that the type and duration of the sanctions for doping offences are provided in a decree, that is, in a sub-legislative Act, seems to contradict the criminal law principle of statutory determination of the penalties. Fine, suspension and lifetime ban for practising certain profession are also penalties provided for in Article 37 of the Criminal Code.[110] Also, Article 45, paragraph 3 of the Law on Sports as the legal basis for the issuance of the decree authorizes the Council of Ministers to determine the conditions and the procedure for the doping control, but no similar authorization is in place with respect to determination of the sanctions for anti-doping rules violations.

647. In the majority of the cases, the anti-doping rules violations would rather have the characteristics of administrative offences. Every deed (action or failure for action) infringing the established order of the State administration, which has been

109. Legal opinion on the conformity of certain provisions of the draft WADC with commonly accepted principles of international law, p. 29, previously available on the WADA official website, 29.

110. Criminal Code of 1 May 1968 in the State Gazette issue No. 26 of 2 Apr. 1968.

perpetrated at fault and declared punishable by an administrative sanction imposed through administrative channels would qualify as administrative offence pursuant to Article 6 of the Law on the Administrative Offences and Sanctions.[111]

648. Doping offences infringe the general prohibition for administration of doping and application of doping methods pursuant to Article 45, paragraph 2 of the Law on Sports and is contrary to the State policy for fight against doping implemented by the Minister of Youth and Sports. Therefore, they would be deemed to infringe the established order of State administration.

649. In order to qualify as administrative offence certain action or failure of action must be perpetrated at fault (intention or negligence). That would mean that the strict liability principle could not apply with respect to administrative offences. In fact, due to the options for eliminating or reducing the penalties under Article 10(5)(1) (no fault or negligence) and Article 10(5)(2) (no significant fault or negligence) pursuant to WADC, the strict liability rule is not longer applicable in its original meaning with respect to fines and bans. The strict liability principle, as such, continues to apply only with respect to sports sanctions (disqualifications).[112]

650. The third element to be established for triggering the administrative liability is the penalization of the action or the failure by administrative sanctions. Those sanctions may take three forms under the Law on the Administrative Offences and Sanctions – public reprimand, fine and temporary ban for practising certain profession. The duration of the latter shall not be less than one month and shall not exceed two years. Further, the temporary ban shall not affect in any manner the obtained licence for practising the respective profession. Obviously the life time ban as well as the temporary bans exceeding two years laid down by the Decree for doping offences would be incompatible with the system of sanctions operated at national level with respect to the administrative offences.

651. In order to guarantee the sports discipline, the Decree provides for different sanctions that could be imposed to the sports organizations. First, the provisions of the Decree specify monetary sanctions. The latter may reach up to BGN 3,000 (approx. EUR 1,500). Thus the offences of the doping rules committed by the athletes and the sports and technical persons registered with the respective sports organization reflect on the property status of the latter. In case an official or a sportsman registered with a particular sports federations is punished for violation of the anti-doping rules, which is third or more for that organization, the Minister of Youth and Sports may revoke the licence of the sports federation.

652. The actions and failures constituting administrative offences and the corresponding sanctions must be established by virtue of the law. The Council of Ministers may be authorized by the law to elaborate the particular *corpus delicti*; however, it cannot modify the type and the size of the statutory defined sanction in Article 2 of the Law on Administrative Offences and Sanctions.

653. Therefore, the very decision for establishment of the system of doping offences and corresponding sanctions by way of issuance of decree of the Council of

111. Law on the Administrative Offences and Sanctions of 28 Nov. 1969 in the State Gazette issue No. 92 of 28 Nov. 1969.

112. *See* J. Houben, *Proportionality in the World Anti-doping Code: Is There Enough Room for Flexibility?*, 1–2 Intl. Sports L.J. 12 (2007).

Ministers appears to be contrary to the law and vulnerable to various challenges on constitutional law, civil law, criminal law and administrative law grounds. The example of other countries such as Italy and Poland, for instance, demonstrates that this matter is regulated by special law or by special chapters included in the general law on sports. It is highly recommendable that similar approach be adopted in Bulgaria too.

Chapter 4. Burden of Proof and Standard of Proof

654. The principle of strict liability as provided for in WADC triggers the effect of shifting the burden of proof to the athlete who is responsible for proving the presence of exceptional circumstances in order to have the period of ineligibility eliminated or reduced pursuant to Article 10(5). This option for the athlete to avoid liability or at least mitigate the consequences of the doping offence, however, does not totally undermine the strict liability principle since the athlete is still considered guilty but merely the penalty is either excluded or reduced.

655. Under Article 3 of WADC, the Anti-doping Organization shall have the burden of establishing that an anti-doping rule violation has occurred. The standard of proof is determined in WADC as lying between the mere balance of probabilities and proof beyond the reasonable doubt. Article 56, paragraph 7, section 1 of the previous decree of 2008 required the Anti-doping Centre, which is in charge for the establishment of the offences, to do that beyond the reasonable doubt. However, the Decree of 2011 harmonized the standard of proof with the one required in the WADC and this situation is maintained under the Decree of 2015.

656. The standard of proof applicable to athletes shall be by a balance of probability in all the cases where the burden of proof is placed on the athlete pursuant to WADC. In the previous decree of 2008, the person alleged to have committed an anti-doping rule violation was required to prove the existence of circumstances that invoke reasonable doubt in the athlete's fault. On the basis of this wording, it was not clear that these circumstances had to be exceptional as required by Article 10(5) of WADC thus limiting significantly the number of cases where the elimination or reduction of the penalty may occur.[113] The 2011 Decree introduced the rule from the WADC that the standard of proof for the athlete shall be balance of probabilities with the exception of the provisions of Articles 66 and 71, which require the athlete to meet higher standards of proof, namely the comfortable satisfaction of the hearing panel. The two provisions referred above are virtually identical to Articles 10.4. and 10.6. of the WADC titled Elimination or Reduction of the Period of Ineligibility for Specified Substances under Specific Circumstances and Aggravating Circumstances Which May Increase the Period of Ineligibility, respectively.

657. The drafters of the Decree of 2008 had experienced difficulties in finding the appropriate standards of the Bulgarian law corresponding to the unfamiliar standards utilized in WADC. However, the differences in the applicable standards might lead to different outcomes and, consequently, to lack of harmonization of the national anti-doping laws with WADC. This problem was overcome with the 2011 Decree, which constitutes virtual translation of the respective standards of proofs as stated in the WADC.

113. Pursuant to the commentary of Art. 10(5) of the Code, said article is meant to have an impact only where the circumstances are truly exceptional.

Chapter 5. Organization of the System for Doping Control

658. The national body in charge for the carrying out of doping control, prevention and fight against doping in sports shall be the Anti-doping Centre established with the Minister of Youth and Sports. The Anti-doping Centre shall be responsible for the distribution of the List with the prohibited substances and methods adopted by WADA. The Anti-doping Centre is an individual administrative body that is managed and represented by the Executive Director. The latter is appointed by the Minister of Youth and Sports through a competition held under the procedure set in the Labour Code. The structure and the functions of the Anti-doping Centre are determined in its Statute.[114] The structure of the Centre includes the Laboratory for Doping Control and three structural departments: Implementation of the Anti-doping Programme, Legal and Administrative Service and Finance and Accountancy Service. The department responsible for the implementation of the anti-doping programme encompasses two activities: medical control and education. The medical control activity is put into practice by a specific commission whose three members shall have medical education with at least three years professional experience. The commission is entitled to carry out educational courses for applicants who want to join the anti-doping teams; to propose to the Executive Director a list of the anti-doping teams; to maintain a register of the members of anti-doping teams; to control the observance of the international standards for doping control, etc. The person responsible for the legal service of the Centre shall have law education with at least three years professional experience. The total amount of the personnel in the Centre including the Executive Director is nineteen.

659. Among the responsibilities of the Anti-doping Centre shall be included activities such as organization of doping control, adoption of a plan for doping control on annual basis, request of data from the sports organizations needed for the doping control, maintaining a registry of the athletes tested for administration of doping as well as the results obtained, notifying the Minister of Physical Education and Sports, BOC and WADA for acknowledged doping offences, proposing before the Minister of Physical Education and Sports sanctions for sports organizations in connection with doping offences, conducting anti-doping campaigns, etc.

660. The Executive Director of the Anti-doping Centre shall manage and control the activity of the Centre and represent the latter before third persons. Further, in the capacity of administrative body, the Director is entitled to enact penal provisions under the terms of the Law on the Administrative Offences and Sanctions, as well as orders and other individual administrative acts. The Executive Director also appoints the General Secretary of the Centre who shall assume the administrative management of the body. The procedure for doping testing shall be carried out by anti-doping teams in compliance with the International Standard for Doping Control. The anti-doping teams shall consist of at least two members who are determined by an order of the Executive Director.

661. The laboratory analysis shall be conducted by the Laboratory for Doping Control with the Anti-doping Centre in compliance with the International Standards

114. Structural Regulations of the Anti-doping Centre of 11 Oct. 2010 in the State Gazette issue No. 82 of 19 Oct. 2010.

for Anti-doping Laboratories. The task of the laboratory shall encompass analysis of the prohibited substances and methods included in the Prohibited List of WADA as well as other substances in accordance with the monitoring programme of WADA. The Laboratory shall comply with the general principles as stated in Article 14, paragraph 1 of the Statute: confidentiality, equity and independence.

Chapter 6. Disciplinary Provisions

662. The Decree of 2015 fully complies with WADC in terms of the type of sanctions and duration of the bans to be imposed on individuals for violation of anti-doping rules.

663. The legal subjects who shall have the right to remit an issue to the Disciplinary Commission are listed in Article 62, paragraph 1 of the Decree of 2015: the athlete or a person authorized by him/her, the respective licensed sports organization, every person that have been established to have committed a violation of the anti-doping rules, the Executive Director of the Anti-doping Centre and WADA.

664. The Disciplinary Commission established with BOC is the body that shall render the decision. Its decisions are subject to appeal before the Bulgarian Sports Arbitration Court in accordance with the latter's Rules for Dispute Settlement. Regarding disputes arisen from international competition or involving athletes at international level, the decision may be appealed solely before CAS in accordance with the provisions applicable for that court.

Chapter 7. Anti-doping Agreements for the Olympic Games

665. According to the General Secretary of BOC, special agreements were intended to be concluded between the athletes who were going to participate at the Summer Olympic Games in Beijing 2008 and BOC. This way the athletes had to declare and warrant that they had not used any prohibited substances or methods and, consequently, had to indemnify BOC for any damages that might have occurred in case of anti-doping rule violation which would have further amounted to a breach of the contract. Signing of such agreements was following the Hungarian practice as was alleged by the General Secretary of BOC.

Part IV. Sport and Commerce

Chapter 1. Broadcasting of Sports Events

§1. Introduction

666. Rights to broadcast sports events are property rights, which nature and scope are to be determined in accordance with the national law.

667. The Law on Sports created the sui generis right of the sports federations to hold the advertising and TV and radio broadcasting rights for the sports competitions, organized by them while providing percentage of the revenues to the participating sports clubs on a contractual basis.

668. Similarly, the Law on Sports envisages the possibility for the sports clubs to hold the advertisement rights, rights of TV and radio broadcasting of sports events, organized by them under terms and conditions specified by the respective sports federation.

669. The ostensible ambiguity of the two provisions with respect to the precise owner of the broadcasting rights whether sports federations or sports clubs necessitates some legal analysis for the purpose of reconciliation of those provisions.

§2. Ownership of Broadcasting Rights for Sports Events under the Law on Sports

670. The issue about the ownership of the broadcasting rights for sports events was rigidly disputed between years 1996 and 2000 due to the even more ambiguous text of the then effective provisions of the Law on Sports. Not only did the Law on Sports at that time recognize the right of the sports clubs to hold the advertising and TV and radio broadcasting rights for the sports competitions, organized by them, but also further extended that right to cover the sports competitions where such clubs merely participated. Another provision, however, was also recognizing by way of reference the very same right for holding the broadcasting rights in favour of the sports federations.

671. In result of this contradiction, both federations and clubs were at a time claiming their right to negotiate with the broadcasters. One of the persons who was most rigidly defending the individual marketing of the broadcasting rights by the sports clubs was the president of FC Neftohimic Burgas. During the season 1999/2000, he was constantly denying the Bulgarian National Television (BNT), having a contract for the broadcasting rights of the national football championship the access to the stadium of his club. In result, the President of PFL filed a proposal for clarification of the owner of the broadcasting rights with the Commission on the Health Protection, Youth and Sports with the then Bulgarian Parliament and for consecutive amendments of the Law on Sports, if necessary. Such amendments took place on 15 June 2000 and in result the above-cited and currently effective provisions of the Law on Sports were adopted.

672. One possible solution of the issue who is the owner of the broadcasting rights under the Law on Sports is hidden in the phrase 'sports competitions, organized by them'. A sports federation holds the broadcasting rights with respect to the sports competitions, organized by that sports federation and a sports club holds the broadcasting rights with respect to the sports competitions, organized by that sports club. It may be, therefore, argued that the individual matches included in a championship, organized by a sports federation, are in fact organized by that sports federation albeit certain role of the clubs in the technical organization of their particular matches as hosts.

673. This way, the sports clubs would hold the broadcasting rights only with respect to other competitions and tournaments, which are not organized by the respective sports federation.

674. The BFU Statute also makes clear this difference. Article 96 the Statute titled ownership of broadcasting rights states the following:

> BFU holds the exclusive rights for advertising, TV and radio broadcasting of football competitions organized and administrated by the union. BFU holds the exclusive rights for advertisement, TV and radio broadcasting, Internet and mobile phone broadcasting, video and audio recordings, CD, DVD, video games, broadcasting via optical means or by satellite, broadcasting via all known means and those means, which will be available in future, and of the games of the national teams. BFU is exclusive owner of the image rights as a team of the national football teams. The rights are exercised in accordance with the law and the rules of FIFA or UEFA. The football clubs are owners of the rights for advertising, TV and radio broadcasting of organized by them traditional and regional football competitions apart from the national sports calendar. In case of football competitions organized by international football organizations the above rights shall be exercised according to the rules of these organizations.

675. Examples of such traditional and regional football competitions apart from the national calendar or sports are the summer friendly tournament organized by FC Levski Sofia and named after the legend of this club Georgi Asparouhov – Gundi – resembling the summer tournament Juan Gamper, which takes place in Barcelona. Likewise, CSKA Sofia in the recent years organizes the international tournament, Playstation, as a preparation for the new championship. The broadcasting rights with respect to these two summer tournaments undoubtedly shall belong to the clubs organizing them.

676. Consequently, the then effective provision of the Internal Regulations of BFU indicating both BFU and participating clubs as owners of the broadcasting rights was substituted by a provision saying that the clubs participating in the championships and tournaments in the system of BFU unconditionally recognizes that BFU, as the organizer of the matches, holds the advertising and broadcasting rights against a certain percentage of the revenues for the participating clubs.

677. The said Regulations including their current version available on the BFU website amplified the legal effect of that provision from mere recognition of the right of the football union to hold the broadcasting rights into unconditional granting of those rights from the clubs to the union against certain part from the revenues. This was most likely done due to dubiety whether the now-effective provisions of the Law on Sports resolves undoubtedly the issue about the owner of the broadcasting rights. This way, even if the owner is deemed to be the clubs, the broadcasting rights would be transferred to the football union by virtue of the cited provision in the Internal Regulations of BFU, which is mandatory for the clubs on the ground of their voluntary membership with the football union.

678. The BFU Internal Regulations regarding the status of its member clubs provide further clues for the conclusion that BFU (and not the clubs) is the organizer of the matches. Article 28 thereof sets the obligation of the member clubs to participate in the competitions in the system of BFU under conditions and procedure set forth in the respective internal BFU regulations. This provision implies that clubs' main obligation is to participate and not to organize the competitions. The above-cited provision on the broadcasting rights also explicitly designates BFU as the organizer of the matches.

679. The above understanding and explanation of the issue about the owner of the broadcasting rights of sports events is not confirmed by an official court decision or derived from the reasoning for the draft of the Law on the Amendment of the Law on Sports in 2000 or any other official opinion rendered by the Bulgarian Parliament. However, it allows these ostensibly confusing provisions of the Law on Sports providing once that sports clubs holds the broadcasting rights and second time that sports federations do hold them to be construed in unambiguous and consistent way.

680. There is also a decision of the Bulgarian Commission on Protection of Competition (CPC) available, which confirms the right of the football union to market centrally the broadcasting rights for the football championship relying on the Law on Sports. This decision shall be analysed in details *infra* in this chapter.

681. On the other hand, finding the ownership over broadcasting rights for sports events solely on the ground of a condition precedent who is the organizer of those events reveals some risks for further misunderstandings. For instance, PFL was designated by the BFU Regulations on the Football Championships and Tournaments for the season 2006/2007 as the body responsible for the organization and administration of the State championships for A and B groups and the tournament for the Cup of Bulgaria. The PFL Statute also includes such organization and administration in the PFL's registered scope of activity, provided that a decision of the Executive Committee of the BFU for that end is passed. This way, FCs will most likely be considered owners of the broadcasting rights as organizers of the matches albeit through PFL as an organization of the clubs. However, PFL would not be able to be such an owner as non-eligible under the Law on Sports to hold broadcasting rights. The now-effective version of the BFU Regulations on the Football Championships and Tournaments proclaim BFU as the body responsible for the organization and administration of the State championships for First and Second Professional Groups with the support and the assistance of the PFL. Regarding the tournament for the Cup of Bulgaria both BFU and PFL shall organize it. Thus, by virtue of the explicit provision of Article 28, paragraph 3 of the BFU Internal Regulations regarding the status of its member clubs the football union is the only owner of the broadcasting rights.

682. The fact that clubs have transferred their broadcasting rights to BFU would not remedy this situation because the way to CPC would be open with significant chances for successful challenge of this granting especially with a view to the absence of an option for central marketing of those broadcasting rights which are deemed to belong to the sports clubs. Such an option is possible only in the case where the sports federation is the owner of those rights by virtue of the law.

§3. Sale of Broadcasting Rights for Football Matches

683. Football enjoys considerable share of the total media coverage of domestic sports events. Consequently, the broadcasting rights for football matches are quite appealing for the broadcasting organizations.

684. Upon the very enactment of the Law on Sports in 1996, that is, upon the first establishment of the possibility for the sports federations to hold the broadcasting rights with respect to the sports events organized by them, BFU assigned its broadcasting rights over the domestic football championship on an exclusive basis to the German company UFA Film – und Fernseh – GmbH&Co KG (UFA). In 1998, UFA reassigned said rights to its official representative for Bulgaria S.V.-RSA OOD[115] (S.V.-RSA). On 22 November 1998, BFU and S.V.-RSA renewed the original contract of 22 November 1996 extending its term of validity up to the football season 2005/2006. This contract was once again extended to the summer of 2008.

685. The scope of the contract included all matches from the domestic football championship, the matches from the tournament for the Cup of Bulgaria from the stage of one-eighth finals on, the matches from the Supercup to be played between the champion and the winner of the Cup of Bulgaria. The price for the broadcasting rights was fixed at USD 620,000 per football season.

686. Article 93, paragraph 2 of the BFU Statute provides that when concluding contracts for centralized sale of advertising and broadcasting rights, BFU acts as a representative of its member clubs.

687. The Law on Sports requires conclusion of a contract for distribution of the proceeds from the sale of the broadcasting rights between the sports federation as organizer of the sports event and the clubs participating therein. The particular percentage is left to be agreed between the parties to the contract.

688. According to Article 77, paragraph 2, section 3 of the BFU Statute the activity for negotiating and preparing contracts for centralized sale of advertising and

115. The acronym OOD stands for Limited Liability Company, in Bulgarian, pursuant to the Law on Commerce.

TV rights for the games in the professional leagues may be assigned to PFL by decision of the BFU Executive Committee.

689. In practice, PFL in its capacity of organization representing all professional FCs concludes on the behalf of its members a contract for the distribution of the proceeds from the sale of the broadcasting rights for the national championship and the tournament for the Cup of Bulgaria. PFL is a non-profit association of the professional clubs which has registered in its scope of activity, *inter alia*, 'providing assistance for the football clubs for the preparation and conclusion of contracts for centralized sale of advertising and broadcasting rights with respect to the matches from the professional football leagues', that is, A group and B group.

690. PFL is entitled to receive part of the proceeds from the football competitions organized by BFU generated from advertisement and TV broadcasts of said competitions as the amount of this part shall be determined by the Executive Committee of the football union. The right of PFL to receive part of the income from the football competitions held in the system of the BFU, from advertising and TV programmes, as well as from other sources is further confirmed in Article 77, paragraph 3 of the BFU Statute.

691. Pursuant to Article 93, paragraph 3 of the BFU Statute, the procedure according to which the FCs exercise their rights for advertising, TV and radio broadcasting of football competitions, as well as the distribution of the money received from the contracts for centralized sale of these rights shall be stipulated by a decree that shall be endorsed by the Executive Committee after agreement with PFL.

692. Under the extended to 2008 contract which was made known to the public by the president of the PFL, the agreed share in favour of the clubs amounted to 90% of the revenues from the sale of the TV broadcasting rights, meaning 90% of USD 620,000, that is, USD 558,000. The 10% remaining with BFU were intended to support the juvenile international team of Bulgaria. A total of 20% of the clubs' share (USD 111,600) was directed to the PFL's budget for the purpose to cover the current expenditures as well as the prizes for the finals of the tournament for the Cup of Bulgaria and the final match for the Supercup.

693. The remainder of 80% (USD 446,400) was to be distributed among the clubs in compliance with a prior agreed formula. Said formula took into account factors like arena (the ratio for distribution is 70:30 in favour of the host of the event), the number of matches shown on the TV and the position of the teams in the final table.[116]

694. During the first couple of years following the acquisition of the rights by UFA and later S.V.-RSA, respectively, BNT was purchasing the rights on an annual basis at the very same price of USD 620,000. However, the so fixed price of the broadcasting rights in the contract between BFU and S.V.-RSA turned out to be quite overestimated with a view to the market value of the rights. The low interests of advertisers and sponsors to the TV broadcasts of the matches made the investment of BNT in the broadcasting rights quite unprofitable undertaking.

116. Pursuant to the official information provided by PFL for the season 2005/2006 professional FCs shared the amount of USD 490,141. The biggest share belonged to the champion Levski Sofia, which received USD 96,390. Levski was followed by CSKA (USD 85,630), Lokomotiv Plovdiv (USD 67,313), Litex Lovetch (USD 65,634), Slavia Sofia (USD 44,612) and Lokomotiv Sofia (USD 34,060).

695. For the seasons 2002/2003 and 2003/2004, BNT purchased the broadcasting rights for USD 350,000 against the condition to share the revenues from commercials and sponsorship with S.V.-RSA. BNT was further entitled to sublicense the right to a third party – a television organization. In season 2003/2004, certain matches were shown on NOVA TV by virtue of a contract on total value of BGN 260,000 (approx. EUR 130,000).

696. The contract for the broadcasting rights for the season 2005/2006 was radically amended. The rights were sold for BGN 200,000 (approximately EUR 100,000) under the condition that all revenues from the sublicense of the rights and sponsorship would be in favour of S.V.-RSA. This condition, however, was valid only until reaching the amount of USD 620,000. Up to that moment, S.V.-RSA was also entitled to receive 60% of the revenues from broadcasting of commercials during the matches, after which the ratio was set at 50:50. Said moment, however, according to the information provided by media did not occur at all.

697. The price of the broadcasting rights under the contract for the season 2005/2006 was increased to BGN 250,000 (EUR 125,000), but BNT received a share of the revenues from sponsorship at the amount of 30% or 40%.

698. The particular price of the contract for 2006/2007 was not disclosed, however, it became clear that the price was again increased. The broadcasting rights for the season 2006/2007 were offered as a main package including thirty matches of the championship and the five most interesting matches from the Cup of Bulgaria and were granted to the BNT. An official open tender for the sale of the rights had not been organized. By 'bidding procedure' as used usually in the mass media, it actually meant the informal negotiations involving television organizations having national coverage of their programmes (BNT, BTV and Nova TV) and the holder of the rights S.V.-RSA. Television organizations such as Nova Television and Eurocom Plovdiv were granted smaller packages consisting of sixteen matches of the championship as well as three matches from the championship, respectively. Other television organizations acquired rights to broadcast highlights from the matches.

699. According to the prices for the broadcasting rights per match to be shown on the TV for the season 2006/2007 as was announced in the media, the price per match shown on BNT varied between USD 10,000 and USD 11,000, on Nova TV it was USD 8,000, and on Eurocom, USD 6,000. If those prices are multiplied by the number of the matches scheduled for broadcasting, the total price will amount to USD 476,000, which is close in the amount as the one from the previous season.

700. It may be summarized that, as a rule, BNT paid a certain amount for the acquisition of the broadcasting rights for the domestic football matches in money and granted S.V.-RSA advertising space before and during the matches, which S.V.-RSA had the right to sell to particular advertisers or to sponsors as consideration under the sponsorship contracts. For example, prior to the summer of 2005, the general sponsor of the Bulgarian football championship (which at that time was the brewery Zagorka) was paying BGN 250,000 per season, and the provision of advertising time for broadcasting of commercials of the Zagorka brand during the games shown on the TV was part of the sponsorship contract. The official importer of Ford automobiles for Bulgaria, the company 'Moto Pfohe', was also paying between USD 100,000–USD

140,000 as a sponsor of the tournament for the Cup of Bulgaria and the broadcasting of commercials during the matches was part of the deal.

701. In July 2005, the financial company TBI Bulgaria, which is a part of the Dutch TBIH Group became a general sponsor of the football championship. The obligations of S.V.-RSA under the contract included provision of advertising billboards at the stadiums as well as advertising time during the TV broadcast of the matches. The price of the contract concluded for a term of three years was not officially announced, but it was stated that said amount exceeds the price paid by the previous general sponsor.

702. Consequently, an increase of the revenues from the transaction with the broadcasting rights was expected. This explains the fact why the amount of TV money distributed among the clubs in 2005/2006 and the expected amount for 2006/2007 exceeded the respective share of the clubs from the fixed price of USD 620,000 under the contract between the BFU and S.V.-RSA. Therefore, the season 2005/2006 was probably the first season where the investment in broadcasting rights brought some profit to their holder after allegedly almost ten seasons of operations with broadcasting rights at a financial loss.

703. The wave of increase reached its highest level in the summer of 2008 when the BFU and TV2 OOD (later renamed to ProBG OOD) concluded a five-year contract for sale of the broadcasting rights for football matches from A group. The rights were sold for the record-breaking price of BGN 50 million (approx. EUR 25 million), that is, 10 million per season. Further, TV2 attached some conditions to the contract that stipulated for some investments, which shall be made by the FCs. The latter were obliged to invest in their home stadia in order to receive their respective share from the fixed price.

704. In the season 2008/2009, ProBG and the affiliated thereto RingBG had the right to broadcast seven of eight matches from the respective round of the championship. BNT kept the right to broadcast the most interesting match from every round in that season because of the previously concluded contract that was about to expire in 2009.

705. However, ProBG experienced some financial problems; the high price turned out to be excessive, and the contract was amended in the summer of 2010 – the term was shortened to three years, and the revenues were decreased to BGN 7 million per season. Soon after that, ProBG and RingBG joined BTV Media Group. At the time of writing, the matches from the spring midseason are broadcast by the recently started TV channel BTV Action.

706. According to the information released in the press, BTV Media Group has paid in advance BGN 700,000 to BFU and S.V.-RSA and BGN 1.5 million to the FCs. Unfortunately, no official information has been provided with regard to the respective shares of the FCs. However, when the contract was concluded it became clear that certain percentage of the amount would be shared equally between the clubs with the purpose of investing in sports sites and facilities. The formula for sharing takes into account also factors like rating of the matches shown on TV and the position of the teams in the final table.

707. The broadcasting rights for football matches from the Bulgarian A group for the season 2011/2012 was jointly acquired by BNT1 and TV7. Season 2012/2013 was marked by total ambiguity with regard to the TV broadcasting of the matches. As a result, the first ten rounds from the A group were not shown on the TV. A new company Football Pro Media OOD was established exactly for the purpose to be assigned with the broadcasting rights by the BFU and negotiate the TV coverage of the matches. Since 2013, TV7 is the single television which broadcasts the football matches from the Bulgarian A group via its channels. In May 2013, the BFU officially announced the sale of the broadcasting rights to the company Football Pro Media against the amount of approximately BGN 15,000,000 with respect to the following three years.

708. The company Nova Broadcasting Group purchased the exclusive rights for TV and online broadcasting of the matches from the Bulgarian football championship, the tournament for the Cup of Bulgaria and the match for the Supercup for the seasons 2014–2015 and 2015–2016. The company started broadcasting the games on its channels Nova, Diema and Nova Sport. Later, special paid channels Diema Sport and Diema Sport2 were created and the matches were predominantly shown on these channels including for the season 2016–2017.

709. In 2015 it was announced on the media that the FCs have agreed on a new contract with the company Football Pro Media, under which the said company will pay BGN 30,000,000 for the period of five years between 2015 and 2020.

§4. Broadcasting of Sports Events under the Bulgarian Competition Law

I. Collective Sale of Broadcasting Rights

710. The issue for centralized marketing of broadcasting rights was addressed by CPC in its Decision No. 40 of 5 April 2001. The CPC concluded on the ground of Article 19, paragraph 1, section 11 of the Law on Sports empowering sports federations to hold the advertising and radio and TV broadcasting rights for the sports competitions organized by them that BFU was the ultimate seller of the broadcasting rights for football matches. Any competition concerns in respect of ownership over exclusive broadcasting rights for the matches from the Bulgarian football championship remained outside the assessment of the CPC due to the fact that this was a power conferred to BFU by the legislator.

711. Nevertheless, CPC made some further points regarding the rationale behind the cited provision of the Law on Sports comparing this provision with the idea behind the Northern American Sport Broadcasting Act exempting the central marketing of TV broadcasting rights from the prohibition of the US Sherman Act,[117] which was to provide source of revenue to small sports clubs, as well as for clubs running not very popular sports. Indeed, in Bulgaria the legislator has opted for a system of central marketing for the broadcasting rights exactly in order to leverage bargaining powers between different sports clubs.

117. The CPC further assumed that the legislative rationale was the same as the one described in Decision 93/403 of the European Commission of 11 Jun. 1993 in the case *EBU/Eurovision System*.

712. Irrespective of the statutory granted power to market centrally the broadcasting rights for the sports competitions organized by them, it shall be noted that sports federations are still obliged to exercise this power in a way not preventing, restricting or distorting the competition.

II. Exclusivity

713. CPC justified the need for initiating ex officio the proceedings, which ultimately led to Decision No. 40 of 5 April 2001, with the fact that usually contracts for broadcasting rights contain provisions for exclusivity and, therefore, might infringe Article 9 of the Law on Protection of Competition (Article 15 of the present law)[118] repeating almost literally the wording of Article 81, paragraphs 1 and 2 of the Treaty of the European Communities (ECT).

714. CPC found that the legislator's decision to confer exclusive broadcasting rights upon BFU fell outside its competence to judge upon. It is the transfer of such rights to another undertaking as a package – a 'complete bundle' for all matches – that may raise competition law concerns. Indeed, CPC has confirmed by a line of case law that exclusive dealing will not per se qualify as infringement of competition law, but in all cases, its impact on the competition should be assessed in order to be determined whether the particular transaction may potentially lead to prevention, restriction or distortion of competition.

715. In Bulgaria at the very beginning when it became clear or at least possible for sports federations to hold the broadcasting rights, the latter were sold on exclusive basis to UFA. S.V.-RSA is actually the official representative of UFA for Bulgaria and after UFA joining the consortium SPORTFIVE GmbH & CO.KG, the official representative of the latter. SPORTFIVE is currently holding the broadcasting rights for the home matches of the Bulgarian national team and some of the rights for the international matches of Bulgarian clubs.

716. In this context, a provision in the contract granting exclusivity for significantly long period of time would definitely have as effect the fore-closing of this market for entrance of other companies to negotiate with BFU for its broadcasting rights. Another concern stemmed from the fixed price of the broadcasting rights under the contract between BFU and S.V.-RSA. BFU was entitled to receive every football season the amount of USD 620,000 without any possibility for bidding for other companies during the period of exclusivity.[119]

118. Law on Protection of Competition of 8 May 1998 in the State Gazette issue No. 52 of 8 May 1998. Said law was revoked by the new Law on Protection of Competition of 28 Nov. 2008 in the State Gazette issue No. 102 of 28 Nov. 2008.

119. Moreover, such a clause may be deemed to result in price fixing, which renders the entire agreement null and void.

III. Abuse of Monopoly Position

717. The potential abuse of monopoly position was among the CPC concerns, which served as a ground for initiating the proceedings. Decision No. 40 emphasizes that usually the undertakings, which hold the exclusive broadcasting rights, are monopolists having 100% market share and this fact necessitates assessment of their conduct with a view to a potential abuse of monopoly under Article 18 of the Law on Protection of Competition (Article 21 of the effective law) setting the prohibition for abuse of monopoly or dominant position.

718. Analysing the market for sales of broadcasting rights for football events, CPC has concluded that a monopoly exists both on the supply and on the demand side. The holder of the broadcasting rights is (at that time, BFU) a *monopolist* de facto as the only person who could offer the product for sale. Likewise, up until 2001 BNT is the only television with national coverage, and, therefore, the only potential purchaser of the broadcasting rights. Consequently, CPC found that both parties have equal market positions and bargaining power, although it was noted that BNT had started to lose its monopoly position after 2000.

719. Notwithstanding the particular reasoning of CPC to investigate or not, certain competition concerns prior to rendering Decision No. 40 and regardless of the particular ambit of the investigation it shall be underlined that all rights conferred to the sports federations by the Law on Sports whether collective sale, exclusivity and monopoly in respect of broadcasting rights, must be exercised in a way which shall not lead to prevention, restriction or distortion of competition.

IV. Impact of the EU Competition Law

720. The accession of Bulgaria to the EU on 1 January 2007 entailed the obligation of Bulgarian courts and competition authorities to apply the EU rules of competition law. Moreover, as part of *acquis communautaire*, the provisions of community competition law (and most notably Articles 81 and 82 of the ECT) shall have supremacy over the national legislation in case of conflicting provisions of the latter. This raised the question about potential different outcome of proceedings having as cause of action infringement of the EU rules on competition instead of the national rules.

721. This question is of minor practical significance since the relevant amendments of the Bulgarian legislation in the field were introduced prior to the accession. However, practical implications may be found in respect of definitions and analytical instruments developed in result of the case law of the European Commission and the community courts, which might affect the line of reasoning of the national courts and competition authorities.

V. Blocked Hours for Broadcasting Football Matches

722. UEFA Regulations governing the implementation of Article 48 of the UEFA Statutes provide the option for each member association to decide on two-and-a-half hours on a Saturday or a Sunday during which any transmission of football may be prohibited within the territory of the relevant member association. The objective of the UEFA broadcasting regulations as summarized by the EU Commission is:[120]

> to provide national football associations with a limited opportunity to schedule domestic football fixtures at times when they are not liable to be disrupted by the contemporaneous broadcasting of football to the detriment of stadium attendance and amateur participation in the sport.

723. This prohibition was contested by various broadcasters arguing that the UEFA Regulations infringe the rules on Competition under Article 81 and do not qualify for exemption under paragraph 3 of said Article. In Decision of 19 April 2001 relating to a proceeding pursuant to Article 81 of the EC Treaty and Article 53 of the EEA Agreement and following a detailed factual and legal analysis, the Commission of the EU concluded that no grounds for action under said Articles was available and the prohibition remained into force.

724. BFU availed itself of the option and introduced the prohibition for a three consecutive football seasons started from 2003/2004 and ended with 2005/2006. However, the application of the prohibition in Bulgaria was an example of a clear-cut infringement of the competition rules combined with total lack of understanding about the objective of the blocked hours. The reason for that was a mistaken translation of the second sentence of Article 3, paragraph 1 of the regulations stating that 'the prohibition shall apply only to intentional transmissions', which in the Bulgarian version of the regulations became 'international transmissions'.

725. This way, BFU construed the prohibition as applicable only to foreign matches and not to the domestic ones despite many other provisions of the regulations proving the opposite. Moreover, UEFA has defined the notion of 'intentional broadcasts' as broadcasts which are specifically produced for a given territory, for example, in terms of language and/or content, which notion was even more present in the case of broadcasting of domestic football in comparison with foreign matches. Nevertheless, relying on the mistaken translation BFU scheduled the most interesting domestic match from every round of the domestic championship envisaged for live broadcast by BNT exactly within the blocked hours and it was coinciding or overlapping with the rest of the matches in the first two Bulgarian football leagues.

726. During the first football season of the application of the blocked hours, some broadcasters were blindly complying with the prohibition not aware of their right to broadcast in parallel to the BNT broadcasts of domestic matches. The Decision of the European Commission has made clear that 'if a Member Association allows the broadcast of a match, including those falling within the above categories (the possible

120. For more information, *see* B. Kolev, *Football Broadcasting Rights – the Situation in Bulgaria*, 3–4 Intl. Sports L.J. 55 (2007).

exemptions), it cannot object to the incoming transmissions of any other match played in the territory of another football association'.[121]

727. For the season 2005/2006, the blocked hours remained to exist only on paper and were not respected by any of the television organizations without any objections on the part of the BFU. For the season 2006/2007, BFU did not notify any blocked hours to UEFA and this put to an end the experience of the Bulgarian football with the blocked hours under the UEFA Broadcasting Regulations.

728. The debate about the correct interpretation of the UEFA Regulations actually removed the focus from the much more serious discussion about the potential benefits for the Bulgarian football championship from the blocked hours. This discussion has never happened in practice. The fact that the prohibition has been frequently introduced by national associations of countries with a quality of their domestic championships comparable to the Bulgarian football championship would probably suffice to prove that such benefits undoubtedly exist.

729. The benefits are not only associated with the attendance of the football matches and larger amateur participation in matches but also even with more legitimate goals like the promotion of public health for instance.

VI. Protected Access of the Public to Sporting Events of Major Importance for Society

730. Bulgaria ratified the European Convention on Transfrontier Television on 4 December 1997, effective as of 13 December 1997. This convention has similar objectives as those set out in the Television without frontiers Directive including the free access to the public of events, which are considered to be of major importance for society (such as sports events).

731. Article 9*bis* of the convention concerns the access of the public to events of major importance, and a party thereto may draft a list of designated events that it considers to be of major importance for society.

732. In addition to this provision of the convention the Bulgarian legislation also contains provisions guaranteeing the access of the public to important events.

733. Pursuant to Article 19(b) of the Law on Radio and Television,[122] radio or television operator who has exclusive right on an important event shall be obliged to provide access of the other radio and television operators for its informational presentation in compliance with the obligations undertaken by the Republic of Bulgaria under enacted international agreements as the convention qualifies as such agreement.

734. The Law on Radio and Television contains definition of the term 'informational coverage', which is the creation and broadcasting within the frames of current publicity broadcasts and the news with duration necessary for the thorough presentation of the contents of the covered event. The systematic interpretation of Article 19(c) of the Law on Radio and Television draws the conclusion that the right to free informational

121. The Decision of 19 Apr. 2001 relating to a proceeding pursuant to Art. 81 of the EC Treaty and Art. 53 of the EEA Agreement.

122. Law on Radio and Television of 24 Nov. 1998 in the State Gazette issue No. 138 of 24 Nov. 1998.

coverage includes the right of radio and television operators to choose freely short extracts of the signal of the operator who possesses the exclusive rights; the right to direct access (unless it is not practicable) and the right to record which can be used solely for the creation of material with a duration of no longer than ninety seconds.

735. The right to information coverage is free of charge. Certain compensation may be provided as an exception. Moreover, the compensation shall not exceed the direct surcharges for the provision of access.

736. Pursuant to Article 32, paragraph 3 of the Law on Radio and Television, the Council of Electronic Media (CEM) shall approve and publish a list of the events of important public significance and ensure measures for protection of the access of the audience to their reflection. CEM has to guarantee that an operator under the jurisdiction of the Republic of Bulgaria having acquired exclusive rights over events with important public significance would not be able to exercise these rights in a way to deprive significant part of the audience in the country from the opportunity to follow these events live, fully or partially and if this is necessary or appropriate due to objective reasons of public interest – reflecting the events after some time, fully or partially on the free of charge TV as well as to deprive a considerable part of the auditorium in a country – member of the EU or a country – party to the European Convention for cross-border television, from the possibility of viewing live, entirely or partially, and if this is needed or appropriate, due to objective reasons of public interest – through presentation after a certain period of time, entirely or partially by the free of charge television, of the events of important public significance, according to the provisions adopted by this other country, under conditions of reciprocity.

737. For important event under section 8 of the Law on Radio and Television shall qualify 'an event of social, political, economic, sport or entertainment nature which regards the interests of the prevailing part of the audience'.

738. The adoption of the list under Article 32(3) of the Law on Radio and Television with respect to sport was last announced by CEM on 12 July 2011 and published on its website.[123] As such important sports events were listed the Winter and Summer Olympic Games, the official football matches of the Bulgarian national football team included in the annual calendar of UEFA and FIFA, the opening match, the semi-finals and the final of the FIFA World Cup, the semi-finals and the final of the European Championship in football, the final of the Cup of Bulgaria for football, the international matches of the national volleyball team for men, the international matches of the national basketball team for men, the World Cup in ski alpine, World Championship in wrestling, World Championship in rhythmic gymnastics and the World Cup. The final matches of the World Championship in football, the European Championship in football and the Cup of Bulgaria for football must be broadcast entirely and live.

739. The issue about the protected access to sports events became pending at the time where Diema Vision was awarded the exclusive UEFA EURO 2008 broadcasting rights for Bulgaria due to the fear that Diema could broadcast the matches on its pay-per-view channel. Only the matches of the international team of Bulgaria are protected for live broadcasting pursuant to the list adopted by CEM, and it is not certain that Bulgarian team will play at the finals. However, the concerns were dispersed after the

123. At hpp://www.cem.bg, English version available.

disclosure of the information that Diema is obliged under its contract to broadcast live on Diema Vision's free-channels Diema2 and Diema and only simultaneously broadcast on the company's pay-TV channel Diema Extra.

740. The issue was again discussed when the satellite operator Bulsatcom and its channel TV+ bought the broadcasting rights for the away qualification matches for UEFA EURO 2012. Thus, the home matches of the Bulgarian team will be broadcast by BNT; the away matches, on the other hand, will be available only for those who have subscribed to Bulsatcom and have paid for the certain package of TV channels because TV is a paid channel.

741. Similar situation can be observed with respect to the national football championship that used to be broadcast by BTV Action. Although the channel was a part of BTV Media Group, it was not public one and could be accessed only if the viewer had subscribed to cable or satellite operator.

Chapter 2. Sponsoring

§1. Introduction

742. In Bulgaria, the income from sponsorship is the most reliable source of money for the professional football and particularly relevant for other collective sports such as basketball and volleyball. All other sports, however, are facing serious difficulties in luring financial support from sponsors. The main reason for the general reluctance of wealthy businessmen to sponsor sports may be found in the absence of incentives provided for in the law like, for instance, tax relieves. Usually, sponsors are companies, generating their profits from the local markets and sponsors from other countries hardly could be lured, although in Bulgaria such examples existed in the past when Italian Cintofarm was for a certain period of time sponsor of the FC CSKA Sofia. Nowadays, main sponsors are the mobile operators and companies involved in petrol, oil and military industries on the territory of Bulgaria.

§2. Definition of Sponsorship

743. Section 1.19 of the Law on Sports defines 'sponsorship' as a direct or indirect financing of athletes, sports organizations and sports events, provided by a physical person or a corporate body, with the purpose of assisting the popularization of his name, mark or public prestige. Sponsorship is further mentioned in Article 62, paragraph 1, section 6 of the Law on Sports as one of the possible sources of financing for the sports organizations having status of non-profit legal entities.

744. Sponsorship contract is not regulated as such by the Bulgarian law, although it has been extensively used in practice in the recent years especially in the field of sport. Therefore, the legal nature of this type of contract is innominate contract based on the principle of freedom of contracts.

745. In absence of specific legal regulation of the sponsorship contract, its definition, legal nature and specifics are best explained by Professor Vitaliy Tadger. He defines the sponsorship contract as a contract whereby one individual or legal entity undertakes with advertising purpose to support financially an activity of sporting, educational, scientific, cultural or social nature exercised by another individual or legal entity whereas the latter undertakes to perform certain action or achieve certain result and indicate the advertisement of the sponsor.[124]

746. Tadger determines the sponsorship contract as a kind of commercial transaction falling within the scope of Article 1, paragraph 1, section 6 of the Law on Commerce. That means that the respective provisions of the commercial law would apply to that contract while due regard should be had for its specific advertising purpose.

747. With a view to the absence of specific legal regulation, every sponsorship contract is necessary to contain detailed provisions governing the relations between

124. V. Tadger, *Sponsorship Contract*, 1 Contemp. L.J. (1993).

the parties as Tadger observed. Therefore, the contract may provide for payment of liquidated damages and other penalties in case of breach. Regarding the matters not specifically addressed by the contract, the general contract law shall fill the gaps.

748. The sponsorship contract may be concluded through intermediary. The role of such intermediary is searching for sponsors and mediating during the sponsorship against payment. This role may be played by individuals or special companies who are aware of the interests of the potential sponsors and offer them conclusion of suitable contracts.

§3. Parties to the Contract and Their Obligations

749. The sponsorship activity may be carried out by one or several natural or legal persons. It is not geographically limited and may be performed outside Bulgaria as well.

750. Parties to the sponsorship contract are the sponsor and the sponsored person.

751. According to Tadger, any natural or legal person whether merchant, non-governmental organization, or foundation may act as a sponsor. He expressed doubt with respect to the issue whether State bodies may be sponsors insofar as they do not dispose of their own funds but rather operate with the funds from the State budget and more importantly that they do not need to advertise their activities.[125]

752. The sponsored person may be a single natural person or a group of persons such as a team, sports club and organizational unit. Legal entities including non-profit association or even public body such as school, choir, theatre, sports club, sports federation, symphonic orchestra may also be sponsored parties under a sponsorship contract.

753. Tadger underlines as the most important feature of the sponsorship contract that both parties have rights and obligations. The one party is obliged to support financially the other party, and the other party is obliged to organize and carry out the sponsored activity whose scope may encompass performance of personal activities, achievement of certain intellectual result or performance of activities for the benefit of the sponsor. Tadger stressed the fact that the sponsored activity may not be of commercial nature (in most of the cases, it is intellectual or sports activity according to him).

754. The main obligation of the sponsor according to Tadger is the financial support provided to the sponsored person. The subject matter of the support may vary from a particular monetary amount given as an award for best sporting achievements or limited in time – maintenance of persons participating in a competition. Certain assets also may serve as subject matter of the support – sports equipment, sports facilities, etc. The sponsor's obligations may be stipulated under condition, for instance if the athlete qualifies for the competition, achieve certain position in the final ranking,

125. Tadger expressed doubt with respect to the issue whether State bodies may be sponsors insofar as they do not dispose of their own funds but rather operate with the funds from the State budget and more importantly that they do not need to advertise their activities. However, in the cases where such bodies do dispose of such additional funds or have realized savings they could become sponsors.

make a world record, etc. In case the condition does not occur, the sponsorship contract may envisage restitution of the funds paid.

755. Tadger specifies two obligations of the sponsored person as major. First, such person may be required to participate in something (competition, concert, etc.) to perform particular action (broadcast movie, sports event, concert, etc.). Second, the sponsored person is obliged to perform certain actions that form the content of the promotion of the sponsor among the general public. These actions are specific and depend on the nature of the activity of the sponsored person. In sport, such actions may be wearing clothes with the sponsor's trademark or logo at certain occasions and for duration specified in the sponsorship contract. The sponsored person may be also obliged to provide advertising space on the TV or areas of stadiums and sporting halls for placement of sponsor's banners.

756. Other obligations of the sponsored person are to refrain from inflicting material or moral damages to the sponsor, from criticizing him since this would be incompatible with the advertising purpose of the contract.

§4. Demarcation Between the Sponsorship Contract and Other Contracts

757. Tadger demarcates the sponsorship contract from the donation contract. He observes that in economic terms, sponsorship tends to replace or set aside donation. However, the legal comparison between the two reveals many differences. The sponsorship contract creates rights and obligations for the two parties unlike the donation contract where this is valid only with respect to one party. The two types of contracts further differ in terms of the purpose of the financial support. In the case of sponsorship contract, this purpose is the promotion of the activity of the sponsor through actions that may contribute for the better acceptance of the sponsor by the general public as well as for the social recognition and social legitimacy of its business or brand. In the case of donation contract, such purpose is absent.[126]

758. Also, the presence of advertising purpose demarcates the sponsorship contract from the patronage contract. Article 11, paragraph 7 of the Law on Patronage[127] explicitly prohibits the use of the name or the brand of the patron for advertising purpose in consideration for the financial support provided. The patronage contract is specific also in terms of the characteristics of the supported party which may be a person having activity in the field of art, literature, music or science.

126. However, sponsorship will trigger the same tax implications as donation in case it is made without consideration from the other party. If there is such consideration provided by a sport company or sport association like, for instance, provision of banner advertising of the sponsor at the stadium or bearing the sport equipment of the sponsor or having its logo thereon, the sponsorship is considered as a commercial transaction and, therefore, the whole amount under such sponsorship contract is accepted as expenditures for tax purposes.

127. Law on Patronage of 23 Dec. 2005 in the State Gazette issue No. 103 of 23 Dec. 2005.

§5. Multiple Sponsorship and Conflicting Sponsorship Contracts

759. One person might enter in several sponsorship contracts at a time. In such cases, Tadger suggests that the sponsors must be notified so that an undesired competition is avoided. Another option according to Tadger is that all sponsors sign an agreement whereby the conflicting interests are resolved via designation of a general (central) sponsor who should have specific rights and obligations vis-à-vis the other sponsors. It is further possible that the sponsorship agreement provides for a single sponsor for particular sporting event for the exclusion of the others.

760. An interesting case of conflicting sponsorship contracts may arise if an athlete from a collective sport has concluded an individual sponsorship contract that turns out to be in conflict with a sponsorship contract concluded by his/her team. Such situation happened during the World Football Championship in USA in 1994. The most famous Bulgarian football player Hristo Stoichkov was obliged to use the sports shoes of Cronos under his personal sponsorship contract and the BFU had similarly undertaken to ensure that all players from the national team would play with the sports shoes of Adidas pursuant to the general sponsorship agreement.

761. The conflict could be resolved in favour of the federation where the athlete is a member or in favour of his/her club if the athlete is deemed to have legal status of employee. In the Netherlands for instance the absence of right of the athlete to determine the sports clothing he/she wears is one of the key elements for establishment of the presence of control and, consequently, for presence of employment relationship. The element of dependence that is typical for the employment would entitle the club or the federation to require the subordinated athlete to act in accordance with the instructions of the employer.

762. However, in Bulgaria several court decisions rendered on the occasion of allegedly unpaid taxes again by Hristo Stoichkov drew the conclusion, among other things, that relations between a football player and the football union concerning participation in matches of the national team are governed by civil law and particularly the service contract referred to in Article 258 and the succeeding article of the LOC.[128] In such cases from legal perspective, the obligation of the player to wear the clothing provided by the federation would be a mandatory condition precedent for the decision of the federation to enter into the civil law agreement with the player.

763. Allegedly, this exactly happened in the situation with Stoichkov prior to the Mondial 94. The then president of BFU, as explained by him in an interview, threatened Stoichkov with going back home in case of non-compliance with the official brand for clothing including sports shoes.

128. This provision concerns a service contract, whereby the contractor undertakes at his risk to do something in accordance with the order of the principal against consideration. The participation of Stoichkov in the football matches of the national team as a player in a team of sportsmen was intended for achieving a result common with all other members of the team. The fact that Stoichkov owed a result and not provision of labour was the key factor for finding in favour of relationship other than employment.

§6. Sponsorship of Sports Broadcasts under the Law on Radio and Television

764. The TV broadcasts of the matches may be sponsored under terms and conditions set forth by the Law on Radio and Television, which defines 'sponsorship' as every contribution by an individual or corporate body who does not participate in the radio and/or television activity or in the production of audio and audio-visual works to direct or indirect financing of radio and television programmes with the purpose of popularization in the society of his name, trademark, reputation, activity or production.

765. Article 82, paragraph 1 of the Law on Radio and Television points out the requirements that the sponsored media services and broadcasts shall meet:

- their content and scheduling shall in no circumstances be influenced in such a way as to affect the responsibility and the editorial independence of the media service provider;
- they shall not directly encourage the purchase or rental of commodities or services, especially by indicating these commodities and services in the broadcasts;
- the viewers shall be clearly informed about the existence of a sponsorship agreement; and
- the media services or broadcasts shall be clearly identified as sponsored by the name, logo and/or any other symbol of the sponsor such as a reference to its products or services or a distinctive sign thereof in an appropriate way at the beginning, during and/or at the end of the broadcasting.

766. The Law on Radio and Television prohibits political parties and organizations as well as religious organizations to sponsor individual broadcasts. Sponsors of broadcasts cannot be also persons whose basic activity is the production or sale of cigarettes and other tobacco products. News and publicist broadcasts cannot be sponsored.[129]

§7. Advertising in Sports Broadcasts

767. Pursuant to the Law on Radio and Television, a commercial is such form of commercial communication which accompanies or is included into an audio-visual or radio broadcast against payment or similar consideration, or broadcast for self-promotion purposes by a public or private company or natural person in connection with a trade, business, craft or profession in order to promote the supply of commodities or services, including real estate or rights and obligations; to promote a cause or idea

129. Article 98 of the BFU Statute provides that in order to satisfy the public interest towards football, the TV and radio operators that have been licensed by the Law on Radio and Television and have not concluded sublicense contract with the holder of exclusive rights can make footage of the football competitions after receiving the mutual agreement of the latter. The footage must have duration up to ninety seconds and can be broadcast only in news and sport programmes. They cannot be broadcast more than three times per week, as well as transmitted to other TV operators.

or to provoke another desired by the advertiser effect against payment. The commercials similarly to the sponsorship shall be settled by written contracts between the radio and television operator and the commercials payer. The rules regarding the observance of copyrights and the neighbouring rights, the prohibition for broadcasting of commercials during national celebrations and religious services; the prohibition for paid coverage during news programmes, as well as the requirements set for the commercials presenting alcohol beverages and medical supplies shall apply respectively to the commercials broadcast in radio stations and to the radio market.[130]

768. The provisions of the Law on Radio and Television on commercial communications, sponsorship and product placement shall apply regarding:

- television programmes dedicated exclusively to advertising and television market; and
- television programmes dedicated exclusively to self-promotion,[131] whereas the provisions shall be interpreted and applied according to the nature and the character of these programmes.

769. The commercials must comply with certain requirements provided for in Article 75 of the Law on Radio and Television. First, the commercials must be clearly recognizable as such. They also must not hurt the human dignity or encourage such behaviour that threatens the health, the personal security of citizens or the protection of the environment. Further, the commercials must respect certain prohibitions, such as, those for commercials containing pornography or inciting violence and disregard of the human dignity or which violates the public peace and the generally accepted moral norms; any commercials containing erotic elements with the participation of children or addressed to the latter are also prohibited; prohibition for broadcast of commercials based on national, political, ethnic, religious, racial, sexual and other discrimination, prohibition for commercials for cigarettes and for the smoking, etc. Concealed commercials are also prohibited.[132] The producers of commodities and the providers of services shall be obliged not to influence the editorial content.

770. Especially relevant for sports broadcasts are the rules regarding the commercials of alcoholic beverages. For a long time, one of the basic sponsors of BFU has been the brewery Kamenitza, which was replaced in October 2006 by its main competitor Zagorka. The breweries are, as a rule, the merchants who are interested in advertising during football matches.

---

130. Article 74, para. 3 of the Law on Radio and Television defines the 'radio and television market' as form of commercial communication which consists of every direct offer to the audience with the purpose of supply of commodities and services, including real estate, rights and obligations in an audio-visual or radio broadcast against payment.
131. 'Self-promotion' under the Law on Radio and Television is a form of advertising, whereas the operator advertises his own commodities, services or programmes.
132. 'Concealed commercial' under the Law on Radio and Television is presentation through words, sound or pictures of commodities, services or the name, the mark and the activity of producers of commodities and services in broadcasts when such presentation is intended by the media service provider to serve as advertising and may mislead the audience about its nature, in particular if it is done against payment or for similar consideration.

771. The commercials for all kinds of alcoholic beverages must comply with the following requirements:

- not to be directed specifically to minors or, in particular, to present children using these beverages;
- not to link the consumption of alcohol to higher achievements or driving of motor vehicles;
- not to create impression that the using of alcohol contributes to a social or sexual success;
- not to maintain that the alcoholic beverages possess therapeutic qualities, have stimulating or sedative effect or that they solve personal problems;
- not to encourage the excessive consumption of alcoholic beverages or present the abstention or the moderation in negative light; and
- not to emphasize that the high alcoholic contents contribute to the good quality of the alcoholic beverages.

§8. Linkage Contract

772. The linkage contract is also innominate contract that has become largely spread in the recent years predominantly in basketball and volleyball. The subject matter of the contract is the insertion of the name of a commercial company before or after the original name of the club or in some cases even replacing the original name of the club with the name of the company against consideration.

773. Many basketball clubs have so far resorted to linkage contracts as a form for fundraising – Lukoil Academic, Euroins Tcherno more (used to be MM Beer Tcherno More; later renamed to Tcherno more Intercom Group), CSKA-Interlogic (used to be even the peculiar CSKA Cool Condoms). In volleyball, Levski Sikonko, Lukoil Neftohimic and Marek Union Ivkoni are examples for name insertions based on linkage contracts.

774. Similar insertions have become typical also for sports tournaments, however, mainly in result of obligations undertaken under the sponsorship contract with the general sponsor. The Premier Football League (A group) bears the title TBI A group after the name of the general sponsor. Similarly, the tournament for the Cup of Bulgaria is called Cup of Bulgaria – Moto Pfohe.

Chapter 3. Merchandising

§1. Introduction

775. In practice, sports clubs registered as companies limited by shares very often sell different merchandise bearing the respective club's trademark. From time to time products such as beer CSKA, lemonade Levski Sofia, chocolate '50 years CSKA', etc. have appeared on the Bulgarian market. Merchandise bearing individual athlete's image also proved to be quite attractive option for raising money.

§2. Registration of Mark

776. The name of sports club as well as the name, picture or figure of an athlete may be registered as a mark pursuant to the Law on Marks and Geographical Indications.[133]

777. Article 9 of said law defines the mark as a sign capable to distinguish the merchandise or the services of one person from these of other persons and could be graphically presented. Such signs could be words, including names of persons, letters, numbers, drawings, forms, the form of the merchandise or its packing, combination of colours, sound or any combinations of such signs. A mark shall be a trademark, mark for services and certificate mark.

778. The right over a mark is exclusive right and shall be acquired through registration assumed from the date of submitting the application. The right to registration shall belong to the first applicant.

779. The right over a mark shall include the right of its owner to use it, to dispose with it and to prohibit to third parties to use without his consent in the commercial activity a sign that:

- is identical with the mark for merchandise or services identical with these for which the mark has been registered;
- because of its identity or similarity with the mark and the identity or similarity of the merchandise or the services of the mark and the sign, there is probability for confusion of the users including a possibility for connecting the sign with the mark; and
- is identical with or similar to the mark for commodities or services which are not identical or similar to these for which the mark has been registered when the earlier mark is well known on the territory of the Republic of Bulgaria and the use of the sign will derive without grounds benefits from the distinguishing character or the popularity of the mark or damages them.

133. Law on Marks and Geographical Indications of 14 Sep. 1999 in the State Gazette issue No. 81 of 14 Sep. 1999.

780. The owner of the right over a mark cannot prohibit a third person to use his name or address as well as instructions concerning the kind, the quality, the quantity, the designation, the value, the geographic origin, the time of production of the merchandise or of rendering the services or other characteristics of the merchandise or services in the commercial activity, under the condition that the use does not contradict with the good commercial practice. The same rule is valid also for use of the mark in cases where it is necessary to be pointed out the designation of the merchandise or the services and in particular if they serve as accessories or spare parts.

§3. Licensing Agreement

781. The right of use of the trademark may be transferred by virtue of licensing agreement between the trademark holder and a third party. The trademark holder may permit its use with respect to all or a part of the products and services, for which it has been registered, as well as for part or the whole territory of Bulgaria by means of signing a licensing agreement in writing.

782. The licence may be exclusive or non-exclusive and in absence of special stipulation regarding its type, it shall be considered as non-exclusive. The licensor of an exclusive license is legally prevented from further licensing the trademark to other parties but may use it unless otherwise agreed between the parties. Licensing agreements shall be registered in the State Registry following an application of one of the parties accompanied by certain requisites. The Patent Office of Bulgaria shall issue a certificate for the registration. The licensing agreement shall become effective vis-à-vis third parties following the registration in the State Registry.

783. Certain aspects of licensing agreement, to the extent not covered by the Law on Marks and Geographical Indications, are governed by the Law on Commerce. Article 587 of the Law on Commerce makes clear that the transfer of the use is made against payment of a licence fee. In case the license fee has been made dependant on the scope of the use, the licensee is obliged to notify the licensor about the precise scope of use within the agreed terms. The licence fee shall be due with respect to the last calendar year unless other has been agreed between the parties.

784. However, there are some aspects which proved to undermine the viability of the trademark registration of athlete's image, such as, the need for registration of a trademark covering certain classes of products and services, the requirement for use of the trademark within five years following the registration, and the possibility for a third party to register the name of a sportsmen in order to assign it later for money. Whereas the first two options are related to practical difficulties, the latter case poses also the question about the available remedies against such conduct.

785. The Law on Marks and Geographical Indications provides for deregistration of a trademark upon interested party's request where the applicant has acted in bad faith upon filing the application. However, the bad faith conduct has to be proven by a court judgment entered into force, which makes this remedy quite burdensome in practice, especially with a view to the time-consuming court procedure. Another option for deregistration exists with respect to trademarks which use may be prohibited on the ground of earlier right of a third party entitled to protection under another law and, more specifically, on grounds such as, *inter alia*, right of name and portrait.

§4. Conclusion

786. As evidenced by this monograph, the conflicting provisions of the laws of different sources in today's sport are quite a number.

787. By way of example, in Bulgaria a dispute having as subject matter a right under employment relationship is prohibited from being resolved by way of arbitration although employment disputes constitute one of the most common forms of the sports arbitration used within the global sports movement. Likewise, in Belgium, except as regards higher paid employees, agreements to submit future employment disputes to arbitration are void. Similar norms exist in Hungary and France and they question the legality of the sports arbitration system in those countries as far as employment disputes in sports are concerned.[134]

788. Currently the conflict in sport is avoided because recognition and enforcement of the arbitral awards are not sought in those countries but at the place of arbitration, which is Switzerland. Thereafter, compliance with the awards in the respective countries is attained through the threat for imposition of disciplinary sanctions on the addressees of the award and this way the assistance of national courts is rendered superfluous.

789. However, ideas about establishment of the headquarters of CAS in Brussels have recently emerged, which could reconcile sports arbitration system with the Community order due to the fact that the concept of public order as a ground for challenging the arbitral award in Belgium encompasses also the Community order of the EU since Belgium is a Member State.[135]

790. The above example illustrates the conflict that would arise between the sports arbitration system and the applicable Belgian legislation thus threatening the enforceability of the arbitral awards in employment disputes in sport.

791. Another problem is the general misfit of the employment legislation in force in the EU Member States governing relations between clubs and players. European Social Law provides for minimum standards of harmonization and do not prevent national laws concerning employment of going too far and rigidly regulating relations regarding provision of labour.

792. In its bigger part, the body of labour law in the former socialist countries now members of the EU has been developed during the socialist times when the economic reality was radically different in comparison with that in the 'old' EU Member States. International regulations of the sports governing bodies cannot be harmonized with the national laws and very often conflicting provisions exist. National sports federations are confused in their efforts to comply simultaneously with the EU law, national employment law and the rules of the respective international federations.

---

134. A. Samuel & R. Gearhart, *Sporting Arbitration and the International Olympic Committee's Court of Arbitration for Sport*, in *The Court of Arbitration for Sport 1984–2004* 323 (Blackshaw, Siekmann & Soek ed., TMC Asser Press 2006).

135. *See* M. Wathelet, *Sport Governance and EU Legal Order: Present and Future*, 3–4 Intl. Sports L.J. 9 (2007).

793. The Bulgarian Labour Code, for instance, provides for the possibility of the unilateral termination of a fixed-term contract by the employee who may give three months' notice. Players' contracts with their clubs are, as a rule, fixed-term contracts, which would mean that a player would be entitled to leave his club at his own discretion without even having completed a single full season with the team.

794. Bulgaria has an interventionist type of legislation with respect to sport meaning that it has adopted a comprehensive piece of legislation regulating various aspects of the Bulgarian sports movement. The interference of the State in sport is desired and traditionally expected by all stakeholders in the sports sector. Albeit the available legal mechanisms for involvement of the State in the development of sport, the State is often blamed for turning its blind eye to the problems of sport. Consequently, the single possible direction of sports development is perceived to be the adoption and effective implementation of a national strategy for sustainable development in sport and more direct engagement of the State with the problems in that area.

795. Sport in Bulgaria is also missing beneficial tax regimes, which are present in other Member States of the EU. The Study on National Sports Legislation in Europe in 1999 which first introduced the terms 'interventionist' and 'non-interventionist' with respect to sports legislations in Europe also concluded that 'the countries formerly under communist regimes have not provided the same kind of tax relief treatment for sports organizations as the other European states under review' and 'it seems that the governments in these countries have not given the sports movement the special social and fiscal status that helps it to function in other European countries'.[136] The need for tax exemptions for sport, as a whole, sports events, and sports organizations should be the real motive for future amendments in the Bulgarian sports legislation. This would place the sport in Bulgaria on equal footing with sport in the 'old' Member States and at least in terms of taxation 'level playing field' for the sports organizations in the EU will be created.

796. The traditional main role of the State regarding sport could be probably best viewed with the concept of physical education. Although translated into English in this way or as physical training, the literal meaning of the term *fizichesko vazpitanie* means physical upbringing. This expression implies something bigger than mere education of youngsters and, in general, the people of Bulgaria – it associates the State policy in that particular field with the relations between parents and children.

136. Study on National Sports Legislation in Europe, Council of Europe 124 (1999).

Selected Bibliography

Anderson, J. 'Recent Developments in Tort Liability for Foul Play'. *International Sports Law Journal*, nos 1–2 (2006): 41.

Archetti, E. & A. Romero. 'Death and Violence in Argentinean Football'. In *Football, Violence and Social Identity*, edited by R. Giulianotti, N. Bonney & M. Hepworth. London: Routledge, 1994.

Caiger, A. & J. O'Leary. 'The End of the Affair: The "Anelka Doctrine" – The Problem of Contract Stability in English Professional Football'. In *Professional Sports in the EU: Regulation and Re-Regulation*, edited by A. Caiger & S. Gardiner. The Hague: TMC Asser Press, 2000.

Colucci, M. 'Italy'. In *International Encyclopaedia of Laws: Sports Law*, edited by R. Blanpain & F. Hendrickx. Brussels: Kluwer Law International, 2004.

Houben, J. 'Proportionality in the World Anti-doping Code: Is There Enough Room for Flexibility?'. *International Sports Law Journal*, nos 1–2 (2007): 12.

Iliycheva, M. *Faithful Until Death: Sport Fans and Nationalist Discourse in Bulgarian Internet Forums*. Budapest: Central European University Press, 2004.

Kedzior, M. 'Effects of the EU Anti-doping Laws and Politics for the International and Domestic Sports Law in Member States'. *International Sports Law Journal*, nos 1–2 (2007): 111.

Kolev, B. 'Football Broadcasting Rights – the Situation in Bulgaria'. *International Sports Law Journal*, nos 3–4 (2007): 55.

Mayer, P. 'Mandatory Rules of Law in International Arbitration'. *International Arbitration Journal*, no. 2 (1986): 274

Mrachkov, V. *Trudovo pravo (Labour Law)*. Sofia: SIBI Press, 2004.

Samuel, A. & R. Gearhart. 'Sporting Arbitration and the International Olympic Committee's Court of Arbitration for Sport'. In *The Court of Arbitration for Sport 1984–2004*, edited by Blackshaw, Siekmann & Soek. The Hague: TMC Asser Press, 2006.

Simov, T. & B. Kolev. 'Bulgaria'. In *International Guide to the Taxation of Sportsmen and Sportswomen*, edited by R. Betten. Amsterdam: NOLOT BV, 2007.

Simov, T. & B. Kolev. 'Players' Contracts in Bulgarian Football'. *International Sports Law Journal*, nos 1–2 (2006): 110.

Soek, J. *The Strict Liability Principle and the Human Rights of Athletes in Doping Case*. The Hague: TMC Asser Press, 2007.

Stalev, Z. *Bulgarsko grajdansko procesualno pravo (Bulgarian Civil Procedural Law)*. Sofia: Ciela, 2001.

Tadger, V. *The Sponsorship Contract*. Sofia: CIELA Legal Information System, 2007.

Wathelet, M. 'Sport Governance and EU Legal Order: Present and Future'. *International Sports Law Journal*, nos 3–4 (2007): 9.

Weatherill, S. *European Sports Law, Collected Papers*. The Hague: TMC Asser Press, 2007.

Nekov, R. (Sports Law). 'Emergence, General Characteristics and Particular Features'. In *Modern Law: Problems and Tendencies*, edited by Krassimira Sredkova. Sofia: SIBI press, 2011.

Bulgarian Sports Literature

Bogdanova, N. *Zeleznite Myze na Bulgaria* (The Iron Men of Bulgaria). Sofia: Medicina I Fizkultura, 1988.

Donchev, I. *Bljasyci na Bulgarskija Sport* (Magnificence of the Bulgarian Sport).

Sofia: Medicina I Fizkultura, 1987.

Djundjulova, I. *Letopis na Sportna Slava na Druzestvo za Fizkultira I Sport 'Levski – Spartak'* (A Chronicle of Sport Glory of the Club for Physical Culture and Sport 'Levski-Spartak'). Sofia: Dr Petar Beron, 1986.

Hristov, G. *Letopis na Sportna Slava 1948–1988* (A Chronicle of Sport Glory 1948–1988). Sofia: Voenno Izdatelstvo, 1988.

Jankova, I. *Vtoroto Pijanstvo* (The Second Drunkenness). Sofia: GerArt, 1995.

Martinski, T. *Vyzhodyt na Fizicheskata kultura I Sporta v. NRB* (The Progress of the Physical Culture and Sport in People's Republic of Bulgaria). Sofia: Medicina I Fizkultura, 1976.

Milchev, S. *Futbolnata Romantika na Bulgaria*, vol. 1 (The Football Romantics of Bulgaria). Sofia: HKIA, 1998.

Nojkov S. *S 'Levski' po Dylgijat Pyt prez Vremeto* (With 'Levski' Through the Long Time Path). Sofia: Trud, 1994.

Petrov, R. *Pojava I Razvitie na Borbata v. Bulgaria* (Emergence and Development of Wrestling in Bulgaria). Sofia: Medicina I Kultura, 1982.

Sokolov, A. *Fizicheskata kultura I sportyt v. Bulgaria prez Vekovete* (Physical Culture and Sport in Bulgaria through Centuries). Sofia: Medicina I Kultura, 1982.

Todorov, S. *Sportistyt – Plamenen Patriot na Socialisticheskata ni Rodina* (The Sports Person – An Ardent Patriot of Our Socialist Country). Sofia: Medicina I Fizkultura, 1987.

Index

The numbers here refers to the paragraph numbers.

Made in the USA
Monee, IL
14 March 2026

46153208R00111